Becoming Places

Becoming Places is about the practices and politics of place and identity formation – the slippery ways in which who we are becomes wrapped up with where
we are. Drawing on the social theories of Deleuze and Bourdieu, the book
analyses the sense of place as socio-spatial assemblage and as embodied habitus.

Through a broad range of case studies from nationalist monuments and
new urbanist suburbs to urban laneways and avant-garde interiors, a range of
questions is explored. What is neighbourhood character? How do squatter settlements work and does it matter what they look like? Can architecture liberate?
How do courthouses legitimate authority? How do rhizomatic practices shape
the meanings of public space? How do monuments and public spaces shape or
stabilize national identity? The thread that ties these together is place identities
in states of becoming: closed becomes open, interior becomes landscape, character becomes caricature, illegal becomes legal, hotel becomes brothel, public
becomes private – and vice versa in each case. *Becoming Places* is a book about
the unfinishedness of place and identity.

Kim Dovey is Professor of Architecture and Urban Design at the University of
Melbourne. He has published and broadcast widely on issues of place and ideo-
logy including the book *Fluid City* (Routledge, 2005) and *Framing Places*
(Routledge, second edition 2008).

Kim Dovey

Becoming Places

Urbanism/Architecture/
Identity/Power

 Routledge
Taylor & Francis Group

LONDON AND NEW YORK

First published 2010
by Routledge
2 Park Square, Milton Park, Abingdon, Oxon OX14 4RN

Simultaneously published in the USA and Canada
by Routledge
270 Madison Ave, New York, NY 10016, USA

Routledge is an imprint of the Taylor & Francis Group, an informa business

© 2010 Kim Dovey

Typeset in Frutiger by
Wearset Ltd, Boldon, Tyne and Wear
Printed and bound in Great Britain by
TJ International Ltd, Padstow, Cornwall

British Library Cataloguing in Publication Data
A catalogue record for this book is available from the British Library

Library of Congress Cataloging-in-Publication Data
Dovey, Kim.
Becoming places/Kim Dovey.
p. cm.
Sequel and complementary volume to Dovey's seminal text, Framing places.
Includes bibliographical references and index.
1. Architecture and society. 2. Space (Architecture) I. Dovey, Kim. Framing places. II. Title.
NA2543.S6D68 2009
720.1'03–dc22
2009000186

ISBN10: 0-415-41636-1 (hbk)
ISBN10: 0-415-41637-X (pbk)
ISBN10: 0-203-87500-1 (ebk)

ISBN13: 978-0-415-41636-8 (hbk)
ISBN13: 978-0-415-41637-5 (pbk)
ISBN13: 978-0-203-87500-1 (ebk)

FOR KESS

Contents

List of figures and sources

All photographs, maps and diagrams not otherwise sourced are by Kim Dovey

Preface and acknowledgements

This book is about places of change, and about hope. It is in some ways a sequel to *Framing Places*, first written a decade ago and recently published in a second edition (Routledge 2008). It extends the interest in the nexus of place with power and includes a number of essays and research projects that have been developed over that period (often with colleagues and students). It also continues the interest I have in grounding theories of place and power in the specific contingencies of case studies. In this regard it also picks up some of the themes from *Fluid City* (Routledge 2005), a critique of the increased fluidity of urban design and planning as seen through the lens of my home city of Melbourne. This book was largely written in the inner-city suburb of Fitzroy, in a room above a garage where the windows are frosted to above eye-level to ensure that no one looks into anyone else's backyard. While I have no desire to pry I have built a platform just high enough to gain the forbidden view across the rooftops and past high-rise public housing to the city of Melbourne in the distance. Fitzroy is a slightly transgressive place (about which more in Chapter 5); a safe place to write about place. The book was completed in November 2008, just before I left on a short fieldwork trip exploring informal urbanism in Mumbai, where over half the population lives in informal squatter settlements on 6 per cent of the land. These room-by-room accretions of anything from one to six storeys high are relatively closed enclaves where the middle classes never venture. Yet many of them line the railway lines where they are exposed to the gaze of several million people each day on commuter trains. The main terminus, where the crowds surge off the trains and into the city, is the most sublime of urban spectacles – rendered slightly ridiculous by a futile attempt to entice this throng to walk through a scattered array of security screens. The trip was soon interrupted by terrorist attacks – random slaughter in the train terminal and a three-day siege of luxury hotels. If hope is a characteristic of open places, fear closes them down. This most vibrant of cities instantly drew its roller blinds, gates and shutters to create an eerie calm where only the most homeless were left on the street. The closure did not last; the terminal reopened within a day and jogging soon resumed along the waterfront where the hotel siege became a middle-class spectacle. Yet on television the terror was still spreading; images of bloodied bodies and hotels on fire were replayed again and again under the banner of 'breaking news' with a global audience glued to the screen. Just as Mumbai was becoming vibrant again, the world was closing it off – trips were cancelled, academics were ordered to evacuate. The capacity of acts of terror to close down places, to construct a world of fear rather than hope, is far more damaging than the threat to life and limb. As we isolate ourselves from difference in the luxury hotel, gated enclave or privileged nation state, the world becomes a more dangerous place. Places of becoming are constructed and sustained by their connections and it is towards an understanding of this open sense of place that this book is dedicated.

Writers are also products of our assembled connections. The most important debt here is to those colleagues and former PhD students who have co-authored five of the chapters and are separately acknowledged in the body of the work. Ian Woodcock and Stephen Wood have also been highly valuable critics and interlocutors for a number of years. Simon Wollan has provided a meticulous critique of the entire manuscript as well as assisting with illustrations and production. Chapter 2 has benefited from a loosely Deleuzian discussion group including those above, plus Steven Whitford, Gethin Davison, Mirjana Ristić, Wing Raharjo and Kate Gamble. I have also learned much from various discussions with Darko Radović, Ross King, Anoma Pieris, Greg Missingham and Kate Shaw. Kess Dovey provided an insightful view of court procedures for Chapter 8. Quentin Stevens and Karen Franck were particularly helpful editors of an early version of Chapter 11. Sandy Gifford remains the most loving and tolerant of critics.

An earlier version of Chapter 3 appeared in: J. Hillier and E. Rooksby (eds), *Habitus: A Sense of Place*, London: Ashgate, 2001, pp. 267–280 (2nd edn, 2005, pp. 283–296). An earlier and shorter version of Chapter 4 was published in: J. Rendell *et al.* (eds), *Critical Architecture*, London: Routledge, 2007, pp. 252–260. The first two case examples from Chapter 7 appeared in an earlier version (co-authored with Scott Dickson) as: 'Architecture and Freedom', *Journal of Architectural Education*, 55 (4), 2002, pp. 268–277. Chapter 9 was first published as: 'Safety Becomes Danger', *Health and Place* (Elsevior), 7 (4), 2001, pp. 319–331. Chapter 11 first appeared as: 'Urban Slippage', in K. Franck and Q. Stevens (eds), *Loose Space: Diversity and Possibility in Urban Life*, London: Routledge, 2006, pp. 168–193. Chapter 5 was funded by the Australian Research Council grants 'What is Urban Character?' (2002–2005) and 'The Character of Urban Intensification' (2006–2010), with additional support from a British Academy grant (University of Nottingham, 2004). Chapter 9 was initially funded by the National Health and Medical Research Council of Australia. Chapter 4 was first written as a Visiting Scholar at the Bartlett (UCL) in 2004. All of this work was underwritten by the Faculty of Architecture, Building and Planning at the University of Melbourne. Preparation and production of the book was assisted by a publication grant from the University of Melbourne.

Part I

Ideas

Chapter 1: Making Sense of Place

Introduction

This is a book about place formation, about places in states of becoming. One could say this does not exclude much because all places are in a state of continuous change. Yet so much of the thinking about 'place' treats it as a somewhat static concept. Places are identified with what does not change; their 'sense of place', 'character' or 'identity' is seen as relatively stable. Places are experienced primarily in terms of stabilized contexts of everyday life and they are a primary means by which we stabilize our identities in that world. Yet just as human identities are in a continuous process of change, I am interested here in the various ways in which places come into being. By this I do not mean what often passes for placemaking – the conscious attempts of designers to create a sense of place which so easily end up as manipulative corporate formulae or nostalgic ideologies written rather literally into space. And I do not mean a quest for an essence of place based in a primordial past. I am interested in an immanent theory of place that is not abstracted from its instances in everyday life, nor deferred to a presumed deeper or higher source.

The concept of place is a highly contested term, definitions of which show little consistency across the academic discourse. It is also a term with a significant role in design and planning practice where a presumed consensual understanding underwrites some dangerous practices. In everyday life we all know what place means, even if we do not experience particular places in the same ways. There is a crucial difference between the terms *space* and *place* in everyday language. To ask 'what kind of place is New York?' may generate a variety of answers but this question has a sense that 'what kind of space is New York?' does not. When we say 'this is a great place' we mean something more social and less formal than 'this is a great space'. A large part of what distinguishes place from space is that place has an intensity that connects sociality to spatiality in everyday life. We can say 'do you have enough space?' but not 'do you have enough place?' While a space may have physical dimensions, it is intensity that gives place its potency and its primacy.

The ways that place makes sense in everyday life is the primary understanding of the sense of place. How we make academic sense of that sense of place is an entirely different matter. In academic literature space and place are often indistinguishable or are distinguished in ways that best suit the theory, abstracted from everyday life. To introduce the range of theory here with any rigour would result in a quite different book and Cresswell (2004) does a commendable job from a geographic perspective. Yet there is something of a conundrum at the heart of such theory that I will briefly sketch because it frames the field from which the rest of this work emerges. As Casey (1997) has shown, the philosophy of place emerges first (as 'topos') in early Greek philosophy (most notably Aristotle) where it was seen as a form of ontological ground, a view of place that is inseparable from being or existence – to exist is to exist in a place. Casey argues that this notion of place was repressed throughout most Western philosophy in favour of the idea of place as an abstract 'location' within spatial coordinates, the 'site' of something. This view can be traced to the rise of a scientific empiricism that privileges an objective and abstract conception of space as a framework for the particularities of place. Under the enlightenment and modernity, space became identified as the primary and abstract context within which place was seen as secondary and derivative (Casey 1997). The ontology of place was revived and developed in the twentieth century by Heidegger through his spatial ontology of being-in-the-world. Both of these conceptions of place – as ontological ground and as mere location – are abstractions in relation to the experience or sense of place in everyday life (Malpas 2008). Lived experience can be rationalized as based in an ontological ground or in an abstract location with meanings added, yet the everyday sense of place is precognitive – we nearly always take place for granted. So what is it that we take for granted? How are we to make sense of the sense of place?

For most structuralist and post-structuralist thinking, the meanings of place are a form of discourse without intrinsic meanings. For Barthes (1973), place is a form of mythology; for Foucault (1979) a form of constructed subjectivity; for Derrida (1974) a text. Such approaches seek to problematize the ways that conceptions of identity become enmeshed with place, naturalized and depoliticized. The conceptual unpacking of the social constructions of place is one of the most useful of research methods and a crucial part of this book (Fairclough 1995). However, discourse analysis will never be sufficient for an understanding of place. The effectiveness of deconstructive method generally relies upon a reduction of place to text that bypasses the question of ontology and strips the sense of place of some of its most fertile complications, most importantly its connection to ontological security.

There is, however, a more significant problem when the sense of place is interpreted in terms of deep and intrinsic meanings based in an ontological ground. This is the view that is generally accused of essentialism – to see the sense of place as deeply rooted in stabilized modes of dwelling (homeland and history) that cannot be changed. This is also what is often referred to by a 'spirit' of place or '*genius loci*' and related to the Heideggerian view of place as a primordial ground of being (Norberg Schulz 1980). Such a view often conflates the sense and the ontology of place into one seamless whole, a reduction to essence that ignores social constructions of place identity.

Casey suggests we can recuperate the primacy of place as an ontological ground without the essentialism and cites many anti-essentialist approaches arising in the shadow of Heidegger (Casey 1997: chapter 12). However, his inclusion of everyone from Foucault and Derrida to the architects Tschumi and Eisenman in this field is unconvincing. The best case for an anti-essentialist theory of place is the avowedly anti-Heideggerian work of Massey in geography. This work centres on the notion of an open, global and progressive sense of place. For Massey all notions of place derived from Heidegger are problematic and regressive:

> Such views of place have been evident in a whole range of settings – in the emergence of certain kinds of nationalisms, in the marketing of places … in the new urban enclosures and … by those defending their communities against yuppification … All of these have been attempts to fix the meaning of places, to enclose and defend them: they construct singular, fixed and static identities for places, and they interpret places as bounded enclosed spaces defined through counterposition against the Other who is outside.
>
> (Massey 1992: 12)

Against such views she proposes an open conception of place where place identity is provisional and unfixed. Massey's progressive sense of place is outward-looking, defined by multiple identities and histories, its character comes from connections and interactions rather than original sources and enclosing boundaries. Her example is a local high street in London to which she ascribes character and identity without the Heideggerian primordiality:

> while Kilburn may have a character of its own, it is absolutely not a seamless, coherent identity, a single sense of place which everyone shares … If it is now recognized that people have multiple identities, then the same point can be made in relation to places. Moreover, such multiple identities can be either, or both, a source of richness or a source of conflict.
>
> (Massey 1993: 65)

Such a sense of place is seen as primarily global rather than local, forged out of its connections with other places rather than local contingencies, privileging routes rather than roots.

There is little doubt that many Heideggerian approaches to place are regressive in the way Massey suggests, but such critiques can involve a shallow reading of Heidegger (Malpas 2006: 18–20). There is an important distinction between Heidegger's argument about the spatiality of being on the one hand, and a much more spurious argument about a primordial sense of place with a singular identity, authentic history and exclusion of difference. There is little doubt that

Heidegger can be read in both these ways, but the one does not imply the other. The claim that place is wrapped up with ontology does not suggest that lived experience is primordial or fully given. If we sever place from ontology then we are left with a weak theory about the relations of place to power, we have robbed place of its potency to construct ontological security and seemingly naturalized identity. The socially constructionist position implicitly generates the illusion that with enough deconstruction we might all live a free life in a meaningless field of decentred space. The reality is that everyday life continues – here and now, in this body, in this space.

In the end the question of place hinges on the relation between spatiality and sociality. Lefebvre (1991: 26) long ago pointed out the curious condition that space is both a means of production and a product of it. To put this recursiveness another way: while space is socially constructed, the social is spatially constructed (Massey 1993). Place is an inextricably intertwined knot of spatiality and sociality. In this context there is a clear need for approaches that cut across the sociality/ spatiality divide. The spatial turn in social theory is very largely due to Heidegger and others deeply influenced by him; place matters to social theory because spatiality is so deeply implicated in sociality. This is the conundrum as I see it: how to move beyond a false choice between place as pre-given or as socially constructed. If place and space are socially constructed then where did this construction take place? If the social is spatially constructed then what evidence do we have of this pre-given place that is not socially constructed? One way through this conundrum is to explore theories that cut across the sociality–spatiality and subject–object divide. The chapters on Deleuze and Bourdieu in the first part of this book are intended to do this. I suggest we replace the Heideggerian ontology of being-in-the-world with a more Deleuzian notion of becoming-in-the-world. This implies a break with static, fixed, closed and dangerously essentialist notions of place, but preserves a provisional ontology of place-as-becoming: there is always, already and only becoming-in-the-world. I also suggest we replace the division of subjectivity–objectivity or people–environment with Bourdieu's concept of the *habitus* as an embodied world.

***

The chapters of this book are not designed to be read in any particular order, although the case studies of Part II often utilize the concepts from Part I: a series of chapters sketching ideas and theories about place and becoming. Theories are both the beginning and the end of research; they are the conceptual tools and methods one uses, consciously or not, to analyse and understand the world. Theories are all too often critiqued according to their consistency with other theories. I judge concepts and ideas on the basis of what they enable us to do and see, and how they enable us to analyse and to think; as the saying goes 'There is nothing so practical as a good theory'. My interests are in thinking sideways across the gaps between disciplinary paradigms and outside the confines of traditional formalist, spatial and social critique. Poor theory in turn can often be identified by a failure to breach traditional paradigms in their application to inter-disciplinary research questions; all place research is interdisciplinary.

Chapter 2, 'Place as Assemblage', sketches a Deleuzian approach to place. While Deleuze never explicitly wrote about 'place', his work (with that of Guattari) represents a pre-eminent philosophy of becoming, of how identities are formed and changed. The framework adopted here is a conception of place as a territorialized assemblage, defined by connections rather than essences (DeLanda 2006). Place is a dynamic ensemble of people and environment that is at once material and experiential, spatial and social. While the language can be challenging, an understanding of assemblages has a great deal to offer to theories of place. Concepts of smooth and striated space enable new approaches to both buildings and settlements that encompass new conceptions of the relations of form to everyday life, and of formal to informal settlements. These are ways of understanding senses of place in experiential, material and representational dimensions without the closed, stabilized and essentialized concepts that have co-opted and paralysed other theories of place. The emergence of rhizomatic theory in urban design enables us to build upon the key but dated insights of Jacobs ('The Self Destruction of Diversity') and Alexander ('A City is Not a Tree') that have long congealed into design formulae ('Mixed Use', 'New Urbanism').

'Silent Complicities' is an account of Bourdieu's conceptions of the '*habitus*' and 'field' as keys to an understanding of place. If Deleuze gives us a sophisticated account of becoming, of how things change, Bourdieu provides a convincing account of why they do not and of how the appearance of change is often the cover for more of the same. From this view the rules and habitual practices and structures of the habitus lock us into a sense of place that is also a sense of one's place in the world. The potency of place lies in the ways it becomes taken for granted as a neutral context for everyday life, its forgotten-ness. The neutrality of place can neutralize becoming. The design of built form involves the production and circulation of non-economic forms of capital. Social capital becomes embodied in places in the best and worst of ways, as mobilization towards a better future and as enclaves of class distinction. Symbolic capital circulates through places and fields of practice; its potency relies on being seen as a form of distinction rather than a form of capital. From such a view, places often camouflage practices of power; distinctions between people are camouflaged as distinctions between places.

Deleuze and Bourdieu provide two key conceptual frameworks for these investigations of place. These are simply conceptual toolkits; I find them useful to an understanding of the ways that places mediate practices of power. There are differences but also some consistencies between them: both begin from the view that spatiality and sociality are integrated, neither relies on a division between subject and object. Both assemblage and habitus are immanent to everyday life rather than transcendent abstractions. The rules of the habitus can be read as codes of the assemblage. The major contrast is that Bourdieu stresses the inertia and inhibition embodied in the habitus while Delueze and

Guattari stress flow and change. The tendency to take sides may not be the most productive position.

Chapter 4, 'Limits of Critical Architecture', is an account of the ways critical theory has been applied in architecture, whereby the architecture becomes a critique of its conditions of production. It traces the ways in which an architecture that is meant to resist a dominant economic, political and social order becomes complicit with it. The conceptual oppositions of form/function and representation/action are seen as clues to understand the ways a supposedly 'critical' architecture is neutralized – contained as form and insulated from life. The illusion of a critical architecture becomes compatible with a specialization in the production and reproduction of symbolic and social capital. This critique is explored through the fields of practice, criticism, publishing and education. Architectural discourse produces a controlled critique that is funded, framed and subtly controlled by advertising. The delivery of 'critique' to architects is the means to deliver architects to advertisers, and the architectural academy often conflates such controlled critique with research.

Theory is the beginning of research and while the end may be better theory it is also a better form of placemaking practice. The second part of the book explores various kinds of research practice through a series of case studies, often undertaken with co-authors as parts of different research projects. These cases have a broad range in scale and place type: from the room to the nation, from squatter settlements to courtrooms and from Western to South-east Asian cities. The case-study approach has been discussed often enough but a few words are in order about the relationship of such methods to place theory. As Flyvberg (2004) argues, Case studies are often wrongly understood as producing only local and contingent knowledge that one cannot use to generalize. From the viewpoint of empirical science this is understandable, no one wants prognoses about cancer or global warming to be based in case studies. Yet research on place within the paradigm of empirical science has proven very limited, largely reducing place to its measureable components and stripping it of its 'sense'. These are simply the wrong conceptual tools; to turn the saying around: there is nothing so impractical as bad theory. Most place theory is ungrounded in the particularities of place. Case studies are peculiarly pertinent to theories of place because any general theory must account for the particulars – differences between places are central to definitions of place. What is generally true of the sense of place is that each place is different – places are cases. Case studies are a testing ground for theory, but not in the normal sense that the test proves or refutes a theory. Rather the theory proves more or less useful in making sense of place. A lot of this research is 'empirical' in that it is strongly based in evidence – mapping, observing, interviewing, analysing. But this is empirical research in the older sense of examining what is available to the senses rather than only what is measureable. Different methods, including interviews, observation, morphological mapping, discourse analysis and spatial syntax analysis, will prove useful in different contexts. In methodological terms research on place is interdisciplinary and spans the humanities and social sciences. Disciplines are institutional schemas that divide knowledges and practices into discrete categories, places for disciplined thought that can become homes for lazy thinking and territorial control. The sense of place is far too slippery to be contained in these ways.

Chapter 5, 'Slippery Characters' (co-authored with Ian Woodcock and Stephen Wood), is an exploration of various ways in which place identity is experienced, understood and created in four different Australian suburbs. Two of these are older suburbs where the 'character' is perceived to be under threat from new development. In one case a closed and purified identity is threatened by difference, yet in the other an open and diverse mixture is threatened by conformity. The other cases are new developments where formularized corporate strategies produce instant place identities based on historical models and marketed for consumption. Such places are strongly bounded to reinforce the production of purified identities, yet such places can paradoxically camouflage social differences. In each of the four cases 'character' is described as a 'feel' of the neighbourhood that is at once social and material, slipping easily from spatiality to sociality. As 'character' becomes coded into either urban design codes or private covenants as a set of formal characteristics, character becomes fixed and reduced to caricature.

'Becoming Prosperous' (co-authored with Wiryono Raharjo) is an investigation of informal urbanism, closely linked to 'slums' and 'squatter' settlements. After a survey of issues and types of informal urbanism, this chapter presents a morphological analysis of one such settlement in Yogyakarta, Indonesia. While the primary policy is to replace such settlements with new housing, the practice is to continue producing them. United Nations figures suggest that over a billion people now live in slums and that this figure will double by 2050. If so then this will be the major form of urban design and development. Yet such settlements are relatively unstudied in morphological terms. Informal urbanism is a global production of intensely local places that are relatively closed and invisible. Such makeshift urbanism is often ingenious and innovative, with a disturbing yet powerful sense of place and urban aesthetic.

'Urbanizing Architecture' explores the work of Rem Koolhaas, who has long been identified with the attempt to break with architectural ideologies embodied in spatial programmes and to resist the role of architecture in reproducing social roles and structures. A key tactic has been to introduce the spatial structures of urban encounter into building interiors. Here I deploy a spatial analysis that reveals both achievements and limits to this emancipatory project in different building types: school, house and library. Each of these buildings succeeds in some important ways yet deeper forms of ideological and spatial control are also reproduced. Ultimately, Koolhaas's work succeeds through a certain 'magic' whereby formal imagery operates as distraction; some real achievements are coupled with illusions of change.

Chapter 8, 'Open Court', is an analysis of the ways that the courthouse is evolving as a building type. Three recently completed courthouses in Melbourne's legal district were each programmed and designed with a deliberate intent to translate judicial ideals such as access, transparency, enlightenment and equality into contemporary architecture. This chapter is an account of what happens when these ideals come into tension with the need to maintain security and to produce a sense of institutional order and authority through architecture. How can architects pursue ideals of natural light, view and equality of access yet also provide segregated access and egress for judges, prisoners, juries and the public? If courthouse design is to avoid an architecture of intimidation and hierarchy, what happens to the legitimation of authority on which the courts rely? While each building is successful in its own ways, each is also infused with contradictions of place and power. Architects are called upon to mediate social relations and to resolve social issues; and the buildings they design are revealing of those conditions.

'Safety Becomes Danger' (co-authored by John Fitzgerald) explores the uses and meanings of a particular shopping strip in inner-city Melbourne which became, for a time, strongly identified with heroin sale and use in public space. It also became the site of many overdoses and deaths in nearby streets and lanes. Drug trading was camouflaged within a diverse streetlife, with injecting sites dispersed through laneways, car parks and toilets. These injecting zones occupied liminal places which slide between categories of private and public, safety and danger. Those who inject in public space are caught in a dilemma, needing both safety from police and exposure in the event of an overdose. The chapter concludes with a discussion of the paradoxical task of bringing such drug use within the medical gaze without bringing it into the public gaze.

Chapter 10, 'New Orders' (co-authored by Eka Permanasari), is an account of changing meanings and uses of Merdeka Square and the National Monument in Jakarta. The monument was conceived by Indonesia's first President Sukarno to establish and stabilize the Indonesian archipelago as a newly emerging nation. A giant obelisk with a golden flame represented a modernist beacon of democracy and enlightenment, the light of freedom and the fire of revolution. The monument stands on the vast expanse of the former colonial 'King's Square', renamed Merdeka (Freedom) Square. During the period of Suharto's 'New Order' the square was increasingly infiltrated by various prohibited users – beggars, prostitutes, illegal vendors and homeless people – disturbing the national image. The monument and square are now enclosed within a high fence, reframed as a middle-class spectacle. The emptiness that is left after the real has been fenced out is at once a fantasy of wealth and harmony and also a collective void from which the search for national identity proceeds.

'Urban Slippage' (co-authored with Kasama Polakit) explores a particular slice of South-east Asian urbanism in Bangkok. Public space is used and appropriated by a variety of proprietors, residents, hawkers and others for a broad range of functions, desires and practices. The use and meaning of public space is subject to both local and global flows of time and space with shifting meanings of secular/sacred, private/public and legal/illegal. The social and formal identity of the place is characterized by slippages through which one place, practice or meaning becomes another. Functions slip from house to shop to factory; from hotel to brothel; from sidewalk to restaurant; and shrine to car park. Hawker trolleys become building additions and exchanges of money slip from a fine to a licence to a bribe. Rhizomatic practices in the deeper spaces – the 'migrating' hawkers and residents, children's play, the homeless, the illicit activities – are strongly linked (for better and worse) to the livelihood of the poor.

The book is an assemblage of essays and case studies with some sharp differences of conceptual approach, authorship and viewpoint – and no conclusion. One idea that resonates in all of these narratives is the quest to rethink conceptions of 'place' and to move on from the views of place as essentially closed and stabilizing. Another is the focus on the nexus of place to power; the ways that the sense of place is inextricably wrapped up with questions of authority and authenticity. In the accounts of places in this book – from squares and streetscapes, squatter settlements and laneways, to courts and libraries – there is an attempt to rethink the idea of place and place identity without the suffocating ideal of place as closed or finished. These places are lived and embodied; they are structured, ordered, transformed, infiltrated and negotiated; they are symbolized, packaged and marketed. In each case they are local places enmeshed in global fields of power: capital markets, nationalisms, design professions, mass media, rural–urban migrations; they are subject to global flows of materials, design formulae, information, capital, heroin, design styles and reputations. They are also fundamentally local – constructed from the contingencies of site and society, climate and economy. In no case are these places, or the critiques of them, finished. In the end this book is nothing more than some assembled attempts at making sense of place. What you make of it is up to you; what I hope you make is more ideas and better places.

Chapter 2: Place as Assemblage

As the title of this book suggests and as argued in Chapter 1, the task for place theory is to move from conceptions of place as stabilized being towards places of becoming. A key theoretical base for this lies in Deleuzian philosophy and particularly in the conceptual toolkit outlined in Deleuze and Guattari's (1987) book *A Thousand Plateaus*. 'Place' is not a concept deployed in this literature, indeed the language of *A Thousand Plateaus* is difficult and esoteric. My aim is to render it more transparent, and to construct a theory of place as assemblage. A key guide in this task is De Landa (2006), whose construction of a Deleuzian 'assemblage theory' is a theory of society rather than of place. This application of such an approach to place is practical as well as theoretical. While I am interested in contributing to better theories of the place–power nexus I am also interested in understanding the ways in which specific places work: the morphologies and socio-spatial networks of boundaries and segments; the flows of everyday life; the narratives that are expressed through them; and the desires, hopes and fears that are invested in them. I have long been of the view that place/power issues require multiplicitous methodologies linking phenomenology, spatial analysis and discourse analysis (Dovey 2008). Place is at once experienced, structured and discursively constructed. It is the contention here that Deleuzian theory has a potential to encompass these complexities and to provide a useful framework for the understanding of place and the practices of urban transformation.

In his translator's introduction, Massumi suggests we treat *A Thousand Plateaus* like an intellectual toolbox (Deleuze and Guattari 1987: xv). A toolbox is not a consistent picture or theory of a world where the tools fit together into a consistent narrative. Different conceptual tools may be useful for different intellectual tasks, even those for which they were not intended: 'A concept is a brick. It can be used to build the courthouse of reason. Or it can be thrown through the window' (Massumi 1993: 5). The test here lies in how such concepts enable us to rethink the idea of place and the practices of placemaking. For these tasks it seems to me we need a relatively sophisticated understanding of this toolkit if we are not to slip into a relativistic practice of throwing new language at old problems or inventing built forms that resemble the theory. In this regard a range of folded and fluid forms in architecture loosely referenced to Deleuze may be best understood as a new round of symbolic capital to service a meaning market (see Chapter 3). My task here is to unravel some of these conceptual tools in a manner that may be useful for the interpretation of place and its intersection with practices of power. An understanding of this work cannot be a simple top-down grasp of a unitary whole; an understanding of Deleuzian thought requires that we enter into this system of concepts rather than contemplate from the outside or from above. We might treat this assemblage of concepts like a strange place – we visit, we explore, we use it; we may or may not get a feel for the game of inhabiting, and we may or may not feel at home.

POWER/DESIRE

One of the key contributions of Deleuzian thought is that it incorporates an understanding of 'power' that moves beyond the Foucaultian conception of disciplinary power to one based more fully on desire. Like 'place', power is used in an everyday manner that presupposes a shared understanding. Yet when we pull it apart we discover how much, and how little, it means. One key and long-standing distinction in the literature is between 'power over' (control of the actions of others) and 'power to' (a capacity to achieve desired ends). These two are clearly not mutually exclusive because the desired end may be control over others and to exercise power over others is to harness their capacities. In the book *Framing Places* I explored some of the ways that 'power over' can be broken down into force, coercion, manipulation, domination, seduction and authority together with the ways these dimensions are mediated in architecture and urban design (Dovey 2008: chapter 1). Simply stated, force removes all agency from the subject (as in incarceration), coercion uses a threat of force (as in the threat of prison), manipulation involves concealment of intent (as in the shopping mall), domination involves the intimidation of scale (the vast open space or tall building), authority uses institutional framings (state, church, school) and seduction involves a transformation of the subject's desires (charisma, art). These dimensions remain important but are largely limited to 'power over' and conceive of power as centred in leaders, hierarchies, institutions and spatial centres.

By contrast, the major theory of power as dispersed micropractices is the one developed by Foucault (1979, 1997) through the concepts of the panopticon and disciplinary technology. The Foucaultian move was to rethink power as a productive practice rather than a resource one held. It is not that the person is simply subject to power, but rather that subjectivity is produced through dispersed micropractices and becomes insinuated into its field of operations. The Foucaultian model of disciplinary power goes a long way to understanding practices of social uniformity and the eradication of difference. In this dispersed sense power is decentred and immanent in everyday life; such power is not held by subjects so much as it produces subjectivity. The Foucaultian model is a theory of 'power to' because it is based in productive capacities and micropractices, however, it retains a negative critique of power as an all-pervasive apparatus of constraint, discipline and oppression.

The Foucaultian notion of power shows how disciplinary power constructs subjects and harnesses the capacities (the power to) of subjects in their own oppression. Deleuze takes this Foucaultian concept of power further; it is not pre-existing beings who hold power or are subject to it, rather power is linked to flows of desire and processes of becoming. For Deleuze, desire is the primary force of life; it is immanent to everyday life and not limited to the human world. The desire of a plant for light and water or a wasp for an orchid is not funda-mentally different from the desire to live in a decent house or a particular neigh-bourhood. Desire does not stem from preformed subjects who lack the preformed object of desire; rather it is a process of connection where one becomes a wasp or a WASP through this connection. From this perspective organisms and things are not subject to practices of power so much as they are produced by desires.

> When a plant takes in light and moisture it becomes a plant through its relation to these other forces; this is one flow of desire. When a human body connects with another body it becomes a child in relation to a parent, or it becomes a mother in relation to a child; this is another flow of desire. When bodies connect and become tribes, societies or nations, they also produce new relations or flows of desire.
>
> (Colebrook 2002: xvi)

The Deleuzian notion of the primacy of desire is linked with a 'sense' or 'sensa-tion' which is seen as a raw experience of perception prior to cognition, language or meaning. For Deleuze sensation is a kind of animal condition strongly linked to desire; in the human world it is the initial impact of a work of art, spectacle, building or landscape that 'passes over and through the body' prior to meaning or cognition (Conley 2005: 244–245). Sensation is linked to the 'affect' of an event or encounter that connects the material and experiential. If one were to speak of a 'sense' of place in this context it would connect the phenomenology of the body to the precognitive encounter with the everyday world as in the work of Merleau-Ponty (1962).

Desire begins as a flow of life, an event of becoming that precedes being and identity. As desires become coded and organized they become identities, organisms, things and assemblages. 'Far from thinking of the world as a collec-tion of beings who then have desires. Deleuze insists that life begins from flows of becoming or desire, which then produce relative points of stability' (Cole-brook 2002: 66). From such a view, all of the places we inhabit can be seen as products of desire. Streets, doors, corridors and freeways are products of desires to connect between places; a corner office with a commanding view emerges from desires for status, light and prospect; suburbs reflect desires for detached identities, distance from the urban and desirable neighbourhoods. To see desire as the basis of power is to see it as positive, productive and as operating at a micropolitical level. A primary product of these flows of desire are assemblages.

ASSEMBLAGE

In the most general sense an 'assemblage' is a whole 'whose properties emerge from the interactions between parts' (De Landa 2006: 5). It is perhaps best seen as a 'state of affairs' in contrast to a 'thing' or a collection of parts. The assemblage is also not an organized system in the sense that its workings are not organic. The parts of an organism such as a branch of a tree, or an organization such as a bank, have an entirely determined and necessary organic role. The parts of an assemblage are contingent rather than necessary, they are aggregated, mixed and composed; as in a 'machine' they can be taken out and used in other assemblages (DeLanda 2006: 9). For instance, a street is not a thing nor is it just a collection of discrete things. The buildings, trees, cars, sidewalks, goods, people, signs, etc. all come together to become the street, but it is the connections between them that makes it an assemblage or a place. It is the relations of buildings–sidewalk–roadway; the flows of traffic, people and goods; the interconnections of public to private space, and of this street to the city, that make it a 'street' and distinguish it from other place assemblages such as parks, plazas, freeways, shopping malls and marketplaces. Within this assemblage the sidewalk is nothing more than a further assemblage of connections between things and practices. The assemblage is also dynamic – trees and people grow and die, buildings are constructed and demolished. It is the flows of life, traffic, goods and money that give the street its intensity and its sense of place. All places are assemblages.

De Landa (2006) sees the concept of assemblage as a key Deleuzian concept, a kind of hinge for what he terms 'assemblage theory'. Philosophically this is an attempt to avoid all forms of reductionism – both the reduction to essences and reduction to text. It is empirical without the essentialism of empirical science; it gives priority to experience and sensation without the idealism of phenomenology; and it seeks to understand the social construction of reality without reduction to discourse. Assemblage theory avoids essentialism through a concentration on the historic and contingent processes that produces assemblages. And it offers an approach to theories of place without the simplistic reductionism and essentialism that has weighed down such discourse for so long.

For Deleuze and Guattari the assemblage is conceived as structured along two intersecting dimensions, a philosophical schema they term the 'tetravalence of the assemblage' (Deleuze and Guattari 1987: 88–89; also DeLanda 2006). The first of these, best understood as materiality versus expression, links the material interactions of bodies and spaces with the expression of meaning through propositions, language and representation. This is not a dialectic – assemblages are always at once both material and expressive. The expressive pole of the assemblage also embodies 'codes' that govern forms of expression. To return to our urban example we can see that the 'street' is an assemblage of material things, flows and spatial connections that co-exist with representational narratives, urban design codes and intensities. The senses or meanings of the place are neither found within the material urban form nor are they simply added to it, rather they are integral to the assemblage. In this regard assemblage theory has the capacity to heal the breach in design thinking that separates questions of expression from those of materiality, a particular problem in architectural theory (see Chapter 3). To see places as assemblages is to avoid the reduction of place to text, to materiality or to subjective experience. What we call 'sense of place' is a phenomenon that connects or spans this materiality/expression dimension; it cannot be reduced to an essence nor to social construction. I will return to this issue later in discussion of the Deleuzian conception of 'sense'. The second dimension of the assemblage is an axis of territorialization–deterritorialization that mediates the degree to which an assemblage is stabilized or destabilized. This dimension intersects with the material/expressive dimension in that territories are inscribed through a mix of material and expressive boundaries. The concept of territory here is broad enough to encompass everything from the rhythms of the urinating dog to nationalism; yet for Deleuze and Guattari (1987: chapter 11) territoriality is creative rather than defensive, a form of becoming at home in the world.

TERRITORIALITY/SEGMENTARITY

The dimension of territorialization/deterritorialization is that through which social and spatial boundaries and identities are inscribed and erased. Territorialization here does not mean anything vastly different from the way the term is deployed in ethology but without the essentialism:

> The territory is first of all the critical distance between two beings of the same species:
> Mark your distance … Don't anybody touch me, I growl if anyone enters my territory, I
> put up placards … It is a matter of keeping at a distance the forces of chaos knocking at
> the door.
>
> (Deleuze and Guattari 1987: 319–320)

Territorialization here can range from the border patrol to Brecht's famous inscription of a chalk circle isolating the self from society, from constructing a gated community to leaving your coat on a chair in the pub. I am reminded of Altman's three-layered construct of primary, secondary and public territories (Altman 1975): primary when we shut the door to the bedroom, secondary when territories are shared by a 'club', and public when territories can be appropriated by anyone (like a park bench). Yet for Deleuze and Guattari there can be no such simple system since territories are subject to deterritorialization – the movement by which territories are eroded: the chalk or the urine is washed away, buildings are demolished, nations are invaded. Deterritorialized elements are recombined into new assemblages through a process of reterritorialization. Territory is a stabilization of the assemblage, establishing a zone of order that keeps chaos and difference at bay. In one key passage Deleuze and Guattari describe the process of territorialization and deterritorialization in three steps: establishing a centre of order; then inscribing a boundary around that centre; then breaching that boundary to venture out:

> home does not pre-exist: it was necessary to draw a circle around that uncertain and fragile center, to organize a limited space ... The forces of chaos are kept outside as much as possible, and the interior space protects the germinal forces of a task to fulfil or a deed to do ... Finally one opens the circle a crack, opens it all the way, lets someone in, calls someone, or else goes out oneself, launches forth.
>
> (Deleuze and Guattari 1987: 311)

Becoming at home is linked to the 'refrain', a form of expression with a different meaning every time it is repeated, as a song ventures forward with each verse before returning to the refrain. The repetitive events of everyday life construct a sense of home through familiarity and order, but this sense of home means nothing without the journey, the connection with difference. 'Every assemblage is basically territorial. The first concrete rule for assemblages is to discover what territoriality they envelop, for there always is one ... Discover the territorial assemblages of someone, human or animal: "home" ' (Deleuze and Guattari 1987: 503–504). Territories are defined not only by boundaries but also often by internal uniformities (De Landa 2006). Those who gain access to a neighbourhood may be a similar class of people inhabiting similar housing types. The assemblage known as a seminar is territorialized in a particular room for a particular time; the boundaries are sharp in space and time, they admit some people while excluding others. The assemblage known as a 'family' is territorialized in a 'house', a 'corporation' in an 'office', a 'community' in a 'neighbourhood' and so on. In each case both spatial and social exclusions operate to enforce spatial boundaries and exclude non-members of the assemblage (DeLanda 2006). A requirement for fees or the more subtle exclusions of social class (feeling out of place) can exclude people from a seminar more effectively than walls or timetables. Bulldozing, burglary, assault and bringing children to a university seminar are all forms of deterritorialization: 'Any process which either destabilizes spatial boundaries or increases internal heterogeneity is considered deterritorialization' (DeLanda 2006: 13). The public space of an urban street is relatively deterritorialized and interconnected with other streets; public territories such as parking spots, café tables and public benches are claimed and vacated; shops and businesses open and close; private housing may overlook from the sides. Territorialization is a synthetic process that enables wholes to form from parts, identities from differences.

One of the key issues for an understanding of place as assemblage focuses on the issue of how boundaries are used to inscribe territories, which Deleuze and Guattari call segmentarity:

We are segmented from all around and in every direction. The human being is a segmentary animal … Dwelling, getting around, working, playing: life is spatially and socially segmented. The house is segmented according to its rooms' assigned purposes; streets, according to the order of the city; the factory according to the nature of the work.

(Deleuze and Guattari 1987: 208)

There are three primary forms of segmentation: binary, circular and linear. Binary segmentation is generally a division of binary social categories such as upper/ lower class, male/female, young/old and black/white. Gated communities, squatter settlements and wealthy nations are class-based, and often also race-based. Retirement villages, school classrooms, student housing and day-care centres are all examples of age segmentarity. Male toilets, girls' schools and men's clubs involve gender segmentarity. Circular segmentation is when segments are nested in hierarchical relation as the room is encircled in turn by the house, neighbourhood, city and nation. These modes of segmentation co-exist with binary segments nested within larger circular assemblages. Linear segmentation is where there is a progression over time through different segments which may or may not be spatially contiguous: preschool > primary > secondary > university. Forms of linear segmentarity embodied in buildings and cities involve a linear movement through a sequence of spaces designed to produce certain place effects. Examples include the the choreographed sequence of the blockbuster art exhibit (entry > gallery > gallery > gallery > shop > exit) and airline travel (check-in > security > shops > lounge > aircraft > shops > security > exit). Each of these segmentation types are geared to microardivicespractices of power. Binary segments not only divide according to race, class, age and gender but also ensure there is no place for hybridity. Concentric segments can operate to ensure a resonance between places at different scales and rungs on a hierarchy: the bank branch resonates with headquarters as the police station resonates with the state. Linear segments can stabilize sequences of identity formation, stimulate consumption and construct a sense of awe – the enfilade used as an approach to centres of political and corporate power is another example. These three diagrams of segmentarity are interconnected and overlapped since segments may be lodged in binary, nested and sequential relations simultaneously. This discussion of segmentarity begs comparison with the spatial syntax analysis developed by Hillier and others which analyses the relationships of spatial segments according to certain genotypes and characteristics such as the relative integration of segments (Hillier and Hanson 1984; Hillier 1996). This connection will be explored further in Chapter 7.

For Deleuze and Guattari there is a distinction between 'supple' and 'rigid' segmentarities. Rigid segmentarities are often identified with the state which is seen to organize a hierarchic structure of concentric segments (nation (city (neighbourhood (house)))) that 'resonate' together (Deleuze and Guattari 1987: 212, 224). Supple segmentarities by contrast involve a fluidity of lateral connections with potential for old segments to dissolve and new segments to form. Rigid and supple segmentaries are inseparable and overlapping:

> It is not sufficient to define bureaucracy by a rigid segmentarity with compartmentalization of contiguous offices, an office manager in each segment, and the corresponding centralization at the end of the hall or on top of the tower. For at the same time there is a ... suppleness of and communication between offices, a bureaucratic perversion, a permanent inventiveness or creativity practiced even against administrative regulations.
>
> (Deleuze and Guattari 1987: 214)

This supple segmentarity is based on the power of networks and a fundamental distinction between tree-like and rhizomatic structures and practices.

RHIZOME/TREE

A Thousand Plateaus begins with a chapter called 'Rhizome' which sets up a contrast between tree-like systems organized hierarchically with roots, stem and branches, and the rhizome (grass, potato, bamboo) which is characterized by horizontal lines of movement, networks and connectivity. The rhizome and tree are primarily metaphors for ways of thinking. Tree-like thinking organizes our world hierarchically under the branches of a transcendent idea (state, corporation, family, church). Rhizomatic thought is identified by lateral movement of network connectivity as opposed to the vertical stability of the stem. There is a connection here with the idea of lateral thinking; Koestler (1964) defines creativity as the production of new connections between previously unrelated ideas – the intersection of different frames of reference. For de Bono (1969) the creative logic of lateral thinking runs against the hierarchic logic of common sense. For Deleuze tree-like thinking stifles creativity and protects the dominant concepts in a field from critique.

The three-part categorization of binary, circular and linear segmentarities outlined earlier is largely a description of tree-like organizations with a focus on the separation of segments in accord with a higher-level order. Thus the corporate office often sets up a binary division between staff and visitors (across a counter?), a nested hierarchy between headquarters and branches of the firm, and a linear spatial sequence to the boss's office. The interconnected permeable network is a spatial structure that is connective and rhizomatic rather than divisive in function. Spatial examples here include places that are structured to maximize exchange, choice and encounter – the open-plan office, city grid or permeable field of market stalls. Yet spatial structures are always a mix of tree-like and rhizomatic. By and large public spaces are more rhizomatic and private interiors are more tree-like. Public life is fundamentally linked to networks of encounter and exchange in permeable spatial structures while privacy is fundamentally linked to enclosure and culs-de-sac. There are, however, many assemblages that embody what might be termed enclosed networks: permeable and open places of supple encounter that are rigidly enclosed on their boundaries. Open-plan offices, shopping malls and enclosed residential developments often embody such a structure where a supple space of flows is constructed inside a rigid segment.

Through their very lack of rigidity, rhizomatic networks are more resilient than tree-like structures. The tree-like structure produces spatial control by channelling flows of movement along spatial stems but it lacks adaptability since there is nowhere else for these flows to go. The resilience of the network structure was dramatically illustrated in 2001 when the planes hit the World Trade Center towers and the Pentagon. The Pentagon building continued to function and was not even fully evacuated while the stems of the towers melted. This example also serves to show that rhizomatic structures such as the Pentagon may house the most hierarchical of social assemblages; there is no one-to-one mapping of the social onto the spatial. Both the Pentagon and the Internet were invented by the US military as structures that resist attack by having no stem.

The two main power structures that we deal with in our everyday lives – the state and the market – are linked to fundamentally different socio-spatial segmentarities. Markets fundamentally rely on exchange and connectivity. While corporations compete to establish tree-like monopolies, consumption relies upon interconnected flows of desire and money. This is why the department store, shopping mall and supermarket are all permeable spatial networks at their centre – choices of products and pathways go together. The state is generally linked to tree-like structures; its power rarely relies on connectivity between elements but rather operates by drawing constituent parts into a tree-like structure and making these elements resonate together. The tree-like state is contrasted in this regard with the rhizomatic town which has the connectivity of parts as its primary function: 'the town exists only as a function of circulation ... it is ... a network ... in contact with other towns' (Deleuze and Guattari 1987: 442). Attempts by the state to control public space, to stabilize memories and histories through monuments and grand statements are generally partial or form only parts of cities. Markets are rhizomatic in that functionality depends on horizontal networks of information, goods and people; monopolies, by contrast, are tree-like. The role of the state in regulating urban form brings two unlike principles together. It is fuelled by desires to order the city in accord with higher goals but can be in conflict with the idea of open markets.

The conceptual contrast between the rhizome and the tree which begins *A Thousand Plateaus* finds a parallel in the penultimate chapter on striated and smooth space (Deleuze and Guattari 1987). The term 'striated' captures the etymological links to the Latin: *stringere* 'to draw tight', linked to 'strict' and 'stringent'. This is contrasted with the 'smooth', which is intended to be understood as an absence of boundaries or joints rather than homogeneous. Smoothness implies a slipperiness and movement where one slides seamlessly from one identity, meaning or image to another. These are not different types of space so much as spatial properties. Striated space is where identities and spatial practices have become stabilized in strictly bounded territories with choreographed spatial practices and socially controlled identities. Smooth space is identified with movement and instability through which stable territories are erased and new identities and spatial practices become possible. The smooth and the striated are not types of space or place so much as conceptual tools for thinking about space. Every real place is a mixture of the two in a reciprocal relation where they are constantly 'enfolded' into each other. 'Folding' is another key term for Deleuze (1993); it involves a focus away from things, elements or points of stability and onto the movements between them as one morphs into the other. This focus on the between is a way to rethink binary and dialectic oppositions as an enfolding of each other; for our purposes here this entails the enfolding of different spaces and functions, of public with private space, and of inside with outside.

Spatial segmentarity is a form of striation and in general terms linear and branching structures are more striated while permeable networks are more smooth. Cellular spatial structures based on socially constructed genotypes can be seen as highly striated spaces with a strict choreography of everyday life and social encounter. Disciplinary institutions such as the traditional school with strict spatial divisions (boys/girls, staff/students, learn/play) are good examples. The architecture of the school in the West is undergoing a major transformation based precisely on the realization that while a strict tree-like segmentarity serves the discipline of *teaching*, learning is a muti-modal practice suited to a more flexible framing of space.[1] All of this raises significant questions about the prospects for spatial structures that are more 'smooth', enabling new kinds of practice.

TWOFOLD

I have begun to outline a range of conceptual oppositions that resonate with each other throughout *A Thousand Plateaus* and Deleuzian philosophy: smooth/striated, network/hierarchy, rhizome/tree. These are part of a much larger cluster of conceptual oppositions that loosely align with the twofold concept of becoming/being and difference/identity. These concepts are binary in the sense that they are twofold, they come in pairs. However, they co-exist in a mixture rather than a dialectic relation; they morph or fold into the other rather than respond to it. In this sense being emerges from becoming, identities from differences. The rhizome grows roots and stems as trees are sustained by forest networks. Lines join points which establish new node points where lines mesh.

What makes this cluster of twofold conceptual tools resonate is the consistent privileging of one side of each with an ontology of 'becoming'. Notice the way in which we normally tend to group these pairs with the stable term first: home and journey, identity and difference. For Deleuze all identities are produced out of differences and the privileging of stable identities is a central tenet of Western metaphysics that needs to be overturned. These twofold pairs form a large part of the conceptual toolkit in the work of Deleuze and Guattari, pairs of binary concepts defined in terms of each other where the focus is on the dynamism between them. They cannot be seen as separate but rather as overlapping and resonating together in assemblages; the striated resonates with the arborescent and hierarchical while the smooth resonates with the rhizomatic and networked (Patton 2000). One side of each pair is consistently and implicitly privileged. This priority needs to be read critically as a reversal of traditional forms of conceptual domination that see the world in terms of pre-existing unities; the goal is not to erase one side of the concept but to rethink which side comes first. In the case of smooth and striated space, these are not types of space, indeed 'the two spaces in fact only exist in mixture' (Deleuze and Guattari 1987: 474). 'Nothing is ever done with: smooth space allows itself to be striated, and striated space reimparts a smooth space … all progress is made by and in striated space, but all becoming occurs in smooth space' (Deleuze and Guattari 1987: 486). Deleuze and Guattari are clear to distinguish these concepts from binary logic or traditional dialectic analysis which they see as rooted in tree-like thinking (Deleuze and Guattari 1987: 5). The denial of any dialectic relation in these twofold pairs is in part an attempt to create a distance from older forms of critique, Hegel and Marx in particular. Yet there is an obvious dialectic component to the description of the movement from territorialization to deterritorialization and then reterritorialization. This is also the case in the earlier description of becoming at home through the establishment of a bounded centre of order and then a breaching of that boundary.

This conceptual opposition between points of stability and lines of flight, between 'wings and roots' to add another metaphor, makes it tempting to add the conceptual opposition of space versus place and to identify space with freedom and movement in contrast with the stability and rootedness of place. I think this is a serious mistake and that place is best conceived as the assembled mix. A key question here is whether place is seen as immanent or transcendent – embodied in everyday life or understood in relation to some *genius loci* or abstract ideal. The explanation of the sense of place, home or roots in relation to some transcendent order is generally related to practices of power, making territories and identities appear eternal – nowhere more apparent than in the tragic story of Palestine/Israel. The danger of such conceptions is that they operate to exclude and repress difference, as legitimation for the defence of home territory.

The concept of place has been widely misrecognized as an organic tree-like concept that organizes spatial meanings around an essentialized stem. This view of place is understandable since it meets a primary human desire for a sense of home and identity. Place can be identified with the axis of territorialization along which assemblages become stabilized. Yet the wholesale identification of place with being, stability and striation, with singular modes of rooted sedentary dwelling and stabilized identities is a narrow, self-deceptive and insular view. Place is an assemblage that stabilizes dwelling but also encompasses lines of movement and processes of becoming. The immanence of place is a field of differences within which tree-like stabilized identities are planted. Places are neither things nor figments of imagination.

The concept of assemblage operates at both micro and macro scales and it shares this independence of scale with the concept of 'place'. At the level of a room, my study is an assemblage of books, furniture, computer, printer, framed by walls, door and window; it connects me to my work, to the world (via telephone, Internet), to the neighbourhood (via window) and to the rest of the house (via stairs). It is an assemblage of spatial practices but also of meanings; more than a location or site it is also distinguished by intensity of experience. Change any of these and it would still be a place, but not the same place. As we rise in scale similar principles apply to both place and assemblage. A neighbourhood is a material assemblage of houses, shops, parks and amenities; it is a discursive assemblage of building styles, forms and names; it embodies certain intensities of interaction and events. The market place in its literal form is a collection of goods, shops, stalls and people assembled to maximize exchange. Cities are assemblages of people, networks, organizations and landmarks. Social assemblages include face-to-face conversations, networks and social hierarchies, all linked to buildings and neighbourhoods over different durations (De Landa 2006: 12).

In all of these senses places can be construed as assemblages in a continuous state of change. Such an approach to place runs counter to Heideggerian notions of place as grounded in an ontology of 'being' rather than 'becoming'. Yet Heidegger is not easily dismissed, particularly his claims about the spatiality of being – the role of place in stabilizing a fragile sense of being and identity. Some of those who adopt a Deleuzian approach to built form see the need to overturn the Heideggerian notion of a spatially rooted ontology. For Rajchman the 'grounding' of dwelling in place is a source of false naturalism and a constraint on freedom: 'we need to get away from the picture ... that the lifeworld is in the first instance a grounded world' (Rajchman 1998: 86). From this view, the gravitas and heaviness of the earth is to be overcome in a Nietzschean spirit of freedom; 'place' is a centre of orientation and identity is an 'anchor' which weighs us down. As Rajchman puts it:

> Once we give up the belief that our life-world is rooted in the ground, we may thus come to a point where ungroundedness is no longer experienced as existential anxiety and despair but as a freedom and lightness that finally allows us to move.
>
> (Rajchman 1998: 88)

There is here a privileging of movement over stasis, of 'wings' over 'roots' which is understandable, but the ideal of severing buildings from the ground on which they stand is wishful thinking that suggests architecture can become something other than shelter for human bodies. In other words this involves the denial of the materiality of the assemblage and of a grounded life on this planet. It also keeps the door open to the nonsensical dream that architecture can be autonomous and free itself from the contingencies of site, gravity, programme and environmental impact. The task is not to decide between an architecture of roots or wings but to understand that it is always both.

SENSE

In his book *The Logic of Sense*, Deleuze (1990) constructs a conception of 'sense' through analysis of the work of Lewis Carroll. For Deleuze, as for Carroll, while we operate every day on a basis of 'common sense' and 'good sense' in a taken-for-granted world, the logic of sense is infused with paradox. Sensation operates at a prereflective level, prior to cognition and meaning. The encounter with a song, painting, poem or place is experienced before analysis can turn it into a proposition. The story of Alice's adventure is a quest for the 'sense' of the world in which she slides deep into the ground, a losing of oneself in an underground world before a return to the surface where all the characters are card figures without depth. For Deleuze: 'Sense ... is an incorporeal, complex and irreducible entity, at the surface of things' (Deleuze 1990: 19–20). But sensation does not exist in things, it is an event that connects the material and expressive poles of the assemblage. The materiality and the meaning of place are two sides of a frontier which is the sense of place. Yet the quest to 'make sense' of place is an impossible task because it leads to paradox; language can name this sense but is powerless to define it: 'the attempt to make [sense] evident is a little like Carroll's Snark hunt. Perhaps ... sense is the Snark' (Deleuze 1990: 19–20).

> They sought it with thimbles, they sought it with care;
> They pursued it with forks and hope;
> They threatened its life with a railway share;
> They charmed it with smiles and soap
>
> (Carroll 1998)

The Snark is a portmanteau word which contracts two words (snake/shark) to produce a signifier without fixed meaning. Its function, however, is to connect two different series – material things (forks, thimbles and soap) with ethereal expressions (care, smiles and hope). When we try to extract the 'sense' from the assemblage in which it is lodged we neutralize it; we are left with the 'smile' without the 'cat' as it were (Deleuze 1990: 32). We say that an event 'takes place', but the event also creates place. When we experience a 'sense of place' it is a very short step to presuppose an essentialized 'place' as the foundation of the 'sense'. This is to confuse the foundation with what it founds. The concept of a 'sense of place' can become what Deleuze calls a 'despotic signifier' that seeks to stabilize meaning in service of a transcendent sense of power (Colebrook 2002: 120). For Deleuze signs are aspects of the production of desire, we should ask not what they mean but what they do and how they work. What the discourse of 'place' so often does is to close down the authentic production of place. What the discourse of 'site' and 'space' so often does is to strip place of its sense.

The idea of a sense of place as an assemblage implies much more than either the materiality of physical form or the spatial meanings that emerge from its construction and use. Places are not just locations occupying a certain extent in space but have 'intensity'. Intensity is a word we use to describe temperature, colour, activity, encounter, character or place where there is a high degree of some quality. Intensity has long been opposed in philosophy to 'extension' – the spatial extent of an area, bulk, height or volume. For instance the temperature of a body of water is intensive while the volume is extensive; to double the volume does not change the temperature (DeLanda 2006). This is an important distinction with regard to urban form because of the complex relationship between density and intensity. It is the intensity that is most strongly linked to the sense and affect of place – the intensity of sunlight; the buzz of conversation; the whiteness of the walls; the vastness of the sea; the sound of birds; the smell of coffee. Intensities are directly desired effects or qualities rather than meanings (Colebrook 2002: 43–45), however, desires become 'overcoded' as everyday experiences are reduced to signified identities as in a tourist brochure. This is what we mean when we say a place has become 'trendy' or commodified – the sense of place is seen to become a cliché, a prepackaged meaning for consumption. Thus white walls are repackaged as parts of certain place styles: the Greek islands, modern architecture and so on. This coding does not determine the sense or affect so much as it constructs place-based identities from desires.

The title of *A Thousand Plateaus* is adapted from a concept in Bateson's (2000) book *Steps to an Ecology of Mind*, where he described the ways in which dynamic cultural systems can stabilize on a plane or 'plateau' between polarities.[2] The concept of the 'plateau' is central to *A Thousand Plateaus* in the sense of a consistent focus on the spaces between levels and things, and it shares more than etymology with the concept of 'place'. Bateson argued that an 'ecology of mind' involves an understanding that the 'mind' is immanent in living systems of organism-and-environment and is embodied in matter as patterns of ideas and information (Bateson 2000: x). A plateau is a culturally constructed system of communications whereby the tendency for a system to run out of control – an arms race, crime rates, environmental degradation – is countered by a plateau or plane of stability that co-exists with constant change: 'a plateau of intensity is substituted for climax' (Bateson 2000: 113). The tendency towards escalation (termed 'schizmogenesis' by Bateson) is linked to what Jacobs (1965) called the 'self destruction of diversity': the tendency for vital urban places to attract their own demise in an orgy of over-development. What we sense as the stability of place is often a plateau of development produced by locally sustainable limits. Yet to perceive place as static is to misrecognize it as a thing rather than an assemblage of differences:

> an assemblage is first and foremost what keeps very heterogeneous elements together:
> ... both natural and artificial elements ... The problem is one of 'consistency' or
> 'coherence' ... How do things take on consistency? How do they cohere? Even among
> very different things, an intensive continuity can be found. We have borrowed the word
> 'plateau' from Bateson precisely to designate these zones of intensive continuity.
>
> (Deleuze 2007: 179)

The sense of place always involves consistency and coherence, often misrecognized as uniformity and regularity. Place intensity is a dynamic intensity where tensions are sustained and sustainable. To see place as assemblage is to incorporate principles of sustainable development into the very sense of the place.

A place-as-assemblage is always a coherent 'multiplicity' of parts, a hotchpotch with no pre-existing whole. Deleuze and Guattari (1987: 33) draw from Bergson the idea that there are two fundamental kinds of multiplicity – extensive and intensive. An extensive multiplicity is where the constituent parts are defined by their spatial extension and are unaffected by new additions. In a bag of jelly beans there may be more or fewer black ones, but no matter how many beans we add it remains a bag of jelly beans, each of which retains its different flavour. An intensive multiplicity, by contrast, is more like a soup with an overall flavour which is changed by each new ingredient. A house, neighbourhood or city is an intensive multiplicity. When different people move in, new buildings or rooms are added, the sense of the larger place changes.

DESIGN

I want to conclude this chapter with a move towards questions of research method and design practice. How are we to understand places in order to be in a better position to manage and creatively transform them? One of the more obscure concepts invented by Deleuze and Guattari is the 'abstract machine' – a 'diagram' or 'map' of the forces comprising an assemblage (Deleuze and Guattari 1987: 141). This diagram produces assemblages but is also part of them; it is a set of relations that operates as both a cause and a framework of possibilities for assembled outcomes (Patton 2000). According to Deleuze: 'the diagram or abstract machine is the map of relations between forces … that is co-extensive with the whole social field' (Deleuze 1988: 36). One example Deleuze (2007: 123) gives is Foucault's notion of the panopticon – a spatial diagram of one-way visibility wherein practices and subjectivities are produced to meet the anonymous gaze of authority. This diagram of seeing without being seen is evident in the many disciplinary technologies of the prison, factory, school, hospital and CCTV network without being determined in each particular instance. It is an abstraction because an 'abstract' set of relations are evident in all concrete examples, and it is a 'machine' because it is productive of subjectivity. I prefer to use the term diagram.

The diagram known as the 'dumb-bell' is an abstract machine of the shopping mall – two large attractors or magnets are connected by a pedestrian mall to channel pedestrian flows to produce impulse consumption (Dovey 2008: chapter 9). The diagram was assembled gradually in the mid twentieth century through a series of experimental projects. This diagram takes the existing desire for the magnet (department stores, supermarkets, cinemas) and uses it to produce desire for something else (jewellery, clothes, food, souvenirs). While the shopping mall no longer resembles the dumb-bell form, this diagram of a spatial structure producing a pedestrian flow past a retail outlet remains and has been applied to many other assemblages such as waterfronts, airports and tourist attractions.

The abstract machine can be conceived as a pattern that connects a wide range of assembled outcomes. Patterns and diagrams have a long history in architectural and urban thought from Howard's 'Garden City' to Corbusier's diagrammatic modernism, Alexander's pattern language and the spatial syntax 'genotypes' of Hiller and Hanson (1984).[3] In many cases the diagram is an image that drives design practices without ever being written down; the serviced floorplate with a view is a diagram of the corporate office that when stacked vertically becomes the corporate tower. The diagram is a 'pattern that connects' (Bateson 1979) one assemblage to another; it is immanent because it is not a transcendent ideal that produces places but an immanent diagram of the forces in similar place types.

In the context of assemblage theory, Alexander, who wrote the seminal paper 'A City is Not a Tree' (Alexander 1965), deserves some renewed attention. Long before Deleuze was popular in architecture, Alexander (1964) argued that a building is not a 'thing' and that what we call 'form' is the product of a pattern of forces. His focus was on the process whereby a set of forces leads to a formal design, on the dynamics of becoming rather than the statics of form. A key insight was to see buildings and cities as embodying patterns that could be abstracted as diagrams: 'Any pattern which, by being abstracted from a real situation, conveys the physical influence of certain demands or physical forces is a diagram' (Alexander 1964: 85). Diagrams then became the constructive components of the approach known as the 'pattern language' (Alexander *et al.* 1977; Alexander 1979). A 'pattern' for Alexander is at once a set of social, spatial, aesthetic and material vectors or forces in a given place and a diagram that resolves them. This resolution is not mathematical or mechanical but is directed towards the production of a 'quality without a name' which has much in common with the ineffable 'sense' of place. Alexander's metaphor is organic rather than machinic:

> if you want to make a living flower, you do not build it physically with tweezers, cell by cell; you grow it from a seed. If you want to design a new flower, you will design the seed and let it grow. The seeds of the environment are pattern languages.
>
> (Alexander 1977)

Alexander's work is much maligned in architectural theory because it has taken on an essentialist and messianic tone. My point here is not to endorse the quality of any particular patterns; they are a mixed bag to be sure and much of Alexander's work is essentialist. However, in some important ways this is an assemblage theory. The patterns are diagrams based in immanent experiences of place and they are not necessarily determinant in their expression. It is interesting that Alexander's work has been more influential in the design of virtual space, where network connectivity is the key driver, than in the design of physical places (Gamma *et al.* 1995).

If we are to take the notion of place-as-assemblage seriously then we need to know a lot more about how places work and how they are transformed. This is the yawning gap in so much of the research applying Deleuzian theory to built form – the actual mechanisms that operate at different scales of room, building, neighbourhood, landscape, city and nation (DeLanda 2006: 31). One of the key tasks here lies in the practice of mapping places. For Deleuze and Guattari (1987: 12–13) mapping is a creative act that they distinguish from a tracing: 'What distinguishes the map from the tracing is that it is entirely oriented toward an experimentation in contact with the real … The map has to do with performance, whereas the tracing always involves an alleged "competence".' The map is more than a simple 'tracing' of an existing form because it is infused with a desire to understand how the place might be navigated or changed. This distinction between a map and a tracing is the basis of Corner's (1999) account of mapping as a form of design agency that mediates between the facts of a particular territory and the potentials for what it might become. Maps reveal 'the various hidden forces that underlie the workings of a given place' (Corner 1999: 214). All maps are at once concrete (because they are grounded in a material state of affairs) and abstract (because they cannot show everything, they select and extract layers of data). Maps mediate between the real and the virtual, they represent and create. Corner sees the prospect of maps that are rhizomatic rather than tree-like, mapping networked connectivities rather than stable territories:

> Mapping as an extensive and rhizomatic set of field operations precipitates, unfolds and supports hidden conditions, desires and possibilities nested within a *milieu*. … Instead of designing relatively closed systems of order, rhizomatic mappings provide an infinite series of connections … *mapping*, as an open and inclusive process of disclosure and enablement, comes to replace the reduction of *planning*.
>
> (Corner 1999: 250)

The potential of such forms of mapping is considerable, but the final distinction implied here between mapping and planning is counterproductive. Consider the relations between the concepts of 'diagram', 'map', 'plan' and 'design'. A 'diagram' is an image or set of lines and points designed to show how something works, not a picture of what it looks like but an abstraction with a focus on function. A 'map' is an image with a certain congruence with an existing territory; it enables a certain cognition of the territory and action within it. A 'plan' is an image that represents a particular territory in either the past, present or future. A 'design' is a plan or sketch for a desired future – more specific than a plan and less abstract. Notice both the overlaps and differences between these terms. Diagrams and maps refer more to existing states of affairs while planning and design are more future oriented. It makes no sense to draw a sharp division between a design and a plan, any more than to oppose the design and planning professions. Design is conceived as more open, imaginative and creative than the more logical and restrictive practice of planning. Yet both are united as practices of inventing the future and they cannot be separated from mapping in this regard.

The conception of place as assemblage outlined here suggests a rethinking of the linkages between diagrams, maps, designs and plans.

Design is another term that receives little attention in Deleuzian theory except as it is subsumed into theories of art. The design of built form, however, is fundamentally linked to desires for a better future. This returns us to where we started with flows of desire as the basis of life and of all forms of assemblage. A public transport plan is based on a multiplicity of desires to get to work, to shop and to visit friends. A house design is based on desires for privacy, security, amenity and aesthetic experience. The concept of place-as-assemblage enables us to overcome simplistic divisions between design and planning, form and function, diagram and design. It enables us to develop a sophisticated approach to concepts of territory and spatial structure, and to see all places as embodying twofold concepts such as rhizome/tree, difference/identity, but also global/local and open/closed. Most importantly it enables us to encounter and understand the sense of place as an everyday experience rather than either an essentialized 'genius loci' or a myth.

Chapter 3: Silent Complicities

Bourdieu, Habitus, Field

> Architectonic spaces whose silent dictates are directly addressed to the body are
> undoubtedly among the most important components of the symbolism of power,
> precisely because of their invisibility...
>
> (Bourdieu quoted in Prigge 2008: 46)

We experience places primarily in states of distraction; we live in the world first
and look at it second. Our contemplative gaze falls upon buildings and cities
within a spatial world we have already silently imbibed and embodied. How to
reconcile this unreflexive embodiment of place in everyday life with the ways in
which our critical gaze turns place into discourse? For this task I want to use the
work of Pierre Bourdieu. The 'habitus' and the 'field' are two key concepts that
form threads through Bourdieu's sociology. The habitus is a set of embodied dispositions towards everyday social practice; divisions of space and time, of objects
and actions, of gender and status. The habitus conflates 'habit' and 'habitat' to
construct both a sense of place and the sense of one's place in a social hierarchy
(Bourdieu 1977). The habitus is taken for granted: 'The most successful ideological effects are those that have no words, and ask no more than complicitous
silence' (Bourdieu 1977: 188). While the use of the term 'ideology' now seems
dated, the role of place as a taken-for-granted construction of everyday life
remains a key to the ways power is mediated in built form. Bourdieu's later work
on 'fields' of cultural production examines overlapping fields of discourse (art,
architecture, urbanism) which are like game boards with certain forces prevailing
and resources at stake (Bourdieu 1993). The resources are forms of capital that
flow between the economic (material) and the cultural (social, symbolic). For
Bourdieu, fields of cultural production, such as architecture, are structured in a
manner which sustains the authority of those who already possess it, those with
the 'cultural capital' and the 'feel for the game' embodied in the habitus.

And attempts by the avant-garde to overturn this alliance of architecture with authority play a key role in reinvigorating the existing 'field' of privileged practices – conservatism reappears in the guise of the ever-new. While Bourdieu's critique has its limits, it offers considerable hope for rethinking theories of place and for a re-engagement of design and planning as social practices.[1]

HABITUS

The term habitus emerges from Bourdieu's early work where it frames the ways in which the everyday world of social practice is constructed and learned in early childhood (Bourdieu 1977; 1990a; 1990b). While habitus is an ancient term, Bourdieu's adapatation derives from architecture, adapted from Panofsky's (1967) 'Gothic Architecture and Scholasticism' which interprets architecture as a form of constructed knowledge (Bourdieu was the French translator). Bourdieu's (1973) account of the Berber house was the basis for the theory of the habitus. For Bourdieu, the habitus is a way of knowing the world, a set of divisions of space and time, of people and things, which structure social practice. It is at once a division of the world and a vision of the world (Bourdieu 1990b: 210). Social practice is a form of 'game' within which the habitus is learnt, not as a set of fixed categories but as a set of dispositions to act; it is a 'feel for the game' of social practice (Bourdieu 1993: 5). When we feel 'out of place' in a social situation it is often that we lack this 'feel' for how to act. The habitus is taken for granted rather than consciously conceived; a form of ideology in the sense of a socially constructed vision perceived as natural; culture seen as nature. Its importance derives largely from its thoughtlessness or *doxa* – its silence (Stevens 1998: 57).

The habitus is not cognitively understood but rather internalized and embodied. Bourdieu refers to the dialectical relationship between the body and space as a form of 'structural apprenticeship' through which we at once appropriate our world and are appropriated by it (Bourdieu 1977: 89). As Bourdieu (2000: 141) puts it: 'We learn bodily. The social order inscribes itself in bodies.' The focus on the dialectic of body and space recalls Merleau-Ponty's (1962) phenomenology where space is primarily a 'gearing' of our body to the world. Yet for Bourdieu this a more socially structured lifeworld. Bourdieu deploys the phrase 'structuring structure' to describe the ways in which the habitus shapes but is in turn shaped by social practice. The habitus is both the condition for the possibility of social practice and the site of its reproduction. There are some parallels with Giddens' structuration theory with its dialectic relations of structure to agency (Giddens 1984) and with Lefebvre's (1991) focus on the production of space in everyday life.

While the habitus is not a synonym for habitat, places are strongly implicated through the ways in which built form frames social practice: 'Social space tends to be translated, with more or less distortion, into physical space' (Bourdieu 2000: 134). The social divisions and hierarchies of the habitus (gender, class, ethnicity, age) become evident in the ways space is divided into suburbs, kitchens, playgrounds, classrooms, cafes, factories and bathrooms. And it is evident in the ways time intersects with such spatial divisions forming situations or events such as meetings, dinner parties, lectures and festivals. There are some important links here to what Hillier and Hanson (1984) term the 'social logic of space', an approach that will be adapted in some later case-study chapters.

The habitus is closely linked to the phenomenology of 'home' as both a form of unreflexive knowledge and of ontological security (Giddens 1990).

> The agent engaged in practice knows the world … without objectifying distance, takes it for granted, precisely because he is caught up in it, bound up with it; he inhabits it like a garment (*un habit*) or a familiar habitat. He feels at home in the world because the world is also in him, in the form of habitus.
>
> (Bourdieu 2000: 142–143)

This depiction of the experience of home resonates with that of Deleuze and Guattari (1987) as a familiar refrain and a sense of order, yet Bourdieu's conception stresses entrapment. His notion of habitus as a division and hierarchy between people and things also parallels notions of the segmentarity of assemblages. Yet for Bourdieu the habitus is a rigid and limiting structure, perhaps even a paradigmatic case of striated space. The habitus is a social world subject to constant change, but these are evolutionary rather than revolutionary changes (Bourdieu 2000: 161). The theory of the habitus is primarily a theory of why things do not change. While it is limited as a theory of social change, it is useful in understanding how identities are stabilized and spatial practices are reproduced through built form. It is the most crucial of concepts in understanding the deep complicities of place with power (Dovey 2008).

FIELDS OF CAPITAL

Unlike the habitus which is a 'feel for the game', the 'field' of social practice is like a game board wherein agents are positioned with certain forces available and resources at stake in any given moment (Bourdieu 1984, 1993). The 'field', however, is a field of endeavour which is not identified with physical space. For our interests here, there are overlapping fields of discourse such as art, education, housing, urbanism and architecture. The definition of the 'field' is often part of what is at stake. The field is a social space which structures strategic action for control over resources which are construed as forms of capital (Bourdieu 1991, 1993). This work extends the concept of 'capital' from economic capital to cultural, social and symbolic capital – significant forms of capital based on the economic but not simply reducible to it. There is a good deal of definitional confusion surrounding these terms in writing both by and about Bourdieu. In one of his clearest accounts Bourdieu (1986: 243) suggest three 'fundamental guises' of capital – economic, cultural and social capital. However, symbolic capital forms such a key part of his later theory that it must be considered a fourth category (Swartz 1997). I will examine each in turn.

Cultural capital is the accumulation of manners, credentials, knowledge and skill, acquired through education and upbringing (Bourdieu 1993). There are three main kinds – embodied, objectified and institutionalized (Bourdieu 1986). *Embodied* cultural capital is the component of the habitus which lends us the capacity to act in a way that shows class or manners. The confidence of bodily language and facial expression that engenders authority in social situations is central here. Such capital is subject to hereditary transmission in the sense that it is often acquired so young that it appears to be innate or natural. *Objectified* cultural capital is the kind of capital contained in things such as art objects, food, dress and buildings. It is more than the ownership of them, it is the capacity to choose and consume them that is important here. The objects can be bought but this capacity cannot. *Institutionalized* cultural capital is the kind of capital that is certified in institutionally recognized educational degrees and academic titles. University fees transform economic capital into cultural capital as an investment in socially valued knowledge.

Social capital is a resource which inheres in social relations or networks of family, friends, clubs, school, community and society. For Bourdieu social capital is based in class membership, institutionalized in the form of exclusive club membership and titles of nobility. Social capital is a collectively owned resource based on reciprocity. It differs from cultural capital by being collective rather than individual; if you leave the group you lose the capital. While Bourdieu depicts social capital primarily in terms of the power of dominant groups, the concept also has currency as a positive resource base of all community networks (Portes 1998; Putnam 1995). A sense of trust, solidarity and community are indicators of high levels of social capital while fear, alienation and isolation indicate its absence. Putnam distinguishes between two primary forms of social capital: bonding and bridging. 'Bonding' reinforces solidarity and identity as it excludes difference; it is somewhat tribal and constructs relatively closed networks. 'Bridging' establishes weaker ties and builds open networks of acquaintances. To say someone is 'well-connected' is to suggest a rich network of bridging capital that can be transformed into political power or 'cashed' as profit.

Social capital is embedded in the built environment where it is sustained and reproduced by architectural programmes as spatially structured patterns of social encounter. Buildings and neighbourhoods both ground and structure social networks, enabling and constraining the development of social capital whether in housing enclaves, shopping precincts, sporting venues, community centres or university departments. Bonding is more common in building interiors (families, clubs, etc.) and bridging more common in neighbourhoods and larger organizations.

Symbolic capital is the most problematic form of capital to define and there is considerable slippage in Bourdieu's use of it. In his early work (Bourdieu 1977) it is defined as the symbolic component of goods which demonstrate the aesthetic 'taste' of the owner. Thus it is a form of 'honour' or objectified cultural capital that accumulates in objects and individuals. In later writings 'symbolic capital' appears to break out of any definition of cultural capital as an individually held resource:

> Every kind of capital (economic, cultural, social) tends (to different degrees) to function as symbolic capital … symbolic capital is not a particular kind of capital but what every kind of capital becomes when it is misrecognized as capital … and therefore recognized as legitimate. More precisely, capital exists and acts as symbolic capital … in its relationship with a habitus predisposed to perceive it as a sign.
>
> (Bourdieu 2000: 242)

Symbolic capital circulates through the 'fields' of cultural production and aesthetic discourse where it melds into practices of 'symbolic domination' and what he calls (rather loosely in my view) 'symbolic violence'. Symbolic domination is the power to frame the field in which symbolic mastery will be determined so that the criteria of taste favour those who have already imbibed a basic disposition towards it through the habitus (Jenkins 1992). To enter a field with any success one must possess the cultural capital and the 'feel for the game' of investing it. Yet symbolic capital is not something one possesses so much as something which infuses the field, similar in some ways to the Foucaultian (1980) notion of power with its capillary actions and micropractices. In Deleuzian terms, symbolic capital is akin to the concept of coding and identified with the expressive dimension of an assemblage.

Symbolic domination involves the power to establish the legitimacy of a particular symbolic order within a given field. In such a context, according to Bourdieu, aesthetic 'taste' is 'misrecognized' – first as a universally legitimate criterion and second as an inner quality of the individual rather than a function of the discursive field. A key part of the definition of symbolic capital is that it is 'denied capital'; it is not seen as a form of capital (Swartz 1997: 43). Its potency in practices of power lies in this masking effect of aesthetic autonomy. Thus the slipperiness of the definition of symbolic capital is not coincidental. The production of symbolic capital is a kind of 'alchemy' through which social class divisions become naturalized (Bourdieu 1984: 172). The base of this alchemy in the everyday dispositions of the habitus is masked – yet if it could be easily 'unmasked' then the misrecognition would not work. Like social capital, symbolic capital infuses a field rather than simply accumulating in individuals. Unlike social capital, of which more or less may be produced, symbolic capital is a fixed resource, a zero-sum game. There is only so much distinction and prestige to be distributed. If everyone gets 'good' architecture, no one wins the symbolic capital.

For Bourdieu, all forms of capital are closely linked and partially convertible into each other. Stevens' (1998) critique of the architecture profession as seen through the lens of Bourdieu's work illustrates many of the concepts outlined here. An architect will inherit a certain disposition towards architecture through the habitus, will develop cultural capital through education and social capital through family, profession and other networks (see also Rüedi 1998).[2] This will enable the architect to play the field wherein the production of symbolic capital is the architect's key market niche.

DeLanda (2006: 63) has pointed out that Bourdieu's division of capital into economic and non-economic forms can be seen to parallel the material and expressive resources of the assemblage. There are also important links to the idea of territorial assemblages outlined in Chapter 2. What is generally known as a 'village' is a place-as-assemblage with high levels of social capital. Everyone knows everyone and information spreads quickly through local networks that are richly interconnected but remain relatively insular. Such tightly knit territories provide a strongly stabilized identity often with a distinct sense of place. Such places are often poor in economic, cultural and symbolic capital; in times of crisis social capital is their primary resource. The 'village' can be contrasted with urban assemblages that are relatively open, characterized by weak links, relative anonymity and high capacity for identity formation (De Landa 2006: 34–35). Urban assemblages are richer in symbolic and cultural capital than in social capital. Suburbs operate in the middle ground without the richness of either village or urban networks. Gated communities and new urbanist suburbs are often an attempt to recapture the ideals of village life in an urban setting.

DISTINCTION

So how is symbolic capital produced and distributed in the field of architecture and what is the role of cultural producers in this field? Bourdieu's (1984) book *Distinction* is an oblique attack on the primary canon of aesthetic philosophy, Kant's *Critique of Judgement* (Kant 1974, 1979). For Kant, aesthetic value is transcendent and universal. Art is not that which simply gives pleasure or serves any personal interests – aesthetic experience transcends human interest to a higher truth which entails a certain 'disinterest' in merely human affairs. Within such a conception the aesthetics of architecture must transcend function and human interest. For Bourdieu the ideal of aesthetic experience identified as universal truth is a paradigm case of ideology – the social misperceived as natural; a conflation of 'taste' with 'truth'. He wants to expose the Kantian view as based in class domination. 'A work of art has meaning and interest', he argues, 'only for someone who possesses the cultural competence ... The "eye" is a product of history reproduced by education' (Bourdieu 1984: 2–3).

For Bourdieu, a primary social function of art is to divide its audience into those who do and don't understand and appreciate it. Aesthetic judgements which appear to mark distinctions between things turn out to mark distinctions between people (Featherstone 1991: 18). The struggle to establish and reproduce status is often based in a series of conceptual oppositions – difficult vs. easy, unique vs. common, original vs. reproduction and form vs. function – wherein the first term is implicitly privileged over the latter. Symbolic capital in a given field is established through difficulty to understand and scarcity. Legitimate taste is characterized by a privileging of form over function – a contemplative distance that only some people can afford. For Bourdieu (1984: 469) these are structures of domination wherein distinctions between people, based in cultural capital, are made to appear as pure aesthetic judgements. Interest is seen as disinterest.

The traditional role of the avant-garde is to overturn codes of aesthetic taste. To place a urinal on display as sculpture (as Duchamp did), or adapt a chain link fence as architecture (as Gehry did), is to invert the schemas of unique/common, original/reproduction and form/function. One of Bourdieu's key arguments is that such inversions can only achieve success within the field as already constituted. Thus the urinal becomes 'unique' when framed for formal contemplation, the chain link becomes 'difficult' as architecture. Within such a discursive field the scorn which falls on those who 'fail' to understand reinforces the social distinction.

For Bourdieu the avant-garde fulfil a key role of keeping the images within a field from becoming stale; they change and enliven the field without disturbing its foundations. In architecture this requires a separation of form from function and a reduction of architecture to text. Popular, vulgar and common imagery can be revalued, the order of social privilege is upturned but only on paper, framed for contemplation and consumption (Bourdieu 2000: 35). The history of 'deconstructive' architecture is a good example. Designs based on Derridean philosophy which appear to be under collapse or erasure, aesthetic attempts to defy the alliance of architecture with authority and social order, were very swiftly appropriated into the architectural canon with considerable symbolic capital. Architects as diverse (and talented) as Eisenman and Gehry graduated to a corporate market and the clashing forms of early deconstruction lost their symbolic capital to be replaced by the fluid and folded Deleuzian images of the new avant-garde (Jencks 1988). A movement known as 'folding' emerged in architectural discourse in the early 1990s (Lynn 1993) together with a new jargon of 'smooth space', 'rhizome' and 'deterritorialization'. Yet much of this was a thin understanding of the concepts coupled to a strong imperative to produce new 'folded' imagery for the market. The cycle from innovation to banal repetition and aesthetic exhaustion was relatively short while the architectural potential of the concept of folding was hardly explored. By the time serious misunderstandings become evident the field has moved on to another French philosopher and the cycle repeats. This is a cycle wherein things do not change but only appear to change; as Benjamin puts it, the 'ever-the-same' returns in the guise of the 'ever-new' (Gilloch 1996: 14).

The purpose of these examples is not to denigrate any particular social theorists or their architectural followers; the point is that any imagery produced in resistance to dominant aesthetic codes can be framed, emptied of subversive power and appropriated. Those who deploy the relative autonomy of aesthetic discourse as a form of resistance to privileged codes of domination must recognize that the field is structured to appropriate semantic inversions or radical images and to use them to reinforce social distinction (Bourdieu 1984: 254).

Bourdieu does not, to my mind, refute Kantian aesthetics so much as he shows its complicity with the production of symbolic capital. The relative autonomy of the avant-garde, its symbolic opposition to the mainstream, is structurally necessary to its role as the primary source of new symbolic capital. Once the market embraces the product, the architect's reputation as avant-garde is in doubt and a gap re-emerges in the 'meaning market'. The apparent autonomy of the avant-garde is geared to its structural role in keeping the field supplied with a stream of new images. While the avant-garde have the key role of overturning arbitrary aesthetic codes, finding or forging art out of that which had been considered artless, they can do this only within the field as already constituted.

ARCHITECTURE AND URBANISM

From Bourdieu's perspective, aesthetic producers such as architects and urban designers seem inextricably enmeshed in practices of symbolic domination. Any design that catches the imagination is available for appropriation as symbolic capital. What then is the scope for engagement with social change – imagining and building a better world? I suggest there are two key questions that are not answered by Bourdieu. The first is about the relative autonomy of the avant-garde – does the 'shock value' of the avant-garde not have a certain surplus value beyond that which is appropriated (and cashed) as symbolic capital? Is there not a residual effect of opening cracks and breaches in the symbolic order of the kind that Delueze and Guattari (1987), de Certeau (1984) and others understand as opportunities for new forms of practice? How does one account for social change and for the role of artists in the initiation of new ways of seeing? The second question is about the universality of aesthetic judgement. Bourdieu's work appears to rule out any kind of universal aesthetic but is less than convincing. To show that taste is socially produced and implicated in symbolic domination is one thing, to show that this exhausts the aesthetics of place is another.

I suggest that the potential of Bourdieu's work for the theory and practice of placemaking lies in an acceptance and articulation of the deep complicity of architecture with social order – the complicity without the silence, a noisy complicity. The practice of imagining and building a better world will always be political. There is no zone of neutrality in which to practice and a primary imperative is to strip the design professions of the illusion of autonomy. Design is the practice of 'framing' the habitat of everyday life, both literally and discursively. The events of everyday life 'take place' within the clusters of rooms, buildings, streets and cities we inhabit. Spatial practices are both enabled and constrained by streets, walls and doorways, the forms of which also construct and frame narratives and meanings. Architecture is mostly cast as necessary yet neutral to the life within, our gaze towards place is oblique. Yet this supposed neutrality of place is its primary power; the more that practices of power are embedded in place the less questionable they become and the more effectively they can work. This is the 'complicitous silence' of place (Dovey 2008: 2).

Buildings necessarily both constrain and enable certain kinds of life and experience – they are inherently coercive in that they enforce limits to action and enable social practice to 'take place'. The control over access to the tutorial room or the bedroom enables freedom of debate or of sexual behaviour, which an open plan would constrain. Designers who believe they are engaged in an architecture of liberation by refusing to segment space or a random segmentation may be engaged in a different form of coercion – an 'enforced' subjection to uncontrolled encounter and disciplinary gaze. The segmentation of space enables and constrains the production of social capital – the resources made available by participation in socio-spatial networks. Enclaves, security zones and boundary-control techniques often generate privileged forms of social capital. The task of design is an inherently social practice of negotiating socio-spatial structures, space allocations, boundaries and formal expressions of identity. If social responsibilities were taken more seriously by the profession then it would gain legitimacy for the production of both symbolic and social capital. Architects inevitably manipulate modes of spatial encounter – the issue is not whether but how they do so.

Architects also necessarily shape a representational world wherein certain forms of identity and place are stabilized and authorized through built form. Architecture engages in imaginative play with our dreams of status, sexuality, security and immortality; our fears of violence, death and difference. While we may articulate theories of fluidity, transparency, virtuality and ephemerality, architecture has great inertia – it inevitably 'fixes' a great deal of economic capital into built form. As Hollier (1989: ix) puts it, architecture is 'society's superego' in the sense that it enforces a social order. Again the issue is not 'whether' but 'how' it does so. The complicities of architecture with social order are to be understood, recognized, theorized, critiqued and debated. But the attempt to avoid such complicity is often fraught with new forms of deception.

Certain directions for research and criticism are suggested by the work of Bourdieu, particularly in terms of an analysis of the spatial structures of the habitus. Bourdieu's work also suggests analysis of the fields of practice and discourse in which transformations of built form are enmeshed. The task is to interpret and articulate the various interests at stake, particularly those which are hidden within the 'disinterest' of aesthetic discourse (Bourdieu 1991: 16). Such research must include discursive analysis of the primary circuits of symbolic capital within the field – architecture magazines and monographs, where the dominant architectural narratives are constructed and sustained. A primary task is to deconstruct the way photographs, drawings and text excise buildings from their habitus and repackage them for the fields of professional discourse. These forms of discourse construct a virtual habitus of desire, the illusion of an artful life of freedom where the traces of everyday life and human labour have been erased (Dovey 2000a).

The field of architecture with its focus on the struggle for symbolic capital between a shifting hierarchy of professional stars has a tendency to reduce academic debate to the issue of how the available symbolic capital is to be distributed – critique becomes reduced to booing and cheerleading. Architectural monographs are often funded by architects who exercise editorial control over their own critique through tame academic 'authors'. Photographic images are often supplied and controlled by the architect, stripped of the traces of everyday life except when used to signify forms of social capital. These books and magazines with their prices discounted by subsidy and their ideas filtered to match the ideology of aesthetic autonomy are crucial to the production of symbolic capital within the field of architecture. And this field becomes increasingly oriented to the pursuit of symbolic capital and disconnected from the lifeworld of everyday experience. Such symbolic capital circulates across coffee tables within privileged social settings connecting the field of architecture to the dominant social classes that are its primary market (Zukin 1991: 47). I shall return to some of these issues in Chapter 4.

The values of the field also permeate architectural education with an increasing specialization in the production of symbolic capital. Why is is that so many architects follow the footsteps of their parents into the profession (Stevens 1998; Reüdi 1998)? What values saturate design juries and which of our students have already imbibed those values? Why is it so difficult to generate rigorous engagement with social and environmental issues in architecture? Students are urged to produce socially and environmentally responsive work, but little of the symbolic capital within the field is distributed on those criteria unless they produce new imagery (Owen and Dovey 2007). To what extent do architecture schools hire and promote on the basis of social and cultural capital to produce graduates with more of the same to invest in the production of symbolic capital?

The early history of modernity in architecture can be read as a heroic but failed attempt to engage architecture as a social practice – a radical attempt to reinvent the habitus in both formal and functional terms. There is not scope here to pursue this history but it was based upon simplistic notions of 'function', easily reduced to imagery and co-opted to the reproduction of privilege. Chapter 7 will explore some more recents attempts in the work of Rem Koolhaas. Social questions in architecture appeared again and again during the twentieth century yet were either resisted or co-opted into new forms of social control. The 1960s unleashed a round of promise for a more socially responsive design through research in human-environment studies (Altman 1975; Rapoport 1982). While such research continues it is increasingly marginalized within architecture schools and is often more useful for the questions it begs than those it answers. If buildings are shaped to match human needs, interests or desires, then whose interests are to prevail and how have they been constructed? Architecture will not progress by getting better and better at the spatial reproduction of the habitus. The reduction of architecture to any kind of programme can begin to approach social engineering. Yet the cleavage between function and form serves ideological purposes. Architecture has found a role for itself whereby the definition of the field is largely reduced to the production of imagery while control over programming is ceded to the commissioning client (Markus 1993). The illusion of 'changing the world' is maintained through the production of ever-new imagery while the reproduction of social practice continues unchallenged.

Bourdieu's work punctures this illusion and suggests that designers who seek a retreat from codes of aesthetic domination in radical forms of representation are engaged in a misrecognition of the field. Architecture is the least autonomous of the arts and even its most radical products operate to supply new images for appropriation. The only way through this nexus seems to be a re-engagement with social practice. And this will require a broad and deep understanding of both the field and the habitus of architecture.

Architecture has long lived with the tensions of being both an art and a profession – it is the most social of arts and the most aesthetic of professions. As an art it carries the obligation to imagine a future world; as a profession it carries the obligation to practice in the public interest. The idea of the 'public interest' irritates many architects with its implications of participation, populism and comfortable consensus. Yet many of the same architects conveniently forget that architecture has always served the interests of those who commission it – participation is a name we use for power when it is distributed evenly. Yet engagement with questions of the public interest need not lead to comfortable consensus at all. Real communities are shot through with differences of identity, ethnicity, age, class and gender. A socially engaged architecture entails the deconstructive and reconstructive tasks of exposing and giving voice to real public interests; unpacking and restructuring the habitus. Such a programmatic deconstruction would entail a systematic engagement with the ways in which the lifeworld has been sliced, its functions categorized, coded, juxtaposed and omitted. The key role of architects is to join design imagination to the public interest; it is to catch the public imagination with visions of a better world. The task, albeit in a small way, is to 'change the world'. It is to keep alive the liberating spirit of design without the illusion of autonomy. We cannot erase the complicity of architecture but we can render it less silent.

Chapter 4: Limits of Critical Architecture

'I Mean to be Critical, But...'

When someone begins a statement: 'I don't mean to be critical but...', then we are forewarned that they do mean to be critical, and they will. In the practice of architecture the reverse is often the case. Architecture that is meant to be critical becomes incorporated into, and complicit with, a prevailing economic, political and social order: the ever-the-same returns in the guise of the 'critical'. In this chapter I will suggest that critical architectural practices can be seen to operate along two semi-separate dimensions: the 'formal' construction of meaning and the 'spatial' mediation of everyday life. The conceptual oppositions buried here (form/function, representation/action), and the separations between them, are clues to understanding the ways a supposedly 'critical' architecture is neutralized. The illusion of a critical architecture becomes compatible with a specialization in the production of both symbolic and social capital. The chapter will also examine the space for critical thinking in architectural magazines, coffee-table monographs and architecture schools. These fields of architectural discourse have become too settled and safe; we have become comfortable with a condition of constant formal change coupled with social stasis. I don't mean to be critical but I want to suggest that a critical architecture may be one that unsettles the architectural field; and one of the tasks of architectural critique may be to expose what might be called its 'critical complicity'.

CRITICALITY

The ways in which a dominant order appropriates, assimilates, neutralizes and marginalizes its critics have been well-explored by social and architectural theorists operating within a critical theory framework, particularly that of Benjamin (1978), Adorno (1974), Jameson (1984) and Tafuri (1976). A good account can be found in Heynen (1999). The 'critical architecture' project was originally conceived and pursued in the United States by critics and architects such as Hays and Eisenman; the 1984 paper by Hays (1984) entitled 'Critical Architecture' has been seen as seminal and a brief critique of it will serve as an introduction to the issues I want to raise. Hays (1984) defined critical architecture as 'resistant to the self-confirming, conciliatory operations of a dominant culture'. He sketched two extreme positions – the compliant reproduction of dominant values on the one hand and formalist autonomy on the other. He identified 'critical' architectural practice with a zone of operations between these poles. This early formulation of a 'critical architecture', however, then focused firmly on form to the exclusion of social meaning; it embodied the promise that an architecture of formal autonomy could resist the dominant order through its very own order of materials, surfaces and forms. 'Critical architecture' was thus confined to the formalist end of the formal/social spectrum where social engagement was conflated with complicity. He used the autonomous modernism of Mies van der Rohe as an example. In one sense this was an alarming case of theory proceeding without history: when he was head of the Bauhaus in the early 1930s Mies depoliticized the school, publicly declared support for Hitler and of one of his designs he wrote: 'This clear and striking language corresponds to the essence of German work ... This hall of honor ... serves to accommodate the national emblems and the representations of the Reich' (Hochman 1989: 226). Mies found more compliant clients in the United States which is also where the project of a 'critical architecture' took off under the rubric of 'deconstruction' in the 1980s and 1990s. In another sense this was also a response to the pessimism of Italian historian Tafuri (1976) who had portrayed an architecture of social engagement as hopeless and deluded. The modernist project for a socially critical architecture was redirected by Hays and others into autonomous formal pursuits (Heynen 2007).

By the end of the century this project seemed to have largely run its course to be challenged in turn by the 'post-critical' (Somol and Whiting 2002; Baird 2004). There is not scope here to cover this ground in detail and I will presume some understanding of it as I explore a little of the social and institutional context of how and why the critical imperative in architecture is so systematically thwarted. I also want to bring in Bourdieu's work on discursive 'fields' of cultural production which shows how aesthetic practices camouflage practices of power, how images are appropriated as symbolic capital, and how aesthetic production reproduces social distinction. While there are some parallels between Tafuri and Bourdieu (particularly on the economic role of the avant-garde), Bourdieu's work is widely ignored by most within the 'critical architecture' project. I suggest this is because it unsettles the social 'field' of architectural practice rather than the formal debates within it.

PRACTICE

I will first explore the question of a critical architecture practice, moving to the field of architectural criticism. I take a critical architecture practice to mean one that engages broadly with the ways in which architecture is enmeshed in practices of power. It does not necessarily mean an architecture steeped in critical social theory nor one that makes critical statements. Indeed, as my title suggests, the intention to criticize may be the first step to complicity. A definition of a critical architectural practice also depends on how the field of architecture is defined. Are all buildings architecture or (as Pevsner would have it) just those produced by an elite? And is architecture limited to the imagination and construction of buildings or does it apply to broader practices of spatial imagination and graphic design?

At risk of oversimplifying I think it useful to conceive of the social critique of architecture operating along two closely related yet distinguishable dimensions of representations and spatial practices. The first of these has primarily to do with the ways in which built form constructs meanings through signs and symbols; architecture as text. Largely stemming from the discursive/deconstructive turn in social theory, the key focus here is on the manner in which identities and subjects are produced and reproduced through architecture. Within this framework a critical architecture often transgresses the codes through which gendered, ethnic, class and other identities are reproduced. A critical architecture may seek to unsettle or disorient its subjects, to transgress the grounded comfort zone of fixed identities and meanings while engaging with new identity formations. However, one thing we have learned from the deconstructive move is that destabilized meanings may be complicit with new forms of domination. A critical architect will be critical of the thoughtless reproduction of identities and will accept the responsibility of the inevitable production of identities – nations, cities, corporations, communities, families and selves – through architecture. The question is not whether architecture constructs identities and stabilizes meanings, but how and in whose interests.

The second dimension involves the ways in which architecture frames spatial practices, actions and events through its spatial programmes. A critical architecture in this regard may pay attention to the structure of social space; the use of boundaries to mediate social encounter; to the standardized spatial fields and types (Hillier and Hanson 1984). The focus again is often on issues of identity and subjectivity as mediated by permeability and segregation, by transparency and opacity, and by the desire lines and rhythms of everyday action. The Foucaultian and Lefebvrian foci on the micropractices of power in everyday life are crucial here: the importance of the spatially structured social gaze in the production of normalized subjects; and the equal importance of transgressive spatial practice (Lefebvre 1996; Foucault 1979). A critical architecture in this regard will engage creatively with the building programme and will resist the mindless reproduction of socio-spatial practices. It will also resist the idea that because power is invested in programmed boundary control, liberation is somehow found in open plans or fractured geometries. Architecture always mediates spatial practices in a semi-coercive manner, it enables and constrains; the question is not whether but how it does so and in whose interests.

These two dimensions are always connected in constructed buildings which simultaneously construct meanings and mediate spatial flows. Architecture is a multiple 'framing' wherein representations are framed by spatial structures that are in turn infused with narrative interpretations. The path into and through a building mediates the encounter with meaning, and meaning in turn is partly produced by the mode of encounter. Represented meanings and spatial practices produce each other through architecture. While representations and spatial practices are integrated in the field of everyday life, they are seriously divided in architectural practice and criticism where avant-garde form-makers and spatial analysts generally operate in quite separate fields. It is the reduction of architecture to representation alone and its separation from everyday life that has facilitated the appropriation and neutralization of 'critical' architecture.

The imperative to integrate meaning and use comes in part from the degree to which meanings are constructed in use – a view with roots in both Heidegger and Wittgenstein. Heidegger distinguishes between an active engagement with the world (*zuhandenheit*) and the more distanced contemplation of it (*vorhandenheit*) (Heidegger 1962). While the meaning of works of fine art is based in contemplation, those of architecture are based in everyday life – of which contemplation is but one part. The point here, however, is not to reduce meaning to action but to integrate the two; in Heidegger's famous phrase, language is the 'house of Being'. For Wittgenstein, language is a 'game' with meanings of words constructed through the uses to which they are put; to paraphrase him: 'let the use of [buildings] teach you their meaning' (Wittgenstein 1967: 220). Again, this is not to suggest that meaning can be reduced to function, but rather that some primary meanings of architecture stem from what and who it is 'for'. A critical architecture will not separate meaning from action; it may be useful to ask the Deleuzian question – not what architecture 'means' but what it 'does' (Colebrook 2002: xxxviii). What are the effects of particular semantic and spatial framings, what flows of desire are produced? Such effects may have little to do with the architect's conscious intentions; architecture is a social art that, as Benjamin (1968: 232) puts it, 'is consummated by a collectivity in a state of distraction'. This oblique contingency of the encounter with architecture, its 'taken for granted' framing of our collective lives, is a key to its potency. Architecture is steeped in habit, it is a production of habitat and of the *habitus* – the social structures of everyday life and the sense of one's place within it. Bourdieu's work is useful to this issue in part because he links the habitus to the discursive *field*; the socially structured practices of everyday life to the production of symbolic capital within institutionally structured fields of power (as discussed in Chapter 3).

I want to step sideways now to illustrate this a little and to look at architecture as a field of power. Peter Eisenman's early buildings, for their time, seemed to many to be paradigmatic of a 'critical' architectural practice. Many of the reassuring certainties of dwelling, tectonics, function and identity were relentlessly transgressed as he inspired a generation of younger architects with the hope for an architecture that could resist and deconstruct a dominant order. Small matter if the architecture was dysfunctional, interrupting prevailing spatial practices was a key point. But clients pay the bills. In practice the project of criticality was only enabled by the deep separation of form from function that enables critical discourse to co-exist with social reproduction. In a 2004 interview, Eisenman was quoted as follows:

> most of my clients are Republicans, most of them are right-leaning…. And I have the
> most rapport with right-leaning political views, because first of all, liberal views have
> never built anything of any value, because they can't get their act together.
>
> (Eisenman 2004)

While there is no suggestion here that Eisenman was necessarily endorsing the Republican Bush administration, his identification of architectural value with this dominant and violent global regime gives pause for thought about how a 'critical architecture' has been conceived. Is this the old story of the critical 'young turk' turning conservative as he reaps the benefits of success, following the oldest professional imperative of doing what it takes to get built? Or is it more of a desperate attempt to regain the limelight by reframing the field of cultural production? I tend towards the latter view. Eisenman's persona, his architecture and his career have been largely produced by the 'fields' of architectural discourse and practice; he has played this field successfully and in a manner that has never threatened broader processes of social reproduction. This is not a new argument, it was most clearly, if rather simply, put by Ghirardo in 1994 when she argued that Eisenman's work creates an illusion of a critical architecture, sustained by staying one step ahead of the audience's capacity to critique it (Ghirardo 1994).[1] I don't mean to imply that his work is not a sophisticated application of some kinds of critical social theory, particularly Adorno and Derrida. My point is to suggest that the illusion of a 'critical' architecture can be constructed by containing it within formalist critique. Consider another quotation from the same interview:

> I believe that art and life are two different discourses, and how I want to live is different
> from how I want to practice architecture. I love living in an old New England house; my
> in-laws have a small sea-side house in Connecticut. I had this 1740s farmhouse …
> where I used to live. What I do not want to do is to recreate a 1740s farmhouse; I want
> the original thing, with the original boards, because you can't get those kinds of wide
> boards any more, the kind of nails that were made.
>
> (Eisenman 2004)

Here we find the distinction between representations and practices that I outlined earlier. Everyday life is first reduced to a discourse and then set aside as separate from architecture as art. But there is also another distinction here that Bourdieu would understand, the social capital available to those with the right in-laws and access to seaside houses; the symbolic capital and 'aura' of the rare and authentic original.

Eisenman has become an easy target but this issue is not about individuals, it is about fields of power. Daniel Libeskind's 'freedom tower' on the World Trade Center site illustrates this is in a different way. This is a commission which Libeskind is well-qualified to carry out in a sophisticated and critical manner. Instead we found him personifying the freedom-seeking immigrant, wearing the stars and stripes, affirming the dominant ideology of the United States as a bastion of freedom and democracy (Goldberger 2004). Perhaps this repetition of the party line, with its simplistic reduction of the 9/11 attack as an assault on 'freedom', is the price to be paid by the architects of the new world order, but it can scarcely be called 'critical'. There is a sense that architecture is permitted to be critical at certain moments and in certain places where that criticality helps to both heal social division and legitimate the social order. Libeskind's Holocaust Museum in Berlin and Maya Lin's Vietnam Veteran's Memorial in Washington each stand as seminal contributions to a critical architecture of this kind; to experience these places is to understand the notion that 'to criticize is to call into crisis' (Barthes 1982: 379). Yet there is also the syndrome that in a real crisis architecture returns to its stabilizing role of overcoming crisis.[2]

For many critics the work of Rem Koolhaas comes closest to a critical architectural practice. Pimlot (2007: 312) argues that:

> For the majority of the architectural *avante-garde* ... there is only a formal dimension to their work: even politics for the majority of the *avante-garde* is reduced to a formal or an aesthetic issue ... Koolhaas' distance from the *avante-garde* is established by his apparent engagement in reality and political issues; his critical rather than projective practice.

Koolhaas engages critically with both dimensions sketched earlier – formal image and spatial practice. Much of his programmatic innovation can be construed as an attempt to import urban models of spatial practice and random social encounter into the interiors of buildings.

Koolhaas understands and accepts that architecture cannot be an autonomous practice and seeks a new path for modern architecture within this understanding. In a critique of one of his unbuilt projects Heynen (1999: 222) argues that: 'In the intertwining of complicity with the system and opposition to the levelling tendencies inherent in it, the project of rewriting modernity is given form.' Yet it is in realized buildings that success or failure in this engagement will become apparent; my exploration of these issues in Chapter 7 suggests mixed results.[3] Ironically, many of his achievements come from the degree to which he recognizes the limits to autonomy and criticality. Instead of encoding critical comment or opposing the effects of power, his work at times accentuates such effects rendering architecture more socially transparent. One could go on deconstructing the deconstructionists, however, my point is not to target individuals who are often producing good work in the more traditional sense of the art and craft of architecture. It is rather to suggest that all this work exists, and all these agents operate, within a field that is structured in a manner that enables a seemingly 'critical' architectural practice to thrive while at the same time reproducing the very social structures, identities and practices that it purports to challenge.

It is interesting in the case of the 9/11 project to consider the proposal by Sorkin which was to turn the site of destruction into a memorial and open space while distributing the required floorspace across a series of sites in Lower Manhattan, where urban regeneration would be of more social and economic value (Goldberger 2004; Sorkin and Zukin 2004). This idea, where void rather than solid signifies memory and social value is married to economic value, was never seriously considered because it directly contradicted the ideological agenda in both symbolic and programmatic terms. The debate was framed around the merits of the various forms proposed for replacing massive volumes of office space and constructing a monument. Once framed in this manner the field is ripe for critique about which forms are more 'critical'. In his critique of the prospects for a critical architecture Baird comments that:

> despite widespread admiration for his critical writings, the substantive theoretical form of Sorkin's 'resistance' is not seen to be centrally embedded in his own design production, as Mies's has been seen to be by Tafuri, or Eisenman's has been seen to be by Hays.

(Baird 2004: 18)

While Sorkin's work is formally engaging it is not easily reduced to formalist critique and does not fit the prevailing definition of the field of 'critical architecture'. The appropriation by the corporate market of the autonomous form-making of both Mies and Eisenman is not accidental; autonomous formalism is a required condition for the production and renewal of symbolic capital in that field.

This narrow definition of the field is the 'straw-man' deployed by Speaks in his much-discussed polemic entitled 'After Theory', where he largely conflates theory with critical theory, and declares it finished: 'I would argue that theory is not just irrelevant but was and continues to be an impediment to the development of a culture of innovation in architecture ... unremitting critique chasing its own tail, without purpose or end' (Speaks 2005: 74). This notion of the end of 'theory' is mere polemic since what replaces it in this account is a different theory about the opportunities for formal innovation opened up by new technologies and information systems. Yet it does ring true that the trajectory of criticality based on Tafuri's pessimism and Adorno's negative dialectics has largely exhausted its formalist possibilities. Baird has interpreted this turn to what he terms the 'post-critical' in terms of the need for a generation of Eisenman's protégés to move out from under his shadow. Yet from the broader viewpoint of the field of cultural production I would suggest that this is a significant move in clearing the field of architecture (both theory and practice) for new symbolic capital; it is a correction in a 'meaning market' which has become saturated by images of criticality. The deeper problem with Speaks' critique of criticality is that it suggests an abandonment of critical social theory while largely preserving the 'field' of critique – a recipe, as Benjamin might put it, for 'more of the same' returning as the 'ever-new' (Gilloch 1996: 108).

These current debates in some ways echo those from long ago between Adorno and Benjamin on aesthetic and social theory.[4] For Adorno the only hope for art was a retreat into a critical, autonomous and esoteric formalism – an art that resists appropriation by politics, markets and dominant classes. Benjamin, in contrast, saw liberating possibilities for collective aesthetic practices, modes of production and reception. For Adorno criticality is embodied in, and protected by, the 'difficulty' of the work; Benjamin seeks a broader audience and is keen to dispense with the aura of the individual genius. A good deal of what has passed for 'critical architecture' in the Eisenman/Hays trajectory can be seen in the Adorno tradition which Eagleton (1990: 362) describes as 'offering up the sickness as cure'. There is a certain subversive potential or shock value in such an approach and the deconstructive movement in architecture has exploited and largely exhausted it. The limits of such an approach lie in its autonomous formalism. The framing of everyday life and the representation of identities within it are reduced to text; critical architecture is reduced to architectural criticism. In their pursuit of 'criticality' such buildings can become signifiers of the idea that nothing can be done beyond the production of architecture as criticism. Beyond the stifling of formal innovation, the deeper problem lies in the stifling of programmatic innovation and therefore of social engagement.

CRITIQUE

A lot of what passes for critical practice can be understood by looking at the context of its critical reception within the field of architectural critique. Yet this field is scarcely an 'ideal speech situation' in Habermasian terms, with all the difficulties of that concept (Habermas 1984). The field is dominated by the major professional magazines where the profusion of glossy colour photographs is largely funded by the advertising of construction materials and products. While these magazines meet a market in the architectural community and genuine debate occasionally breaks out, there is too much at stake for much more than a generally positive promotional critique. Such architectural critique is framed by the imperatives of the promotion of products to the profession that effectively consumes them. Architects occupy a key node point in the flows of capital for urban development; while they have little power over the volumes of capital, they have enormous discretion over choice of materials and products. It is this market that largely frames and limits the critical discourses of architecture. In some ways it is the symbolic capital circulating through the images of new buildings that is converted here into economic capital for the advertisers. Photographs and drawings are the most potent parts of this discourse since they circulate the symbolic capital; they are in turn conceived, cropped, framed and digitally altered to construct a promotional story – generally stripped of everyday life unless a choreographed version is useful to the narrative.

My experience in trying to write against the grain within this field shows some of the ways in which the field operates. In 1996 I became interested in the way a house designed by Glenn Murcutt for an Aboriginal client was being funded by a major steel corporation. It was widely advertised in journals and through a television film as a steel-based solution for both Aboriginal housing and cultural reconciliation (Hyatt 1993, 1994). At the same time, the same company were fighting a compensation claim from another indigenous community over the environmental destruction of an entire village due to mining operations.[5] My critique was published in the professional magazine *Architecture Australia*, although the editor changed the title and added some contentious illustrations (Dovey 1996). A certain outrage followed in the letters column and I was not asked to contribute to the journal for over a decade. A subsequent site visit suggested to me that this was a very fine building but it was not the one portrayed in the international magazines where a single set of authorized photographs were used to construct a particular narrative. A further paper (Dovey 2000a) in a refereed journal analysed the ways that photographs were controlled, cropped and digitally altered to edit out the context of social disadvantage on the one hand, yet posed to simulate fictional forms of Aboriginal life. As architectural critique retreats, or is banished, to the refereed journal it becomes insulated from the field of practice.

Then there are the coffee-table books and monographs. A number of years ago I was asked to review a book on the architecture of Harry Seidler, the innovative modernist who is famous in Australia for taking his critics to court. He once unsuccessfully sued a newspaper cartoonist who mocked his architecture. The book I was asked to review was a coffee-table hardback with some fine photography and an introduction by Kenneth Frampton (Drew 1992). Often funded by architects and developers, coffee-table publishing operates as advertising for architects, developers and projects. It can come perilously close to architects writing their own history; certainly one does not expect to find critical comment (even from a critical regionalist). When I was asked to review the book I also received a call from Seidler who very politely asked whether I felt qualified to review his work and what kind of review did I think the book might receive. I didn't have an answer but I got the message and passed it on to the journal editors who decided they could not afford to review the book.

For about a decade I critiqued the development of Melbourne Docklands, a large stretch of post-industrial public land adjacent to the central city (Dovey 2005). When a large coffee-table book was commissioned to promote the development I was asked to write an account of its integration with the city. When it became apparent that I saw it as un-integrated the offer was withdrawn; the 'book' is a state-funded advertising brochure. This problem of distorted communication and contained critique extends to newspapers. During the early design phase of Melbourne Docklands, local newspapers were keen to debate the merits of different options in a relatively open manner; public debate sells newspapers. Yet once the projects were under way and the newspaper was full of advertising for the new housing, the space for critical debate largely dried up. Critical debate cuts across the advertising (Dovey 2005: chapter 10).

All these forms of discourse – magazines, monographs and newspapers – are enmeshed in a dialectic movement between conflicting desires for credibility and advertising revenue. In many architectural magazines, advertising constitutes about 40 per cent of the content; with project reviews increasingly linked to product advertisements on the same page there is a blurring between culture and commerce. As the advertising content goes up, however, credibility goes down. Coffee-table monographs cannot carry advertising because they would lose credibility as conduits of cultural and symbolic capital; in other words their advertising value is linked to their misrecognition as genuine academic books. Academics who write under conditions of 'controlled critique' weaken the credibility of research in architecture and therefore the position of architecture within the universities.

EDUCATION

One of the places we look to for a field of communication open to critical debate, undistorted by the imperatives of the market and the advertising of professional identity, is in the universities. Such institutions have the capacity to frame and fund critical architectural debate with a high level of credibility. Some magazines such as *Harvard Design Magazine* and *AA Files* avoid advertising and are instead funded by schools of architecture; yet the imperative to promote the programmes, staff and students of the school often overwhelms critical discourse. Architecture schools are increasingly competitive and corporate, drawn into the market as producers of symbolic capital. The production of symbolic capital is the primary market niche of the architecture profession. The professional ideal of architecture as a social practice is displaced by a reification of architectural imagery, exacerbated by the increasing global competition between schools and the image-driven advertising this produces.

While the production of imagery will always be crucial to the practice of architecture, the issue of a critical architecture hinges on the rigour of critical debate about the value of those ideas. Most architectural work remains rooted in the deliberations of design juries for its legitimation – the production of a consensus that this is (or is not) good work, perhaps even 'critical', as certified by those agreed to have a 'good eye'. The Kantian ideal of disinterested aesthetic judgement, as Eagleton (1990: 96) reminds us, is particularly vulnerable to ideological construction:

> Part of what we enjoy in the aesthetic ... is this experience of pure contentless
> consensus where we find ourselves spontaneously at one without necessarily even
> knowing what ... we are agreeing over ... we are left delighting in nothing but a
> universal solidarity beyond all vulgar utility.

How do we know that architectural education is not simply drawn into a role of servicing a 'meaning market' through a quest for new imagery; where is the line between the 'critical' imagination and the merely 'radical' image? The field of architecture is particularly vulnerable to the idea of a comfortable consensus wherein the style of the debate at times becomes more important to its participants than its content. In this context the position of the discipline of architecture within the top research-based universities is not particularly secure, a condition underlined in 2004 by the proposed closure of Architecture at Cambridge University. Such universities house architecture schools not because of any tradition in teaching artistic practices, but because of what is at stake in the future of the built environment. It is only a high level of critical thinking and the production of critical practitioners that will ensure the ongoing presence of architecture near the top of the academic tree.

In all architectural work under critique the most crucial question is 'what is at stake?' My short answer is that to be classed as 'architecture' there must be some idea about the future at stake. This is not the end of critical debate but it is necessary for it to begin – a critical architecture must at least plant seeds of desire for a better future. It follows that the image on the screen, the studio wall or the magazine is but a means to architecture and not its end; the end is the future which is at stake. One of the ways in which we 'mean to be critical, but...' is that architecture becomes separated from its consequences; the image becomes an end rather than a means. One can critique the image, its antecedents, style, facility and critical social content but there can be no debate about aesthetic, social or environmental futures if there is no future represented. Architecture is rendered safe for critical attention by reducing social content to representation and by the severing of architectural discourse from any possible future. When the image becomes the end rather than the means it loses critical potency as architecture.

The issue here is not whether the project has a real site, client community and budget, nor whether it is necessarily buildable, sustainable or affordable. The first question is whether it is understandable as a possible future that could be inhabited; and the second is whether it catches the imagination and nourishes the desire for change. I am not suggesting the eradication of forms of aesthetic production that do not represent possible futures. Developments in computer-aided graphics are unleashing a flood of seductive imagery and there is no need to clip these wings of spatial imagination. The question is: if the work is unimaginable as full-scale built form then to what degree does such work come to substitute for 'critical architectural practice' and does this substitution become a form of complicity? The architectural imagination, at its best, produces the desire for a better future; it contains the potency of the possible. The potency of architecture, its politics and its power, lies in keeping the future always at stake.

Part II

Places

Chapter 5: Slippery Characters

Defending and Creating Place Identities

Kim Dovey, Ian Woodcock and Stephen Wood

The quest to protect and create urban or neighbourhood 'character' has become a key issue for residential development and for our theoretical understandings of place. In the front gardens of older suburbs signs appear saying 'We Oppose Inappropriate Development' as residents become mobilized to defend the special character of their neighbourhood. Meanwhile the creation of character is a key marketing strategy for developers of new residential areas under slogans like 'come to your senses' and 'creating special places'. What does it mean to say that a place has character? How is such character protected by planning codes or created through legal covenants? This chapter explores four case studies in Melbourne.[1] Two of these cases are older neighbourhoods where an established character was seen as under threat; the other two are new suburbs where the creation of character and place identity was a key design strategy. Interviews with residents show that the experience and discourse of character encompasses a broad range of understandings of place identity and embodies important contradictions. While character is often defended as a pre-existing state of affairs, it is also constructed in debates over new development. The character of new developments is often designed in architectural styles that signify an instant tradition. A number of key questions are raised by these places: To what degree does manufactured diversity embody a desire for uniformity, whether physical or social, and how does that play out against the realities of an ethnically mixed suburb? To what degree can urban character be embodied in urban design codes or planning rules? To what extent is this quest for character a quest for a deeply rooted, essentialized and enclosed sense of place and to what degree might it be open to change?

The dual movements to protect and to create urban character are global, as are the place types in our case studies, however, they also have a particular local context. Melbourne is a former colonial city less than 200 years old; a low-density and fast-growing metropolis of almost four million people. The discourse of 'character' first came to prominence during debates on streetscape conservation in the 1980s, a period also marked by a proliferation of academic literature about 'place'.[2] It was incorporated into the planning literature in the 1990s when a combination of market-led development and state policies of urban consolidation produced a reactionary movement called 'Save Our Suburbs', determined to defend what is often referred to as 'the world's most livable city' (Lewis 1999). The resistance focused on the perceived destruction of urban character in the older and leafier suburbs. The definition of 'character' was never clarified but was, at least in part, circular – this place has a 'character' that is being threatened and the 'character' is that which is threatened. The state's response was to require that new developments respect the neighbourhood character. It was no accident that the state seized upon such a highly flexible concept as useful in a period of radical deregulation. The task of characterizing specific places was left to local councils who commissioned studies and by the turn of the century much of the metropolitan area had its character superficially defined. However, these studies did not reflect the experiences of residents and any decision based on them could be appealed to a legal tribunal where the lawyers became the final arbiters of what character means.[3] At the same time market-led developments on former industrial sites and on the urban fringe were engaged in meeting the desire for 'character' through the production of instant place identity. New suburbs, often influenced by 'new urbanism' and based on historic themes, were designed, built and marketed as having a strong sense of 'place', 'community' and 'character'. Largely driven by global formulae, the urban form was tightly controlled and legislated in the form of covenants that insulated residents against change to the form of their surroundings.

We will briefly present here four case studies: two older suburbs and two new ones. The sites were chosen specifically because issues of sense of place and urban character were at stake in either their protection or production. Camberwell is an established upmarket suburb where character is broadly described in terms of comfort, taste, uniformity and modesty; this is a place where a prevailing order is defended against new developments and new people are required to conform. Fitzroy is a largely nineteenth-century inner-city district with an edgy and diverse mix of both people and buildings. Here the character is defined in terms of a physical and social mix that is defended against conformity. Beacon Cove is a 1990s development on a former industrial site where housing is clustered around a series of 'greens' in new urbanist style – it is inward-looking, backward-looking and semi-privatized. Caroline Springs, on the urban fringe, is a series of 'villages', each marketed as having a distinct sense of place and identity. In both new developments the private covenant between resident and developer replaces the public urban design and planning code, and both are more socially diverse in reality than the conformist ideology suggests.

The larger project here is that of understanding the ways in which character is experienced by residents, constructed in the discourse of urban politics and marketing, and legislated through planning controls and covenants. The methodology we deployed was to approach the concept of character from three directions with the aim of understanding it as experience, as discourse and as urban morphology. All quotations are from extended interviews with residents who were at the forefront of resistance or community involvement. In particular we seek to unpack some of the ways in which the meaning of character slips between spatiality and sociality as urban form becomes hinged to social identity. This connection is already apparent in the definitions residents give of character which is generally understood as the 'feel' or 'atmosphere' of a place:

'character is almost the, the feeling it creates in you … you walk through an area and you feel comfortable with it.'

'to me urban character … is actually what's the general atmosphere, ambience of an area.'

'[urban character is] the feel of a place, what it represents to you; the people, the buildings, the things that happen there are all part of the urban character.'

'I'd say urban character is you go to a place and you just have a feel for it, it's how that place feels.'

Beyond this general agreement, the ways in which character plays out in different case studies is more diverse.

MODEST TASTES: CAMBERWELL

Camberwell is a leafy and upmarket middle-ring suburb, on a hill about 10 km from the city centre of Melbourne.[4] It was developed initially in the 1880s as 'Prospect Hill', a railway suburb with detached Victorian- and Edwardian-style houses on large blocks with a prospect towards the city. With few exceptions, residents are upper middle-class with a relatively low level of ethnic diversity. House prices in this particular area are about five times the Metropolitan median. The Character Study undertaken by the local council describes the area as 'notable for quality Victorian and Edwardian period houses, its gardens and quality streetscapes'.[5] The character elements flagged as significant are walkability, single-family houses, visible exotic front gardens, heritage streetscapes, period-style buildings and dense canopy trees. About half of all houses date from the Victorian or Edwardian periods but the streetscape character is complicated by the fact that many of these are hidden from the street behind walls, fences or hedges, and there is a significant new layer of neo-traditional houses designed to 'blend in'. The precinct is almost entirely one to two storeys in height, with buildings in the commercial precinct ranging up to six storeys. In 2003, the residents' association became intensely mobilized against a proposed redevelopment over the local railway station and its associated marshalling yard. While this station precinct is part of the commercial strip and not immediately adjacent to residential areas, the proposed development was seen as a threat to the broader character of Camberwell. Our interviewees are among the most active of resident objectors.

When defining the existing character, interviewees often begin with emphases on the idea of uniformity applied at once to the spatial and social attributes of the neighbourhood:

Figure 5.1
Camberwell.

'its character has been reasonably consistent in the type of people living here. Their type of domicile is similar as well, they'll generally like reasonably nice, well-kept houses, separate houses, gardens, trees, street trees etcetera and I think that's really what ... to me creates what is generally referred to as ... urban character.'

'[Character] really is the benefits you get from living in a particular area, how you feel about it, how people react to you, how you react to the people in the area, what you get from it ... the lifestyle. Most important thing I think for me ... is that I'm surrounded by PLUs – people like us. I see that as a comfort zone.'

This 'comfort zone' is easily punctured by formal and social differences and this identity is largely constructed from what it is not:

'Around the area [one can find] what might be described as "nice" houses, not, not new modern monstrosities, not totally derelict old places, not high-rise, low-cost type housing. I think that's where residents in this area fight very strongly against anything like that as they see it changing the general feeling ...'

Underneath the quest to avoid difference is a desire for a place that reflects ideals of modesty and taste:

'There aren't any extreme architectural forms really that really says "Well, look at me" sort of thing. I just think it's a very pleasant neighbourhood with its tree-lined streets and architecturally speaking very modest but elegant houses.'

'A lot of people here around the area are reasonably affluent [but] they're not flashy about it, they don't … flaunt it, rather they are comfortably affluent.'

The idea of comfort is an assemblage of social, economic and spatial dimensions and is defended in part against the perceived crassness of new money: 'the trouble is we're getting all these people in who all they've got is money, you see,

Figure 5.2
Camberwell – typical
streetscapes.

no taste.' Ostentatious display of wealth is a key signifier of social pretension and such lack of taste is held in disdain.

> 'most people ... fit in the Camberwell tribe ... without sort of standing out too much ... if a guy drives a bright gold Mercedes or BMW ... [people] would walk past and say what a tasteless individual ... and that again I think is part of the character.'

Camberwell's architectural character is often identified with its housing from Victorian and Edwardian periods: 'a lot of people like to think of the area as being almost, even though it no longer is, but almost as a Victorian–Edwardian bastion.' This quotation reflects the fact that while architectural styles are now mixed, Victorian- and Edwardian-period buildings represent the core character for residents. The demand for uniformity tends to produce neo-traditional designs as the only style acceptable in new housing. Yet there is considerable ambivalence in the interviewees about this approach: 'They don't stand up to the original.... In some ways you're better to go with a new design ... they fit in but they're not, they're not the same.' The problems associated with taste and new money are also found with ethnicity: 'Some of these Chinese monied people ... they come in and they build this wall to wall thing, no garden, just concrete because they're not used to gardens in Hong Kong, they're not. So they change the character.' This is in some ways a familiar view of an older suburb defended against differences of race and class. While Camberwell is not gated nor even bounded it has some subtle and sophisticated ways of keeping difference at bay. Part of the rhetoric used against the railway station proposal concerned fears that it could increase crime, particularly associated with drugs and Asian gangs.

Camberwell's urban character is portrayed as a series of intertwining threads – comfort and uniformity, modesty and taste, class and ethnicity, community and security. Yet there are some contradictions here. The 'comfort zone' suggests an easy-going and relaxed lifestyle, yet the interviews display a certain anxiety about fitting in accompanied by vigilance to ensure others do likewise. The demand for 'modesty' means that houses that are invisible from the street due to high fences or hedges are seen to contribute to the character as signifiers of modest wealth. The more the neo-traditional architecture tries to fit in, the more pretentious and tasteless it becomes. The politics of forcing all new development to fit with the existing framework leads to a repression of differences. Those who fall on hard times are required to keep up appearances. Chinese gardens may not be welcome but the Chinese may be if only they will garden like locals. Camberwell is much more diverse than it looks or is portrayed by its defenders. Like Procrustes of Greek mythology who would tailor his visitors to fit the guest bed, Camberwell has a Procrustean character, open to difference but only under condition that differences be renounced.

GENTRIFIED MIX: FITZROY

Fitzroy is a small, inner-city suburb housing a mix of residential, retail, light industrial and cultural uses within walking distance of the central city. As Melbourne's oldest suburb, Fitzroy dates from 1839 when speculative subdivisions produced a cheek-by-jowl mix of row housing and factories. Initially of mixed social classes, Fitzroy became notorious for a rather seedy history of crime and poverty and is an important site of urban heritage. After the arrival of post-Second World War migrants from southern Europe, the mix was altered again in the 1970s with high-rise public housing followed by an influx of artistic bohemian life, and then gentrification from the 1980s onwards. Row houses were renovated and industrial buildings converted to residential. The ethnic mix changed as the post-war Greek and Italian migrants moved out of the row housing and migrants and refugees from Asia and Africa moved into the public housing.

The urban morphology shows a small-grain mix of shops lining busy main streets with a residential and industrial mix in the hinterlands, protected from traffic by a complex system of one-way streets. The older 1–2-storey streetscapes of Victorian row housing are mixed with larger-scale industrial or institutional buildings and new residential developments. The industrial buildings include several former factories of up to seven storeys that have become heritage landmarks. Most have been converted to housing with one or more additional storeys

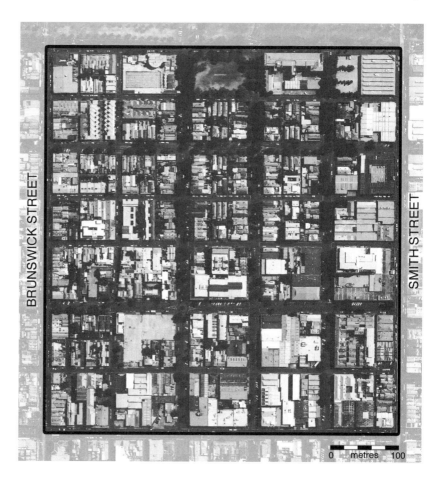

Figure 5.3
Fitzroy.

extending above the street parapet, generally in a quite different style. Against this, the council describes Fitzroy's urban character as 'an area noted for the consistency of its Victorian streetscapes'.[6] As with Camberwell residents, broad understandings of character again focus on the notion of a 'feel', yet in Fitzroy the feel of the place comprises a mixture of buildings (type, lot size, style, age, height), functions (retail, residential, industrial), mixed practices (artworks, graffiti, streetlife) and mixed people (appearance, age, household type, sexuality, social class): 'It's a mixture. This block is a mixture of very old cottages and these warehouses, and there are warehouses and cottages in lots of blocks, they have to co-exist.' Interviewees generally approved of such juxtapositions and of the creativity in the conversion of industrial buildings to residential use: 'I think it's fascinating to see the different types of warehouses and how creative people are, and generally they keep in well with the look or feel of the suburb.' Conceptions of character in Fitzroy were much more than heritage; the mix is a result of different layers of development over time: 'it's not violating an industrial character to make it into a 21st century dwelling, that's adding a layer.' The taller factories are accepted as an important component of the mix, even when sharply juxtaposed with much smaller dwellings. However, similar heights to the old factories are often seen as unacceptable in new developments:

> '[Fitzroy is] … predominantly 2–3 storeys and I think that's really important to its urban character, the scale … I think scale is more important than anything … we have some large buildings, we have five or six, but they're landmark buildings, they're not the norm.'

This idea of character as differences also means a social mix of classes and ethnicities, and a place where character is also found in edginess and seediness:

> '[Fitzroy] is different, it is … it has that 'edge' that people are interesting, that it has a good atmosphere. It has a sort of a seedy side, a sort of an underbelly that is in a way a little bit scary, but it also has a community, it has character and it has depth.'

The edginess is linked to both the cutting edge of change but also the edge or fringe of mainstream culture. Character is seen as more than a constellation or set of juxtapositions but involves connections, consistencies and associations between elements of the mix: 'a hive of coffee shops is consistent with a hive of political activists and fringe politics sits well with fringe music.' The word 'consistent' is used here in a different way than in Camberwell where it referred to 'uniformity'. In Fitzroy it is a kind of congruence or fitting in between spatial and social aspects of the place. The social diversity is generally portrayed positively with a tolerance of difference and a sense of liberation from conformity:

> 'you don't get the sense that people really care what you look like or what you say or how you act because there's so many different people doing so many different things … there are so many different sorts of people and it wouldn't matter who you were you'd fit in there.'

Figure 5.4
Fitzroy – typical
streetscapes.

However, this idea of 'fitting in' embodies some ambivalence, an enjoyment in being in a place of difference while also maintaining a certain distance; the same interviewee says: 'it's different, it's probably things that I would like to be, but probably aren't.' An edgy sense of difference creates an aura of creative authenticity within which even conservative tastes can safely 'fit'.

The idea of Fitzroy's character as seedy, transgressive and edgy has become part of the way in which Fitzroy now markets itself. Fitzroy is at times referred to as Australia's graffiti capital, and the blank walls of industrial buildings and the newer infill housing provide the canvas. Resident attitudes to graffiti are often ambivalent: 'I admit that when I see it on my own wall here, you know I have a flitter of irritation.... But there's a big wall there ... No, I don't mind the graffiti. I like the graffiti.' Residents who are attracted by this seedy authenticity will defend it in principle as an iconic thread of Fitzroy's character while removing it from their own property. The presence of graffiti is seen by some as a bulwark against further gentrification:

> 'eventually [Fitzroy] will become maybe cleaner and smarter and nicer and it will lose some of that character that was actually the reason we moved there ... and that's why I don't complain about ... the graffiti, because I don't want it to change.'

While Fitzroy's mixed character is valued, some interviewees express a desire to keep parts of the mix at a distance. This apparent contradiction is linked to another where gentrifying residents who are attracted to Fitzroy's mix are also the market for the taller buildings that they regard as threatening that mix. The opposition to height coalesced in 2002 around a proposal for an eight-storey building: 'It will change the character of the street as it is now, it's just a huge monolith sticking up ... This will make everything else look very small.' This opposition to height was also linked to a preference for the more social street frontages of the row housing: 'I think there's a big difference between sort of row-living and stacked-living ... you know what's going on with all your neighbours in a row, you hear them you smell them...'

One of the effects of this idea of character as mix is that it focuses attention on the ways in which the boundaries of a particular character zone are inscribed. Since the mix is spread across the urban fabric it makes a big difference whether the place is defined as a particular streetscape, several blocks or a whole suburb. Does a mix of heights, functions and social classes mean a mix in every street or a mix across the neighbourhood? In this case the boundaries proposed by residents, council and developer were quite different. In the end, the character zone was defined by a member of the state planning tribunal where the project was finally approved.

The character of Fitzroy is an edgy 'mix', a contested place characterized by difference and change rather than uniformity or stability. Its identity is forged from juxtapositions and oppositions to mainstream conformity. It is home to a range of people and activities that are often identified with the ideal of the creative city and an ethic of tolerance (Florida 2005). Yet it is also a gentrified community that is increasingly home to a population whose values transform the place. Part of what interviewees fear is the dominance not only of tall buildings but of residents who enter and leave via the garage door, more comfortable looking down on Fitzroy than living in it, who want to clean up the graffiti and remnants of transgression. That the resistance is primarily from the gentrifiers is a paradox; they are defending Fitzroy against more of themselves.

Both Camberwell and Fitzroy have recently been the subject of major disputes over urban development and are being defended on the basis of a preservation of character. In both cases the resistance is to new developments that are seen as 'out of place' and yet are supported by densification policies. The contrasts are also interesting – a spatially and socially uniform comfort zone contrasts with a spatial and social mixture with an edgy sense of difference. Camberwell's place identity is largely defined through what it is not. Nothing stands out, neither houses nor people call attention to themselves. In Fitzroy it is social and spatial differences that comprise place identity; quirky people and buildings are seen to contribute to the character. We now want to contrast these two cases with two newly built places that are examples of market-driven development incorporating a self-conscious creation of place identity.

LOVING LEGOLAND: BEACON COVE

Beacon Cove is an inner-city bayside project developed in the 1990s on a 30-hectare former industrial site adjacent to the originally working-class town of Port Melbourne. Here the desired 'character' was a key driver of the design process, an instant place identity derived from a global mix of Garden City, New Urbanist and gated-community models. A limited number of primarily two-storey housing types are replicated with small variations to enclose a series of small parks or 'greens'. The development is largely protected from through traffic, turning inwards to construct a uniform appearance with a sharp physical and social contrast with its surrounding urban context.

This site was originally slated in the 1980s to become a gated canal development, a proposal that produced furious community opposition and a battle to save Swallow Street – a residential street embedded in the midst of the site. The gated proposal finally collapsed and while the battle to save Swallow Street succeeded there was no further community participation. The market-driven project known as Beacon Cove was built around it. The urban design is organized into a series of precincts, each centred on a park or 'green' surrounded by 2–3 storey housing.[7] The vehicle network excludes through traffic and reinforces the external boundary while encouraging internal pedestrian networks. All car parking is hidden as the housing faces inwards onto the small parks, which are in turn largely privatized by the spatial structure. Yet the closure is by no means complete – in the middle of the project the traditional mixed housing of Swallow Street has been saved with some new public housing integrated.

A small series of house types are used to generate 600 houses with minor differences of colour, materials and entry design. They are mostly row houses with façades articulated to look like detached houses. Each of the precincts was given a different treatment in terms of colour and form to give each 'green' its own identity; as the architect put it:

'There's a family of colours … If you purchase the house in the white precinct … you actually can't paint that house brown. It's felt that once you paint that house brown you're destroying the character of that green space.'

Every detail of the project including the landscaping (coastal natives, no roses) was controlled by the developers and locked into covenants. The design of identity through colour also applies at the level of individual houses which the architect describes as if dressed in a uniform: 'In general there's the issues of having darker colours on the base, it's like the trousers and pants that you wear might be darker and the shirt might be lighter.' The repetition of housing types and the protected 'greens' led initially to Beacon Cove being labelled by outsiders as 'Legoland', 'Disneyland' and 'Pleasantville', suggesting socially engineered identities rather than 'real' urban character. Resident attitudes to the rather strict uniformity of the housing vary: 'Aesthetically, [it] just doesn't particularly please me. It's just all the same. Why would you buy ten jackets the same?' Others residents are not bothered: 'People have said to me … it looks like a stage set, a film set … well "legoland" perhaps … We love living in Legoland!' Residents have traded individualized housing for a stronger collective identity invested in neighbourhood rather than house and garden. The highly restrictive covenants are a key part of the marketing strategy for the development, as the architect put it:

'if you control the entire public/private realm – build everything and say to your purchasers "what you see is what you get and it won't change for ten years" – there's a certain level of comfort that you give … he knows that his investment is actually protected.'

Figure 5.5
Beacon Cove.

Figure 5.6
Beacon Cove – typical
streetscapes.

Beacon Cove was developed during a period of radical deregulation in state planning when many prevailing certainties about urban development, particularly
density controls, were being swept away. It paradoxically meets a market for
those who want a property that is protected from the uncertainties of a deregulated market. Beacon Cove is a comfort zone of urban character that is both
instant and eternal, like an instant heritage zone. The response of residents to
the uniformity and the rigidity of control is decidedly ambivalent:

> 'I guess on the social side of things you sit there and say: "oh my god we're all the
> same". On the other side of it … there is a particular image that Beacon Cove the
> development portrays. And to have everyone go off and do their own thing would raise
> the potential to undermine the inherent value-add of that … I think the uniformity is a
> double-edged sword.'

Aesthetic consistency is linked to property values; individualism is a threat to that image and therefore to the price; as another resident puts it: 'Beacon Cove is part of an image and that's what people buy into.'

Despite the uniformity of the architecture, residents were quick to suggest social heterogeneity within Beacon Cove. The development has proven popular with Asian-Australians and among upwardly mobile second- and third-generation migrants:

> 'if you look at neighbours, across the road, we have a Croatian taxi driver from Mill Park,
> Maltese motor mechanic … insurance broker next door, a couple of gay women have
> moved in next door. Good mix of professional, working-class mix within the street itself.'

Such affirmations of social heterogeneity are perhaps exaggerated given the price of housing in Beacon Cove, but they operate as an affirmation of authenticity and a counterpoint to the epithets of Legoland, Disneyland and Pleasantville that portray it as an unreal community. One resident of non-Anglo background suggested that Beacon Cove constructs a social space where ethnic difference is more difficult to read and where such differences matter less than in other parts of the city. The complex spatial and social codes that establish conformist identities in places like Camberwell do not operate here – the houses and gardens are predetermined and the cars are hidden. The taste and the mix are provided by the developer as a product that you either consume or go elsewhere. The sense of comfort is not found in 'people like us' but in protection from new development and the comfort of having the rules for fitting in clearly established by law.

While the development is upmarket it is relatively ethnically diverse and has attracted residents without the class connections of traditional Melbourne, 'people came here from [places] … where they weren't accepted into the character of that area unless they'd been there 30 or 40 years'. One interesting dimension of Beacon Cove is that the market was more open, diverse, mixed and contemporary than the developers initially thought. The first stage began with a neo-Georgian theme but moved from neo-traditional to contemporary styles in later phases. The retention of Swallow Street in the heart of the development, so bitterly fought by the developers, is now seen by residents as a positive component, lending the project both diversity and authenticity: 'I love Swallow Street. I will take our visitors around there to show them that in amongst Legoland exists a semblance of what used to be, so it's the old part of the history and people power.' The real street in the heart of 'Legoland' becomes a legitimating image and a counterbalance to the idea of a shallow instant identity. Residents recognize that property values are based in a clear distinction from the former working-class suburb yet they also want to be a part of the larger mix that constitutes the place: 'we've got Housing Commission backing onto those houses there. There is a diversity here … You see it, but it doesn't affect you much. But it's there, and that's nice.' This market for diversity at a distance has some elements in common with Fitzroy, difference plus comfort produces character. Residents attracted to Beacon Cove are more socially progressive than the developers anticipated and many are opposed to socio-spatial closure: 'When it started off, the original plan for Beacon Cove was a canal area, even a gated community, which is a terrible thing, I would never have participated if it was a gated community.' Not wishing to be identified too much with the idea of a Pleasantville, residents often find their pleasures outside the neighbourhood and even in resisting its suffocating aesthetic codes. The market turned out to be more diverse than the anticipated uniformity of empty-nesters – more tolerant of diversity and density, with a taste for contemporary rather than neo-traditional styles. The closure and uniformity of the urban form belies a more complex social reality as the place attracts diverse residents and embodies conflicting desires for retreat from as well as engagement with the city.

SELECT FAÇADES: CAROLINE SPRINGS

In 1995 Caroline Springs was a flat and featureless field of thistles adjacent to a freeway on the urban fringe of Melbourne's traditionally disadvantaged western suburbs. By 2000 it had been transformed by the Delfin corporation into a suburb with a grand entry boulevard, a lake and a series of 'villages' focused on waterways and parks with names like 'Brookside', 'Springlake', 'The Bridges', 'The Grove' and 'Cypress Views'. These 'villages' are neighbourhoods of semi-separated street networks, each with entry gateways and planned around shared open spaces and waterways. Marketed as the 'best of both worlds', this is a suburb on the urban fringe with 30-minute car access to the city yet claims to escape the stereotypical conformity and uniformity of suburbia with a stronger sense of place and community. Caroline Springs is a market-led development with a focus on a discourse of 'place', 'atmosphere', 'lifestyle' and 'home'. This is a place that appeals both to desires for stability ('the ideal place to put down roots') and social mobility ('move your lifestyle up a notch'). Delfin have a progressive role in residential development in Australia and regard their understandings of character to be forms of intellectual capital they were reticent to share.[8]

The concept of 'character' as understood by Caroline Springs residents echoes the notion of a 'feel' found in other case studies, but here there is an emphasis on the event of entering the estate for the first time:

'You know you drive in some places and it makes you feel at home, and you drive in other places it makes you feel – I really can't explain it … as soon as you enter it you know what it is…

Just as soon as you drove in, a welcoming feeling, maybe because of the way it was set up. Something about it, yeah, something that will be growing, and will hopefully grow into something that is pleasing and welcoming to others. Not just a sort of normal suburban place.'

Again, the 'feel' is at once social and physical; while the initial encounter (from behind the wheel) is spatial it embodies the social promise of a welcome. Character is presented as something created by the developers ('because of the way it was set up') and it is future oriented rather than stable ('something that will be growing'). In this sense character is paradoxically both instant and yet deferred as a dream or aspiration: 'Character doesn't just happen. You don't know when you buy what's going to happen.'

The identity of Caroline Springs is constructed in both the advertising and in residents' comments as a step up the social ladder: 'I see it as a step up, we certainly felt we'd achieved something, gone the next step.' Yet there are also many steps within Caroline Springs since each village has its own sense of place: 'I'm Chisholm Park. It's how it's marketed to you when you buy, you have your identity … they've bought into this village that's got a theme about it, there's a sense of place about it.' Each village has a self-contained street network with

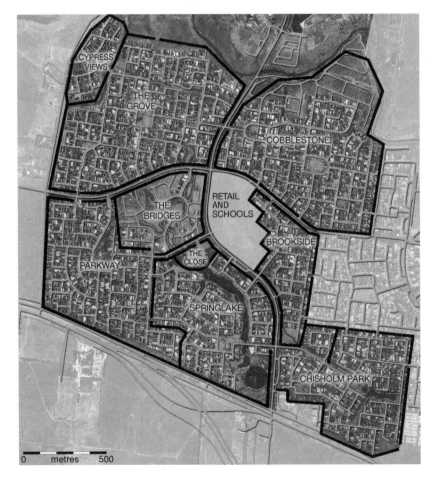

Figure 5.7
Caroline Springs.

substantial entrance gateways that signify a sense of identity and arrival as well as names that construct place narratives, particularly about nature ('Springlake', 'The Grove') and history ('Chisholm Park', 'Cobblestone'). The villages have become identified with status: Springlake and The Grove are more upmarket while 'Cobblestone', 'Chisholm Park' and 'Brookside' are more affordable. Interviewees both affirm and deny the importance of such neighbourhood distinctions but they are always alert to them:

> 'Even, out here, people can be snobby, that whole "I live in Springlake or The Grove", they are areas where there probably are bigger and better houses. But within the community, no one makes those sort of class distinctions … What have other people said?'

The corporate strategy is to ensure that socially mobile residents will see the next step without leaving Caroline Springs: 'We don't walk in the shoes with the people who can afford to buy in the Bridges.... I must admit I like it in there.'

Unlike Beacon Cove, Caroline Springs is a small-lot subdivision and all housing design and construction was left to those who purchased the blocks. A strict set of covenants control height, setbacks, landscaping and materials; every house is required to have a verandah, porch or portico as the street entry; high fences are prohibited and flat roofs need special permission. This code establishes a uniformity of streetscape, but it also requires a diversity of building style including some stridently contemporary designs among the neo-traditional styles:

> 'in some ways you think why did Delfin let them put this great big yellow thing in the middle of these more traditional ones. But again, I think it does show a bit of the character of Caroline Springs that we're not all the same, we don't all want the same.'

In marked contrast to Beacon Cove, the choice of house style at Caroline Springs is central to issues of marketing; one billboard invites residents to 'Choose your look, select your favourite façade'. The passion for period-style houses is widespread and is often linked to issues of character and a desire for the traditional housing of the upmarket eastern suburbs such as Camberwell: 'You can't really beat a row of period homes. You can go into really nice streets around the eastern suburbs, lovely array of period homes together.' While recognizing that the neo-traditional is not the same as a real period house there is some belief that in time the neo-traditional houses will become like the periods and traditions they imitate: 'The old, traditional, Federation, traditional areas is what appeals to me. The leafy streets, big trees, established areas.... It'll take a long time for that to happen.' Another interviewee sees the choice of a period-style house as a mistake:

> 'We pretty much just built a display home … "Springwood 290". All done fairly unemotionally at the time. The façade we chose, a Georgian one, is well and truly overdone. In retrospect it's been well and truly done to death, should have done something different.'

Figure 5.8
Caroline Springs – typical streetscapes.

The suggestion here is that the choice of style is not always an investment in the 'feel' or 'character' so much as a fashion chosen off the rack as it were, only to discover that too many others are wearing the same outfit. Note the contrast with Beacon Cove where everyone in the same 'village' wears the same outfit.

There is abundant evidence in the marketing brochures and in the street life that the market for Caroline Springs is multicultural; residents generally celebrate this ethnic mix:

'a lot of Philippinos, Sri Lankans, few South Africans, few English like myself, Croatians, Maltese, Macedonians, my neighbour's Italian, more Philippinos around the back. Bit of everything. So it's nice for the kids to have that exposure but not have one group dominating, which is nice.'

Some residents defend the mix against a perceived threat of ethnic concentration:

'as much as it sounds awful, there's a huge amount of Asians, a lot of Asians wanting to come in here … I don't care what nationality it is, I don't like to see a glut of one … that can totally change … the character of the area.'

Ethnic differences are not evident in the architecture despite a broad range of both neo-traditional and contemporary styles.

'The houses are very much like each other. I mean different varieties, but you wouldn't walk past this one and say "oh this one belongs to Indian, this one belongs to Maltese". Nothing stands out for me that says that that belongs to a different nationality.'

This quotation suggests a limited suite of surface differences operating as a way of unifying a potentially greater degree of deeper differences; the choice of a façade is broad enough that identities become detached from these choices, as if the choice between different Anglo-Australian building styles is all that stands between different ways of fitting into contemporary Australian life. It is important that each house look a little different from its neighbours but these are differences that effectively affirm or proclaim underlying similarities. Caroline Springs is designed to meet the market for neighbourhood character and recognizes that this market is not unified or simple, and that while it is mixed in values and taste cultures, social classes and ethnicities, there is some desire for commonality among differences that is satisfied by the promise of a future secure against change.

DIFFERENCES AND COVENANTS

The quests for urban character outlined above show a cluster of intersecting and often contradictory desires: for a sense of security, comfort and order; for stabilized identities geared to nature and heritage; for encounter with difference in everyday life; for status and property values. In each case character is identified through experiential words such 'feel', 'sense' or 'atmosphere'. In the new projects of Beacon Cove and Caroline Springs, character is seen as a spectacle, an instant creation and a product for consumption. In such cases there is also the promise of a depth of character over time, a surface that is acquiring depth. In the older cases of Camberwell and Fitzroy the 'feel' was portrayed as less the immediate effect of the spectacle and more of an acquired taste – whether the spicy soup of Fitzroy or the modest taste of Camberwell. Here character is defended as depth that cannot be reduced to surface, yet is threatened by taller buildings.

In both older cases, conceptions of urban character are blurred with heritage as something inherited from urban and social history – a place has urban character because it is old. Yet in both cases certain layers of urban history are chosen as valued characteristics and written into the planning codes as highly selective and essentialized versions of physical character. On the other hand, interviewees' conceptions of urban character were largely constructed as part of the politics of resistance and have a much looser relationship with the material urban form. By contrast, the proliferation of neo-traditional styles of new developments construct an illusion of history, albeit one that many interviewees do not particularly identify with.

The balance between unity and diversity is an ideal that runs through all depictions of character. In Camberwell unity is seen as under threat from difference, yet resident activists portray its character as uniformity and conformity. Meanwhile, the architectural uniformity of Beacon Cove is criticized by its residents as belying a real social diversity that is a better key to the character of the place. In Fitzroy a diverse mix is seen as under threat from the uniformity of gentrification. Residents defend the 'consistencies' in the mix but this is a different use of the same term – not a repetition of the same type of building or person but a consistency between people, practices and places that allows for juxtaposition and creativity. A similar view of character seems evident in the attempt to mix styles in every street in Caroline Springs.

The overall uniformity of urban form in the new developments seems to operate as camouflage for difference. The mix of building forms in Fitzroy is defended on the basis of its edgy sense of social differences, yet it can also be construed as a place where uniformity is camouflaged within difference. While the character of Camberwell has been forged through resistance to diversity on the basis of history, modesty and taste, in other cases diversity is encouraged but carefully contained. It is worth comparing the degree to which place identity is conceived as open or closed, spatially and socially, with the actual degree of openness or closure that operates. The character discourse among Camberwell's defenders is far less open than the appearance of its streets. This discourse and political activism operate together with property values and heritage codes to exclude difference. In Fitzroy, the streets appear radically open and tolerant, and this is reflected in the character discourse of its resident activists. But as in Camberwell, property prices render it closed to some social classes. In contrast to Camberwell the heritage codes in Fitzroy tend, to some degree, to preserve the stock of low-rent housing and its social mix. The new suburbs of Beacon Cove and Caroline Springs are more physically closed behind entry gates and closed spatial structures. While Beacon Cove has high property values, both are more socially open than they appear. The concept of character can thus be mobilized both to pursue difference and to protect against difference.

It is clear that 'character' is a loaded term and a very slippery one, with a propensity to allow conflations between physical and social attributes of places. It follows that there is a strong tendency for the promotion or exclusion of certain kinds of building to slip easily into the favouring or exclusion of certain kinds of people and behaviour; built-form controls can easily become social controls. There is also another kind of slippage: the imperative to define character as a form of planning and design codification can entail a reduction of character to physical characteristics, without concern for how places actually operate as social milieux. The desire for protection and creation of character as a complex assemblage of place attributes slips into the production of caricature – a fixed and superficial mask that makes a mockery of place.

The proliferation of private covenants in new developments is interesting in this regard. In Judaeo-Christian theology a covenant is an agreement that establishes commitments between God and his people; in the cases discussed here covenants embody legal commitments from developers that the place will develop and be maintained according to set rules and a commitment from residents to abide by that code. Covenants are private planning and design rules that differ from public planning regulations by being set as part of the land title. They are not negotiable or subject to democratic processes. When residents buy into Beacon Cove or Caroline Springs they are promised that the rules will not change in the future. Private covenants offer the ultimate comfort zone as protection from the threat of unruly or higher-density development; they embody the paradox of a market-led antidote to free-market economics. By allowing such rules to be written into the land-title system the state takes on the obligation to police these urban codes in perpetuity. Developers move on but the place abides.

North American residential developments of this kind are generally termed 'Common Interest Developments' or CIDs (McKenzie 1994); the private common interests of residents are legislated to take precedence over larger public interests. The argument from those who defend private communities is that residents become members of a club rather than citizens of a society: 'Cities naturally fragment into many small publics, each of which may be thought of as a collective consumption club. The club realm may, therefore, be a more useful – and theoretically more powerful – idea than the public realm' (Webster 2002: 397). Here social fragmentation is treated as 'natural' and the retreat from the public realm is framed in terms of collective consumption rather than citizenship. The state is attracted to such developments because the infrastructure costs are privatized, but this is a Faustian bargain because it also paralyses further change. At Beacon Cove the local government authority was locked out of the original development process yet has now inherited a range of secluded, high-maintenance and effectively private parks. Caroline Springs is a low-density car-based suburb with a similar range of parks and many water features. These are but two examples of the kind of development that now covers extensive areas of Australian suburbia and is even more extensive in North America. To what degree is the state obliged to maintain unsustainable urban areas under conditions of peak oil and climate change? Covenants are designed to produce an instant – but also final – place identity; in doing so they close down processes of becoming.

Character is a highly problematic term to use as a basis for urban development decisions. Yet the aspects that make it so problematic – particularly the slippages between physical and social issues and conflations thereof – give it a currency and vitality that are crucial to urban design practices and theories of place. In Camberwell and Fitzroy the issue of character is more alive because it is threatened, contested and defended in public debate. While character in such public suburbs may at times be constructed in ways that are narrow, closed and essentialized, the question can never be settled. In the end it is not the neo-traditional styles or spatial closure that most characterize the new developments so much as the closure of debate – the character is settled. The character of place, like the sense of place, cannot be reduced to its characteristics without producing caricature. But it is not the desire for character that causes trouble but the belief that it can be defined and contained in urban codes and covenants. The only real characters are slippery characters.

Chapter 6: Becoming Prosperous

Informal Urbanism in Yogyakarta

Kim Dovey and Wiryono Raharjo

INFORMAL SETTLEMENTS

Over one billion people now live in 'squatter', 'slum' or 'informal' housing settlements globally; this population is expected to double by 2030, making it the major form of urban design and development globally (United Nations 2003). Yet informal settlements are the black holes of urbanist discourse – largely invisible and unstudied in morphological terms. Squatter, slum and informal are problematic and negative words, defined in terms of a lack: a squatter lacks land tenure; a slum lacks space, durability, water or sanitation; and informal implies a lack of control over planning, design and construction. This chapter is an attempt to understand such settlements in terms of how they work as places or assemblages. While it is easy to regard such settlements as unsustainable, they are the way in which one in every six people sustain themselves globally and they are in no way temporary. Many such settlements have developed over time into well-serviced neighbourhoods – no longer 'slums' and with varying levels of tenure and formality. The prospect is to understand how informal urbanism works as a basis for the transformation from 'slums' to decent housing and from squatting to secure tenure.

Informal settlements can be defined as urban assemblages that operate outside the formal control of the state. While it is impossible to separate them from issues of slum housing and legal tenure, it is important to define informality separately from slums and squatting. While a squatter settlement implies a blanket lack of tenure, most informal settlements involve a range of rental, squatting and informal entitlements. A slum is defined by the United Nations as any dwelling with more than three people per room or without access to clean water, sanitation, security and durable shelter (United Nations 2003) – yet many dwellings in informal settlements have most or all of these.

Informality is a framework or paradigm for understanding urban cultures of infiltration, the 'quiet encroachment' of informal markets within formal economies (Alsayyad 2004). Informal settlements involve the unauthorized and unregulated occupation of land and construction upon it, coupled with a condition of tenure insecurity. They are best defined as irregular rather than illegal since the tenure is generally in dispute rather than clear. As Jenkins (2006: 94) puts it:

To consider informal solutions as being illegal means putting the majority outside the law and in effect undermines the law. Many informal systems, while inadequate in various ways, are more legitimate and more functional than formal systems – especially when these formal systems have been inherited from another period or imported from another context.

It is also misleading to see informal settlements as unplanned, as Evers and Korff (2000: 153) put it:

The difference between the neatly zoned business district or upper class and the rest of the city is that the former is planned by architects, city planners and other government agencies, whereas life in the slum is based on the planning and strategic action of the slum-dwellers themselves.

Most of the theorizing on the informal sector is based on informal economies; all economies have an informal sector which exists alongside, while integrated with, the formal sector. In wealthy economies the state penetrates the economy and the city deeply and the informal economy is largely limited to the household. In poorer economies the informal sector generally dominates. When the formal system cannot meet demand for shelter the informal system fills the gap. In most lower-income areas of developing cities with market economies informality has become the norm.

The proliferation of such settlements over the past 50 years has been market-driven – employment opportunities generated in cities have not been matched by the capacity of either the state or the market to provide affordable housing for the millions of poorer people attracted to those cities. Half a century of state intervention has failed to halt the growth of informal settlements (United Nations 2003). While the state sees such settlements as a problem to be fixed it is important to note that such settlements have long been an integrated economic part of nearly all developing cities (Perlman 1976). While governments frame informal settlements as places needing to be fixed or formalized, there is a need for approaches that recognize the validity and the values embodied in them (Jenkins 2006: 87).

Martin and Mathema (2006) describe three primary process models for the formation and growth of informal settlements. The first involves the unauthorized occupation of unused land by a small group who may then take a role in overseeing further development as others join in. In some cases the first squatters charge a fee or become slum landlords to those who follow. The urban morphology in such cases tends to be that of piecemeal development. The second model is the overnight land invasion organized by a group of community leaders, sometimes with informal 'rights' of use bought from the 'owners'. Such settlements tend to be roughly preplanned in grid layout with plots allocated. A third model is where the owners of a title develop it in an unauthorized subdivision where plots or houses are then sold or rented for profit – a model that is sometimes called pirate housing (Davis 2006).

Mapped against these processes are territorial types within which informality develops. These are characterized by a certain level of marginality to the space of the formal city, often an interstitial zone or a crack between the formal zones of urban space. First and perhaps most common are urban waterfronts, marginal land between the formal city and the water. Such space may be subject to flooding and often has an economic and ecological connection to the water. Such settlements tend to be more common in the tropical wetlands of South-east Asia. In more mountainous terrain (as in Latin America) key locations are often escarpments or steep margins between the formal city and mountains. Such land is often too steep for vehicles and may be subject to landslides. A third major settlement type infiltrates the marginal land around and under major urban transport projects such as railways and freeways. Informality also tends to locate in the deeper spaces of formal urban blocks where a formal street façade gives way within a few metres to informal alleys and dense informal housing. In some cases informal urbanism is attracted to sites of religious or monarchic power because of the protection offered from eviction. Another settlement type involves the unauthorized occupation of the interior of large disused buildings or institutional compounds such as Cairo's necropolis (El Kady and Bonnamy 2007: 257). Some informal settlements encompass entire districts of the city rather than developing within the margins. Smaller-scale examples include Indonesian kampungs; at a larger scale, famous slums such as Tondo (Manila), Dharavi (Mumbai) and Kibera (Nairobi) are of this kind. Some informal settlements are temporary, particularly those linked to major construction sites where they may be temporarily protected by the construction company. A final territorial type is the sidewalk urbanism of pavement dwellers who built directly onto sidewalks or simply sleep in public and store their belongings somewhere for a price. This typology is intended to sketch the range of settlement types rather than be definitive of all examples. Many settlements occur in hybrid locations such as riverbank escarpments or waterfront railways. Such settlements often have no clear boundaries in space or time; informality is fluid and paradoxically 'unsettled'. As Appadurai (2000: 637) notes in the case of Mumbai:

> there is a vast range of insecure housing from a six-foot stretch of sleeping space to a poorly defined tenancy situation shared by three families 'renting' one room. Pavements shade into ... shacks ... which shade into semipermanent illegal structures.

The responses of the state to urban informality range from upgrading (Turner 1976) and increasing the supply of urban housing (Payne 1999) to neglect and demolition/eviction (Meldrum 2006). There is not scope here to describe these responses but a brief introduction to land tenure issues is necessary to any understanding of informal urban form. A first point to make is that urban land-ownership systems in developing countries are often informal, without clear cadastral maps or legitimate titles (Evers and Korff 2000: 169). What is known as 'squatting' often occurs on land without clear and legitimate ownership. The tenure issue has been addressed by granting individual titles, temporary rights and collective rights (Huchzermeyer 2006). The major threats to security of tenure come from forced eviction and coercive displacement. Forced eviction is generally coupled with demolition of the settlement; it may or may not involve compensation and resettlement. The reasons for forced eviction may include cleaning up the image of the city, clearing dangerous land such as flood plains, or clearing sites for new development. One such reason may be used as the cover for another. However, forced evictions attract both local and global media coverage and are politically unpalatable outside the most totalitarian and least democratic regimes. Resettlement schemes generally involve relocation to technically higher-quality housing with higher rents and less access to employment. Many of the economic advantages associated with the morphology of the informal settlement are lost in resettlement; these include the complex social use of public space, sub-letting of rooms and electricity, incremental improvement of buildings, and home-based industries. One common result of relocation schemes is to stimulate the development of more informal settlements as residents move back into the employment markets.

Over recent decades forced evictions have declined but have been replaced and outstripped by what can be called coercive displacement – informal settlers are led to a situation where they are enticed to leave, often within the framework of tenure reform and the formalization of land titles (Durand-Lasserve 2006). This is a variation of gentrification – informal settlements are often on prime urban locations where uncertainty of tenure and slum conditions depress the value of the land well below what it could be if those conditions were removed. When individual titles are granted or bought by informal settlers the property market escalates due to speculation and residents are offered a windfall profit if they agree to sell. Yet if they do then they can only keep that profit if they move to another informal settlement at a lower level of development.

A key debate in recent years has centred on the ideas of Hernando de Soto, an economist who argues for the legalization of individual land titles so that poor people have a stake in the market, can raise capital and use capital to leverage further capital. For de Soto, informal property is 'dead capital' because it cannot be leveraged to produce growth; capitalism cannot work its wealth-creating magic in the informal economy and the task is to formalize extra-legal tenure (de Soto 2000). He makes a distinction between extra-legal (or informal) and illegal (criminal) activity based on the criteria that if the end (housing) is socially desirable then the means should be legalized. While de Soto's celebration of the entrepreneurial skills of residents and his economic arguments against both eviction and state intervention are often sound, there is considerable evidence that instant formalization does not work. De Soto's cure is to incorporate residents into a market that does not function in their interests but instead displaces them back to lower levels of informality (Huchzermeyer and Karam 2006). Newly formalized properties flood onto the market creating cheap housing in key locations; many former squatters sell their title to take the profit and end up moving to informal settlements elsewhere. Market-based legalization of informal settlements can be seen as a form of coercive eviction with the unintended effect of stimulating new informal settlements elsewhere. Such instant formalization may be a greater current threat to informal settlements than forced eviction. Such market-driven displacements operate at a far larger scale than forced evictions and are much more politically palatable. The prospect of simply granting land tenure to informal settlers also poses a dilemma for the state since it stimulates the development of new informal settlements.

The proposed response to tenure issues from many experts in the field suggests moving incrementally through the middle ground between informal tenure and formal individual titles. The key task is to secure tenure and prevent displacement; the specific form of land title should be seen as the means rather than the end in this endeavour (Huchzermeyer and Karam 2006). Some suggest that formal collective titles rather than individual titles are the best way to achieve this (Durand-Lasserve 2006). Jenkins argues that informal land purchase with informal title can be enough to sustain investment and pass on inheritance without displacement (Jenkins 2006: 93). The task is one of how to maintain some of the productive aspects of informality, especially capacities for entrepreneurial flexibility, without displacement. There is a need to see informality as part of the answer rather than the problem. The distinction between formal and informal is not a dichotomy but a highly dynamic continuum whereby formal and informal processes constantly interact (Jenkins 2006: 88). The research task is to understand these interactions and to design interventions that work with them rather than simply replace one with the other.

VISIBILITY AND MORPHOLOGY

Informal settlements are often largely invisible within the cities in which they are located. This is at once an advantage and a problem. On the one hand governments are embarrassed by the image of informal settlements as signifiers of failure and lack of state control. The image of the city is an iconic signifier of the nation; it stands for the sense of order, or lack thereof. There is a tendency to target high-profile settlements that are visible from major transport routes for eviction. This is a particular problem when the city is host to major tourist or political events; road widening often provides the excuse. On the other hand informal settlers need to be visible in the eyes of those who allocate resources if they are to get a fair share (Royston 2006). State budgets for roads, services and infrastructure tend to be distributed across the formal sector, while informal settlements maintain and upgrade their own public infrastructure. Visibility can attract upgrading schemes but the focus on image can lead to superficial or ad hoc approaches (Huchzermeyer and Karam 2006).

Many parts of informal settlements remain deeply invisible even to those who live or pass nearby. This invisibility operates to protect informal people and practices within. It follows that formalization processes can threaten those who wish to remain invisible (Royston 2006). Informal settlements generally have high levels of social capital due in part to the solidarity of poverty but also to the bond formed by collective opposition to the state and the formal sector (Martin and Mathema 2006). The dilemma is that residents are both trapped and protected by this invisibility. Invisibility enables residents to be left alone and enables the state to abrogate responsibility.

Informal settlements are seen as a blight upon the city and nation, they have negative symbolic capital. While the state carries the burden of blame, there is also considerable political capital available for those involved in slum improvements. Indeed when elections approach there is often a spurt of ad hoc slum improvements (Jenkins 2006). Informal settlement upgrading is a highly politicized process and most of the barriers to successful upgrading are social and political. However, some of them relate to a lack of understanding of informal urban morphology.

Our task here is to try to understand more about the specific ways in which informal settlements work with a focus on the urban morphology and architecture. In some ways this is a paradox, to focus on form as a means of understanding informality. Very little of the literature on informal settlements has much to say in detail about built form which is treated as a somewhat neutral background to issues of process, economics, tenure, employment, infrastructure and politics. Most architects and urban planners who have specialized in the area have abandoned the production of plans and designs for an engagement in policy and process. We have no cause to argue with this since there is little doubt that the key issues of security of tenure and poverty alleviation seem to have little connection to the shape of buildings or urban spaces. Yet there are some reasons for wanting a more detailed morphological study.

Most researchers suggest that solutions must be found that do not simply replace the informal with a formalized system. While there are many ethnographies of informal settlements we know very little of how informal settlements work in detailed spatial and morphological terms. What are the densities, forms of construction and spatial structures? How are private/public interfaces managed? How is space negotiated, how are rooms designed and built? How is space used, demarcated, bounded and upgraded? How are building materials chosen, acquired and stored? What symbolic codes operate in terms of identity, status, materials and forms? What are the social meanings of building location, materials, form and size? We know much more about the social, economic and infrastructural components than about the spatial.

A second point is that the neutrality of built form to practices of power is, in this case, relatively untested. It has been shown in other contexts that the ways in which we relegate built form to a taken-for-granted context of everyday life is one of its most potent connections to power. What if the urban morphology and spatial practices of informal settlements is fundamental to their success in housing the urban poor? We know a great deal about upgrading yet it is generally implemented as a top-down process. Informal upgrading is a continuous practice in terms of public space, public buildings, private houses and private enterprises.

There are good reasons why informal settlements and their social, spatial and economic practices are largely unmapped. The informal sector is, by definition, not part of the formally documented community and there is a serious lack of data. In demographic terms there are rarely accurate records of who lives there and under what conditions. In terms of population densities there are often strong urban–rural linkages whereby residents move back and forth on seasonal or employment cycles (Smit 2006). While many residents rent rooms or houses and many of those sub-letting have informal 'ownership', this information is held in the community and is not formally mapped. Only the residents have the data and while there are community-based methods of data collection, fear and resistance on the part of residents means it is hard to gather (Huchzermeyer and Karam 2006). Since much informal life is technically illegal it may not be in residents' interests to divulge accurate data.

In physical terms there are rarely accurate land titles, street layouts or house plans. Formal land-title maps often do not match the morphology of settlements on the ground. Advances in the analysis of aerial photographs can show something of the urban morphology and the dynamism of such settlements over time (Abbott and Douglas 2003). However, these do not show the functional mix, house size or density. Not all houses are numbered and a single entrance can serve several households. Accurate pedestrian networks are not evident on aerial photographs because dwelling entrances and pathways between buildings are often covered by eaves. While the informality of the urban morphology is largely visible, other forms of informality are not. There is generally an informal market in electricity with some houses paying the bills and subcontracting informal supplies to others. Refrigerator space, storage space or industrial space may be sub-let to neighbours.

Informal settlements are extraordinarily complex socio-physical assemblages about which we know very little. While they seem chaotic and haphazard they have a socio-physical order that is often highly sophisticated, efficient and occasionally beautiful. It is worth reflecting on the fact that the labyrinthine forms of medieval cities that now attract tourists in great numbers were originally informal settlements. This is mostly a rhizomatic order of accretion rather than hierarchical control; its sophistication comes from many years of trial and error and from the incapacity of poverty to tolerate waste. The physical morphology is closely integrated with social networks, domestic economics and employment prospects (Smit 2006: 109). There is a very complex use of open space and innovative trade-offs between private and public space. Martin and Mathema (2006) have argued that, when compared to formal housing, informal settlements in Lusaka had a closer fit of form to function, a more efficient use of space, greater flexibility for change and better value for money. Such settlements, however, are not free of hierarchical control. Site-and-services developments, pirate subdivisions and organized land invasions often bring a strong level of order to the spatial layout. Some such developments speculate on future formalization by matching lot-sizes to the minimum necessary for future legalization. Some communities organize building locations in straight lines and limit materials to concrete blocks in order to raise the legitimacy of the settlement (Martin and Mathema 2006). We will now ground this summary of some of the issues regarding informal urbanism in a particular case study.

SIDOMULYO/KRICAK

Sidomulyo-Kricak is a *kampung* (urban village) lining the Winongo River in north-west Yogyakarta, about 5 km from the city centre. The community is accessible by car but only through a series of single-lane (but two-way) streets. The primary means of connection with the larger city are motorcycle and pedicab (*beçak*), the nearest public transport is about a kilometre away. The land, which is subject to flooding, was first settled by squatters in the 1950s and 1960s when a local industry developed in crushing the small river rocks to supply concrete aggregate; the entire area was called 'Kricak' which literally means 'place of the rock crush-ers'. Early in the Suharto regime, in 1966 a state policy known as *Razia Gelan-dangan* (Homeless Drifter Sweeping) removed large numbers of homeless people from the streets and housed them in bamboo barracks in an institution adjacent to this site known as Bina Karya. A decade later these people were evicted from the institution and moved onto the northern riverbank where they mostly became tenants of one of the original squatters. The name Sidomulyo literally means 'Becoming Prosperous'. These informal neighbourhoods are divided for administrative purposes into what are known as RTs – small local government areas with local community leaders. A small shelter known as a *Pos Ronda* (Watch Post) is built by the community at the main entrance to each RT, a relic of a system of self-surveillance instituted by Suharto's regime in the late 1970s (Kusno 2000: 110). The area known as Sidomulyo is enclosed by the loop of the river; Kricak to the east is a more developed settlement.

The material that follows was the result of a student field trip that spent a week in this community in 2007, a collaboration between an Australian and an Indonesian university and a local NGO.[1] The field trip was timed to coincide with a community festival with a range of activities; our primary involvement was in the production of public artworks and mapping of the settlement. There were (hitherto) no accurate maps of this settlement and a key goal of the field trip, in collaboration with the community and NGO, was to produce maps and analyses that might be of use in struggles for land tenure and ongoing development. These maps were produced in a series of layers that are described and illustrated below. We have grouped the maps (Figures 6.1, 6.3, 6.5) to enable contrasts and comparisons between them and to illustrate a range of issues to follow. The photographs are also grouped to provide a spread of images with the more public sites (Figure 6.2) followed by those showing semi-private spaces (Figure 6.4) and other spatial and material aspects of the settlement (Figure 6.6). Much of the informality is hidden from the main street, anchored by the bridge (Figure 6.2 lower) and lined with shops and several *Pos Ronda* (Figure 6.2 upper).

Figure 6.1 shows the building footprints and the ways various functions are distributed throughout the settlement.[2] Unlike a planned city, the spatial structure emerges as an accumulation of bottom-up acts mediated by a field of spatial, economic, social and political opportunities. These processes are informal but not random or chaotic. Each house that is built contributes to the overall plan without any formal systems of control in place.

While houses are generally constructed individually and in stages, dwelling units are often clustered, sharing common walls or even roofs. These clusters of dwelling units can house up to about six households, are often irregular in form and built from multiple materials. There are many different spatial patterns

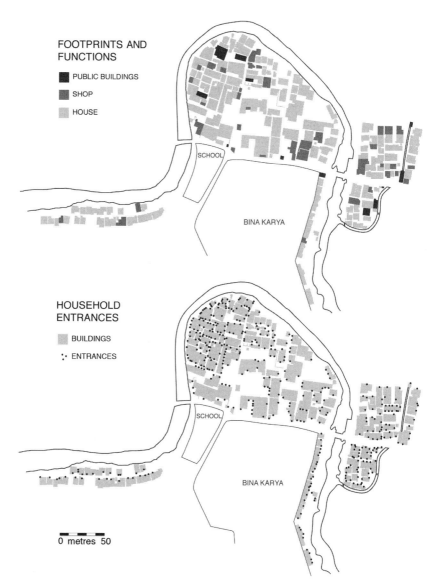

Figure 6.1
Footprints, functions and densities.

Figure 6.2
Public spaces.

evident in different parts of this footprint map, from linear riverbank patterns to a dense labyrinth. As in any city, social conditions are reflected in the location and size of dwelling units with sharp differences of housing quality, income and tenure security. While this map plots the building footprints at ground level, the wide eaves of most houses creates a condition where many of the smaller pathways between houses are completely covered. One effect is that interior light and ventilation are often poor; another is that the public space is a richly differentiated network of light and dark.

About 90 per cent of all buildings are residential and even the shops (*warung*) are often part of a house. Shops are rarely larger than 10 m² and while the main street is lined with shops, some open onto access lanes of less than a metre wide. Every neighbourhood has at least one shop. Public buildings (marked in black) include community rooms, security booths (*Pos Ronda*), a mosque and two small Catholic churches.

Figure 6.1 (lower) also maps the locations of dwelling entrances onto public space. Houses are not generally numbered yet every household is identified through small pads that hang near the front door. The pads record the payment of an informal social security 'tax' (collected and distributed within the community), and indicate the number of households that enter there. The density of different parts of the settlement, as measured by the security pads, ranges from about 60 to 260 households/hectare. This variety reflects large differences of interior space standards and of wealth throughout the settlement. Densities are fluid because there is no simple one-to-one ratio of households to houses and a proportion of the population is 'floating' at any given time.

Figure 6.3 maps the network of publicly accessible space and the typical volumes of streetlife distributed across it. The distinction between public and private space, however, is highly ambiguous. In the most crowded parts of the settlement where people have little interior space, domestic life spills permanently into 'public' space. For this reason large amounts of publicly accessible space are better considered semi-public (Figure 6.4). While the public space is a richly interlaced network, these pathways can be categorized by means of access by car, small vehicles and pedestrians. There is very little access for cars and most vehicle traffic is by motorcycle; other small vehicles include *beçak* and trolleys for food or goods. Pathways for pedestrians only are generally less than 800 mm wide. Many of the smaller paths and some of the open spaces are unpaved; the soft ground is covered with bamboo matting when needed for seating. Paving is often linked to government grants and symbolizes both permanence and state control; it formalizes the public space.

The deeper networks of publicly accessible space are appropriated both functionally and symbolically by local residents. Our access to and photography of these areas was negotiated with the community by the NGO and was for the duration of this visit only. The public/private status of pathways is often unclear to outsiders; some paths covered with symbols of domestic life may be publicly accessible while others are not (Figures 6.4 and 6.6). The appropriation of public

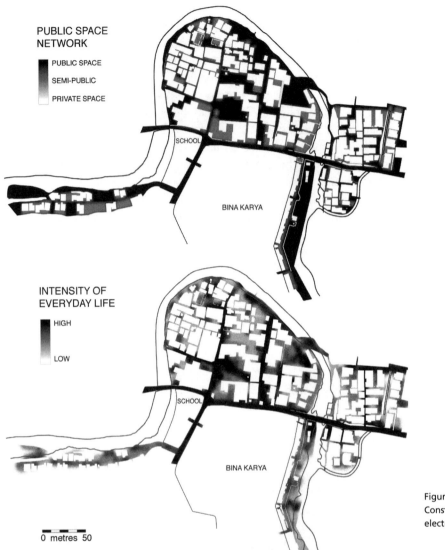

PUBLIC SPACE
NETWORK

■ PUBLIC SPACE

SEMI-PUBLIC

PRIVATE SPACE

SCHOOL

BINA KARYA

INTENSITY OF
EVERYDAY LIFE

■ HIGH

LOW

SCHOOL

BINA KARYA

0 metres 50

Figure 6.3
Construction and
electricity.

space for domestic, social and industrial uses is an integral part of how this community functions. Areas of high internal density also have a markedly higher use
and appropriation of public space. Despite the high densities the public/private
interface is generally mediated by an interstitial porch space used for display and
social activity. There are a range of small public open spaces in the settlement but
most are informal and provisional. The most active is a shady unpaved area that
is 'owned' by residents from adjacent properties who are happy to see it used as
public space (Figure 6.2 centre). All open spaces are ambiguous in that they are
widely used and appropriated for both domestic and public functions. The river is

the largest public open space (Figure 6.2 lower); access changes with the height of the river but is generally as shown on the map.

Everyday life in the kampung is far too dynamic and fluid to map in detail but the general intensities of public activity are shown in Figure 6.3 (lower). There are many differences over time and according to the age and gender of the population. Volumes of activity ensure continuous co-presence, one is rarely alone in any public space during the day. The greatest volumes of streetlife occur in the main street and lanes that connect with it. In the denser and poorer areas domestic and other productive activities largely take place in public space – from cooking, cleaning and laundry to scavenging, aquaculture, construction, rock gathering and rock crushing. Most of this work occurs around the house, along the river or in specific locations. Children's play is widely distributed with a mix of genders, generally in small groups and with a wide spatial range from a young age. All children have access to the river and there is a lot of swimming. Boys play soccer wherever there is a few square metres of open space. Children were also engaged from time to time in organized activities such as library, music and drama sessions in the open spaces (Figure 6.2 centre). Teenagers are sharply divided by gender; groups of boys hang out on the nodes of the main street while girls are much less visible. Most leisure activity by adults is linked to

Figure 6.4
Semi-private spaces.

Places ■

domestic space and comprises socializing on porches and tending gardens and birds. Activities related to the exchange of goods and information are primarily linked to shopping, transport, reading public newspapers and public events. These activities mostly take place in the main streets, however, there are female networks of information exchange integrated with laundry activities along the river.

Figure 6.5 maps the use of different construction materials as well as access to electricity. The common housing type is derived from the traditional double-pitched gable of the Javanese house with a tiled roof and bamboo walls. In this settlement there are a range of types, many houses are reduced to a single room

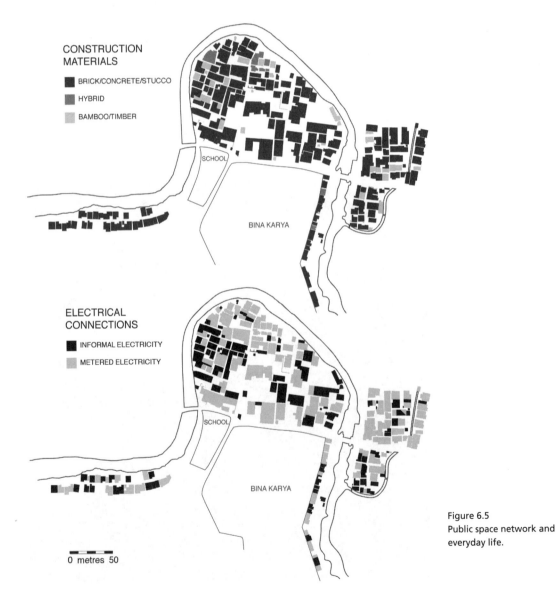

Figure 6.5
Public space network and everyday life.

92 ▢

and most walls are brick and concrete block (Figures 6.4 and 6.6). Design is based on the accretion of single rooms depending on site conditions. Construction mostly begins with a single room on plots of about 3 m by 3 or 6 m. While most houses are detached they are also constructed very closely to neighbours – very few houses are identifiably detached. Interiors and plans of houses were not accessible for this study. The design and construction of most dwellings is flexible and economical, based in the availability of local expertise and materials. Designs are flexible to accommodate gradual changes over time as more materials are acquired, often extending vertically (Figure 6.4 upper left). Construction is rapid and a large range of small construction sites show changes every day. In the absence of secure land tenure residents pursue symbols of permanence and security through house form and materials – the quest for secure tenure is transferred from the legal field to that of urban semiotics. The heavier the material the greater the image of permanence. While woven bamboo screen walls offer better ventilation, brick and concrete block are higher status. A hybrid wall (*kotangan*) with a brick or concrete lower half and bamboo screen above is a common compromise which symbolizes permanence and promotes cross-ventilation. Well-established houses are often rendered and painted with façades and front porches clad with ceramic tiles (Figure 6.6 upper).

The morphology and spatial structure of Kricak and Sidomulyo is the most stable part of this urban assemblage, but it cannot be understood in isolation from a large range of loose parts that circulate through it. Cars, motorcycles, bicycles, pedicabs and food trolleys are parked throughout the site. A range of stored construction materials – bamboo, roof tiles, bricks – are placed between overhanging roofs, against solid walls and in vacant corners of public space where they are 'banked' until resources are available for the next phase of upgrading or construction (Figure 6.6 centre). Miscellaneous domestic resources spill around the entries of houses: bird cages, buckets, planters, mattresses, furniture, children's play equipment, bamboo mats, cooking equipment and stoves. Public space is widely used for drying clothes, sometimes on lines hoisted above the eaves. Roof edges are often used for drying food. Garbage tends to collect in leftover spaces that are not territorialized. There is one large open public garbage container on the main road and a general attention to cleanliness across the settlement.

The various layers of loose parts give the settlement an image that may appear chaotic at first glance, especially in the poorer neighbourhoods. However, the placement of loose parts is determined by an underlying logic: a lack of interior space and a need to spill both resources and activities into public space; a constant need for solar clothes drying; the need to accumulate construction resources over time. Very little of the dynamism can be captured by the two-dimensional cartographic representations here – the use of public space is highly negotiable; public–private boundaries are blurred and the ownership of loose parts is often not apparent. This informal logic produces a public space network saturated with individual inscriptions shaping its identity in both the short and longer term.

Figure 6.5 also maps access to electricity. A good portion of the houses have a formal electricity supply – identifiable by a meter near the entrance – those without meters negotiate an arrangement for informal supply from neighbours who then pay the collective bills. A significant number of public wells have been provided through slum upgrading programmes; carrying buckets remains the primary water supply to most houses (Figures 6.4 lower). The public wells are generally co-located with public washroom/toilets and the sewage flows to septic tanks and then back into the water table and the well. Some houses are connected to the city's water system and again neighbours often have informal connections. Raw sewage often flows directly into the river.

The river Winongo plays a central role in daily life. It is a place to collect building materials, such as sand, gravel and rocks, and also a place for ablutions, bathing and cooling off from the humid heat. A major flood occurred in 1984, washing away the former wooden bridge and many houses. The current concrete bridge was then built by the state, enabling car access for the first time. This bridge has become a major icon with its ship-like pylons as symbols of a permanent connection to the city (Figure 6.2 lower). While many of the riverbanks are now reinforced with retaining walls, some parts of the settlement are likely to be flooded again in time. The river has two primary industrial uses – gathering stones for crushing into concrete aggregate and fish cultivation in sandbag ponds. The fish ponds comprise a dynamic landscape with new ponds and levels being added as the river rises and falls. The river is the primary laundry for the community, conducted on a range of flat rocks or concrete slabs that are also very social spaces.

While there are parts of this settlement that are clearly 'slums' by the UN definition, it is a highly dynamic community with a hopeful future. The public spaces are materially poor but socially rich, without the signs of idleness, despair and disease that mark so many disadvantaged communities. Words such as informal, slum and squatter tend to label a place according to a series of conceptual oppositions of formal/informal, wealth/poverty and legal/illegal tenure, yet most of this settlement negotiates a set of ambiguous zones between these poles. These oppositions align to some degree with those outlined in Chapter 2: striated/smooth, tree/rhizome, territorialization/deterritorialization (Deleuze and Guattari 1987). The urban morphology has been created primarily through processes of rhizomatic assemblage, yet it is also a cluster of territories with administrative boundaries inscribed. It would be easy to cast this settlement as primarily 'smooth' space, yet like most places it is always becoming striated. One way of characterizing it is to say that it is everywhere striated but profoundly smooth; another is that it has an excess of smoothness when it comes to land tenure. One of the challenges and opportunities in the understanding of informal urban morphologies and systems of control is to inform a rethinking of developed cities and their trajectories. While it is important not to get romantic about the difficulties of informal settlements, the ways in which public space shows the traces of many individual and collective acts has lessons for the over-determined and replicated dullness of so much formalized urbanism.

Figure 6.6
Loose parts.

Sidomulyo/Kricak has relatively high levels of social capital and low symbolic capital. This has been a relatively closed place where the deeper alleys of the spatial structure are rarely traversed by outsiders. Leadership remains a male preserve while women work behind the scenes; there is a sense that any change is a threat to current practices of power. The community is subject to internal division into a range of sub-groups based on tenure, class and sexuality. Social capital is highest within the sub-groups but tensions remain between them. Building solidarity between groups and connections with a larger world are key priorities. The festival that coincided with our visit was designed in part to open up the community and to generate connections locally and globally. It was the subject of three television programmes and while there were concerns about how the place would be portrayed, the programmes were generally positive with a focus on the urban artworks. While all residents have access to television and radio, and many work across the city of Yogyakarta, there are few links to other informal settlements locally or globally.

Land tenure remains a key issue for residents, but it is more informal and deeply labyrinthine than the morphology. The informal sense of 'ownership' is everywhere ambiguous and contentious – subject to the play of politics, time, usage, materials, architectural form, rental and 'lease'. Most residents depict themselves as 'owners' or 'renters'. Yet there are few formal land titles and 'tenants' have often built their houses, paying ground rent to 'owners' who in many cases hold no formal title. While the mapping of existing land tenure is crucial to the quest for tenure, such clarity can serve a variety of interests. A key dilemma is that the system is based on conflicting and contradictory systems of legitimation of ownership. Squatter housing is like a game where the rules are unclear and the primary goal is security of tenure. Ownership is widely believed to be legitimated by lengthy occupation and by the investment in 'permanent' housing. In the absence of formal land tenure, housing plays a key role in the signification of permanence – hence the hierarchy of materials from bamboo and timber to brick, concrete and stucco.

While we have mapped the urban morphology as best we can, to map the tenure accurately is at once difficult and contentious. Difficult because of the ambiguities outlined above; there are so many categories of tenure and none of them can be regarded as 'freehold'. Very few residents feel at risk of eviction yet the quest for security of tenure is an important issue. The rock-crushing community with some of the least 'permanent' housing are fearful that the 'owner' will sell the land to someone who will evict them. Others in Kricak feel relatively secure and only lack the legal 'title'. The Government Lands Office, however, is reluctant to grant new titles since this is seen to encourage more squatting. Pressure on the government in this regard runs the danger of triggering retaliatory evictions. In other words any attempt to formalize and legalize territories can lead to deterritorialization and reterritorialization as government land. The ambiguity over ownership operates in the interest of the landlords whose lack of formal ownership could be exposed by detailed study. It also suits the state whose agencies have no desire to engage in forcible evictions and whose officers can sometimes extract a profit for their tacit agreement to do nothing. Thus the ambiguities of formal tenure are not so much residual characteristics of a traditional or rural land system but more a highly functional aspect of the squatter settlement as a formal modern assemblage. Squatters have an interest in more secure tenure but they tend to pursue this through symbolic rather than legal means, and the design and construction of more permanent housing is one dimension of securing tenure.

POLITICS OF REPRESENTATION

We move now from this case to the broader issues of informal urbanism and to the question of how the forms of informality play out in larger assemblages. Roy (2004) calls attention to the politics of representation of informal settlements, and she relates the responses of students from two Berkeley design studios when they returned from field trips in Mexico City. In the first group, an architecture studio:

> students recorded the sounds of poverty, collected the dirt of poverty, acquired discarded objects of poverty, and returned to Berkeley to make a montage of their excavations ... For one student the experience of the squatter settlement was embodied by a battered drum she came across in her wanderings there. Returning to Berkeley, she placed gravel collected from the settlement on the drum, and played it to create contours and shapes that would then determine the topography of her design.
>
> (Roy 2004: 295)

No one who has taught architectural design studios will be particularly surprised by this since it reflects the ideology of Western architecture as an autonomous aesthetic practice. It is important, however, to understand that it is not student behaviour that is at issue here but the field of cultural production and critique within which the student is enmeshed (Bourdieu 1993).[3] A transposition has taken place whereby the squatter settlement is not the end of the design process but the means, the symbolic resource for aesthetic production. The use of images of underdevelopment as symbolic capital can also be understood as the aestheticization of poverty. The second studio related by Roy involved environmental planning students who were focused on the protection of agricultural land from rapid urbanization:

> In the multilayered model that had represented every gradient of the topography, every flow and ebb of the watershed, the land that had been represented as blank and empty, as frontier, was in fact the living fabric of the site, inhabited by squatters.
>
> (Roy 2004: 295–296)

This erasure of the social reflects a desire to hold squatting at bay as a threat to a natural order. Perhaps this approach reflects a more benign ideology, but neither of these approaches engages with the existing conditions of informal settlement.

Roy has several concerns here. The first is to counter the very focus on environ-mental transformation as a response to poverty: 'What is redeveloped is space and buildings rather than people's socioeconomic experience' (Roy 2004: 298). This ideology is seen as linked to the aestheticization of poverty:

> the aestheticization of poverty is the establishment of an aesthetic and aestheticized
> (rather than political) relationship between viewer and viewed, between professional and
> city, between First and Third Worlds. It is an ideology of space. Such a relationship is
> expressed primarily in the form of nostalgia ... a pastoral nostalgia that craves the
> rurality of a magical countryside in a rapidly urbanizing world.
>
> (Roy 2004: 302–303)

The broader concern is that a focus on aesthetic issues serves a neoliberal polit-ical agenda by turning attention away from transnational struggles over poverty (Roy 2004: 304). This is a legitimate issue but any separation of aesthetics from politics and commerce is quite untenable. In our view the interests of the resi-dents of informal settlements are best served by entering into the complex inter-sections of aesthetic and social issues. The ideal of a pastoral nostalgia is a good place to start. In the case of Sidomulyo there was a small public well, located deep within the most dense part of the settlement (Figure 6.4 lower). After a large number of images and maps of the settlement were exhibited at our Uni-versity, this image was chosen and used to promote the Faculty and its field trips. The image evokes a notion of traditional social capital but here it was turned into symbolic capital. This is not a pastoral image but one of deep labyrinthine space. A good deal of the aesthetic response to informal settlements is not nostalgic but is rather a perception of beauty in abjection and dereliction, and in the dialectic imagery that juxtaposes dream images with poverty. Yet the aesthetic of squatter settlements has a potency beyond symbolic capital. Peattie (1992) has argued that images shape politics and policies; she points out the way that an image of informal *favelas* on an escarpment in Rio de Janiero was used in Perlman's seminal study to legitimate squatting (Perlman 1976).

An even more interesting case can be found on a riverbank redevelopment project in Yogyakarta known as Gondolyu (or *Kali Cho-de*) led by the architect/priest Romo Mangun (Khudori 1987, 2004).[4] During the 1980s this project led to an upgrading of about 40 houses from a settlement of cardboard and plastic to brick, concrete, timber and bamboo. It saved the community from eviction and involved a colourful practice of public artworks on the buildings (Khudori, 2004: 44–60). Over 20 years later this project remains a demonstration project for slum upgrading in Indonesia and the community is safe from eviction.

The larger socio-political context of development in Gondolyu has not markedly changed. While the housing has been successfully upgraded, residents do not have legal tenure and many remain stuck in cycles of poverty (scavenging rubbish from the river). Yet this is an informal settlement in a process of becom-ing prosperous; construction has continued long after Mangun's involvement and so has the painting of houses with artworks; visits in 2005 and 2008 show

Figure 6.7
Gondolyu.

substantial transformations in both built form and artworks. This settlement is highly visible from a major traffic artery across the Chode River (Figure 6.7). Prior to redevelopment this visibility was a major reason for the targeting of the community for eviction. The focus on aesthetic considerations, particularly the painted artworks, has worked as a form of political legitimation that has protected this community from eviction. In other words they have turned visibility from a problem into an asset, wearing a colourful place identity (their difference) as a badge of pride. In this case there is a very clear connection of aesthetics to tenure, today Gondolyu is one of the most secure of squatter settlements in Yogyakarta because of the highly visible sense of community pride.

The Gondolyu imagery is interesting in this regard because it does evoke the ideals of Javanese tradition in much of its building typology, materials, colours and painted images. These traditions are part of the reason why this upgrading has been sustained and continued. Yet it is also a highly urbanized settlement with dynamic images of painted houses juxtaposed with McDonald's and other advertising signs on the skyline above. The politics of representation here relies more on urban context than tradition. The imagery legitimates squatting as a signifier for do-it-yourself upgrading. Squatter settlements have a lot in common with both rural tradition and nineteenth-century industrial slums, but they emerge in the latter half of the twentieth century as distinctively modern settlement types. This is not the pure ideal of modern architecture but the modernity of capitalism; the modernism of cardboard, steel and plastic.

PROSPECTS

Some of the issues outlined above came to the fore during our field trip in Sido-mulyo/Kricak which was framed as a research exercise rather than a design studio; mapping the existing conditions was the focus of the study. The question of what to map was developed over the first few days, informed by our under-standings of the place and of urban design issues. It soon became apparent that there were significant opportunities for change in spatial form. The most signifi-cant of them was the existence of a large amount of derelict land immediately adjacent to the settlement. This was officially part of a social institution for the homeless and mentally ill called Bina Karya, separated from the informal settle-ment by a high wall. This is the same institution from which the poorer residents of Sidomulyo were originally evicted in the 1960s. It also became apparent that there was some serious overcrowding in the denser parts of the settlement where these families now live – 'rental' properties where upgrading *in situ* is very diffi-cult. This zone is already high density with poor light in some public spaces and second-storey additions would further lower the quality of public space.

While there are dangers in offering design ideas after a short field trip, there are also dangers to remaining silent in the light of opportunities for change. We asked students to envision a prospect for the derelict land to be developed for open space, community facilities and new housing to ease the most crowded slums (Figure 6.8 upper). These sketchy ideas and images were presented, along with some of the maps, to community leaders and at a final community gather-ing. The forms of the design were less important than stimulating the collective imagination of the community. The official response was that the derelict land was 'government land' and its use was unthinkable. While it looked to us like smooth space or *terrain vague* (Sola-Morales 1994), everything behind the wall was identified with a strict institutionalization and even incarceration of the social 'other'.

A return visit to this settlement a year after the initial fieldwork trip showed evidence of many changes. Notably, the boundary wall between the informal set-tlement and the expanse of derelict land had been reinforced with a high brick wall and barbed wire (Figure 6.8 lower). This was undertaken by the state author-ities at considerable expense and very clearly designed to stop squatting. Outside the wall a new section of riverbank was being prepared for more squatter housing – in this case existing renters seeking home ownership.

This settlement is just one in a million and each one will be different; how different we do not really know in terms of urban morphology because there are very few comparative studies. After five days of fieldwork this is scarcely a defini-tive study but it opens a window onto forms of urban morphology and trans-formation that are rarely studied in this way. It also opens questions about the relationship of built form and design to social change. Settlements such as this are growing at a faster rate than any other form of urban development; they cannot be demolished or replaced as a totality. The United Nations prediction is

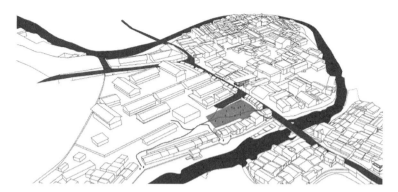

Figure 6.8
Integrating and
defending derelict land.

that the population of urban slums will reach two billion by 2030; their target is to improve the lives of 100 million but there is not much confidence about that. The only real possibility, short of a very major redistribution of global resources, is that such places will become prosperous through the same informal processes by which they were invented – an assemblage of speculative acts from those who have little to lose. The prospect is that they develop through a similar process into healthy, well-serviced, well-connected, if relatively informal neighbourhoods.

Chapter 7: Urbanizing Architecture

Rem Koolhaas and Spatial Segmentarity

Koolhaas' designs are blatantly straightforward ... one and only one cultural aim drives the work ... to discover what real, instrumental collaboration can be effected between architecture and freedom.

(Kipnis 1998: 27)

The success of the work of Rem Koolhaas and his firm OMA rests strongly on the implicit or explicit claim to be an architecture of emancipation. Koolhaas can be interpreted as resuscitating the early modernist imperative to develop an architecture of social relevance through a mix of programmatic and formal change. He seeks to challenge practices of social reproduction as they are embedded in architectural ideology and spatial programme. Programmatic innovations include the production of fields of social encounter, new functional juxtapositions and forms of spatial segmentation designed to resist social reproduction and enable certain 'freedoms' (Zaera and Koolhaas 1992). This chapter is an examination of such claims through a critique of three well-known buildings.[1] The primary lens for this critique is an adapted method of spatial syntax analysis filtered through a Deleuzian framework of assemblage theory (see Chapter 2). Spatial syntax analysis, as developed by Hillier and others (Hillier 1996; Hillier and Hanson 1984), is a largely structuralist critique of spatial structure that would surely be anathema to Koolhaas. Despite a positivist and reductionist bias, spatial syntax analysis has a significant linkage to conceptions of place as assemblage and as habitus, particularly in its interrogation of the 'genotypes' or 'diagrams' embodied in buildings as forms of social reproduction. While Koolhaas rarely mentions or cites Deleuze, the influence is clear (Rajchman and Koolhaas 1994: 99; Kwinter 1996; Speaks 1994). It is at least an interesting congruence that both Hillier and Koolhaas deploy the 'machine' as a primary metaphor in their approach to architecture and space. For both this is a critical response to the Corbusian notion of architecture as a 'machine for living'. Hillier's major book is entitled *Space is the Machine* and Koolhaas' work often deploys machines both literally and metaphorically. Both approaches privilege the idea of buildings being produced systemically through generic (in the case of Koolhaas) or genetic (Hillier) codes or structures; both treat buildings as forms of infrastructure that variously accommodate or constrain flows of life. The loose adaptation of spatial syntax methods here is unlikely to be accepta- ble to either Koolhaas or Hillier; it is not intended to be reductionist but is intended to bring a more rigorous critique to some of the claims for programmatic innovation in Koolhaas' designs. To do this I will first set aside the formalist aesthetic critique of Koolhaas' work except as it informs this task. This does not suggest that form and programme can be easily separated – I argued in Chapter 4 that such a presumed separation is one of the deepest complicities of architecture with power. It is also not because the aesthetic dimension of his work is less interesting or innovative, Kool- haas is a master form-maker and major producer of symbolic capital (see Chapter 3). The problem is that architectural critique is so skewed towards the formal that it is all that many critics see of his work; a problem to which I shall return.

FIELDS

The works of Koolhaas/OMA have been termed the 'social condensers of our time' (Graafland 1998). This reflects a return to the early modernist imperative towards an architecture which would remake the habitat of everyday life. This is not, however, a return to the social engineering reflected in ideas like the 'social condenser' of the Soviet constructivists. Rather it is a vision of an internalized 'culture of congestion' fuelled by the formal and social multiplicities of urban life (Koolhaas 1978). This vision is reflected in the name of Koolhaas' firm – Office for Metropolitan Architecture – which can be read as both an 'architecture *of* the metropolis' and an insertion of the 'metropolis *into* the architecture'. Koolhaas' work is strongly ordered by trajectories of movement through the building. The role of vertical movement via escalators, stairs, ramps and lifts is a key to the order which is set up, as they become the modes of access to fields of event and encounter. Koolhaas is inspired by the notion of an architecture of liberation in terms of the multiple 'freedoms' for new forms of action which architecture is seen to make possible (Zaera and Koolhaas 1992). Space is programmed for indefinite function and chance encounter. Koolhaas seeks an architecture that can resist the imperative to become a diagram of social and institutional struc- ture. For Kipnis, Koolhaas' version of freedom is not an overt resistance to authority but rather a form of programmatic sabotage:

> More like a sadist than a surgeon, he has begun to knife the brief, hacking away its fat,
> even its flesh, until he has exposed its nerve ... the focus on these reductions is always
> on *disestablishment*, that is, always on excising the residues in the project of
> unwarranted authority, unnecessary governance and tired convention. Reductive

> *disestablishment* provides the crucial stratagem in each of Koolhaas' recent projects, the intellectual *modus operandi* by which the architect begins to transform the design into an instrument of freedom.
>
> (Kipnis 1998: 29–30)

Koolhaas seeks an architecture that encourages an eruption of 'events', social encounters and opportunities for action. Rather than designing with a particular hierarchy of spaces and narratives of spatial movement in mind, he generally works towards a spatial structure that allows a multiplicity of choices for pedestrian flow and encounter. Koolhaas wants to 'liquefy rigid programming into non-specific flows and events ... to weave together exterior, interior, vestigial and primary spaces into a frank differential matrix that rids the building of the hackneyed bourgeois niceties of cosmetic hierarchies' (Kipnis 1998: 30).

Koolhaas often designs interiors as if they were exteriors, importing the randomness of social encounter from exterior urban space into interior space. These interiors are often designed as 'fields of play' or 'artificial landscapes' which dissolve boundaries between inside and outside, between architecture and metropolis. Such spaces are often functionally open and visually transparent to maximize social encounter. Jameson situates Koolhaas' work in the context of the prevailing social dialectics of publicity/privacy and freedom/control in what he terms the 'post-civil' society. He suggests that Koolhaas' work enables patterns of free play within a rigid spatial order:

> the originality of Koolhaas is that his work does not simply glorify differentiation in the conventional pluralist ideological way: rather he insists on the relationship between this randomness and freedom and the presence of some rigid, inhuman, non-differentiated form that enables the differentiation of what goes on around it.
>
> (Jameson and Speaks 1992: 33)

There is an interesting connection here with what Allen (1997) suggests is a shift in architectural thinking from a focus on the architectural object to a focus on field relations paralleling the development of field theory in mathematics. A field consists of contingent relations, forces, trajectories and patterns of movement such as those which govern a 'flock' of birds. Field conditions are described as: 'any formal or spatial matrix capable of unifying diverse elements while respecting the identity of each ... Field conditions are bottom-up phenomena: defined not by overarching geometrical schema but by intricate local connections' (Allen 1997: 24). The field is a material condition rather than a discursive practice. Allen draws analogies between field theory and architectural attempts to encourage a spontaneity of 'action'. He suggests that systems with 'permeable boundaries, flexible internal relationships, multiple pathways and fluid hierarchies' are capable of responding to emerging complexities of new urban contexts (Allen 1997: 31). A major innovation in Koolhaas' work lies in the extent to which he has utilized such strategies in the interiors of buildings where they contribute towards the emergence of new kinds of social space. The promise here is that the field-like nature of Koolhaas' work opens up the work to multiplicities of experience and action. This idea of the building as a field rather than an architectural object entails a shift in critique from form to spatial analysis. We must then ask, to what extent do these designs restructure social space or reproduce familiar spatial structures?

SEGMENTARITY

Methods of spatial syntax analysis, first developed by Hillier, represent an attempt to reveal a deep social structuring of architectural space (Hillier 1996; Hillier and Hanson 1984). For Hillier, buildings operate to constitute social organizations as spatial dispositions; architecture mediates social reproduction through spatial 'genotypes'. These are not formal 'types' or 'archetypes' but clusters of spatial segments structured in certain formations with syntactic rules of sequence and adjacency. Genotypes are seen as institutionally and epistemologically embedded – schools, offices, libraries and houses are reproduced from a limited number of spatial genotypes. Each of these is linked to specific social institutions with forms of knowledge, production and reproduction. Hillier's work is widely perceived within the field of architecture as positivist and reductionist. While I share some of these concerns, Koolhaas' programmatic innovations demand critique in terms of the link between spatial structure and institutional authority and the spatial syntax approach is the most sophisticated available. There are consistencies between syntactic analysis and aspects of both assemblage theory (Chapter 2) and theories of habitus (Chapter 3) with some important limitations – it seeks a 'social logic' in the materiality of spatial relations and does not address issues of expression or symbolic capital.

Within the theory of spatial syntax analysis there are a range of analytic techniques and there is not room here for more than a cursory account.[2] This analysis is a loose adaptation of syntactic analysis which translates the building plan into a diagram of how life and social encounter is framed within it. Figure 7.1 shows how similar plans with different access points yield quite different syntactic structures and illustrates three primary cluster relations – the line, net and fan. Each displays a differing level of spatial control and freedom: the line (or enfilade) controls the choice of pathway; the fan (or branching) structure controls access to a number of segments from a single segment; and the net is a ringy or permeable network with multiple choices of pathway. The three may seem a limited set, but all spatial structures can be understood in terms of combinations and additions of them. These are abstract diagrams, akin to Deleuze and Guattari's abstract machines; they are at once immanently embodied in particular places or assemblages yet remain as abstractions with a causative impact across a wide variety of place types.

All architecture involves combinations of the line, fan and net, including a range of decisions regarding how spatial assemblages are interconnected and linked to external space. The linear assemblage is an enfilade of spaces with

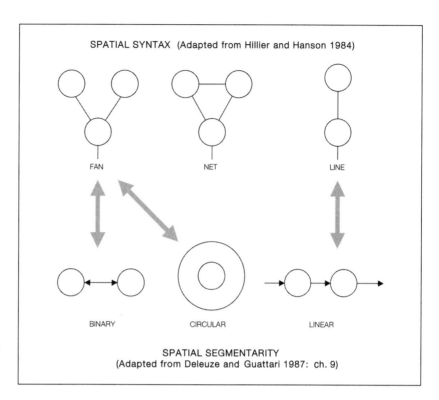

Figure 7.1
Syntax and segmentarity.

controlled movement – it may or may not be a cul de sac. It is common in traditional centres of power (such as Versailles) and in some modern retail buildings
(like Ikea) and blockbuster art exhibitions with an entry at one end and an exit at
the other. The network syntax is defined by a ringy spatial structure and a choice
of pathways as in a department store or shopping mall. Networks are characterized by limited control of spatial flows but may be sealed from adjacent assemblages. The fan is characteristic of bureaucratic organizations with large numbers
of cells controlled by a hallway.

There are important links between these diagrams and the theoretical concepts of *habitus* and *segmentarity* outlined in Chapters 2 and 3. For Bourdieu the
habitus is both a socio-spatial division between people, things and practices as
well as a 'sense of one's place' within this world.

Bourdieu's early structuralist account of the Kabyl (or Berber) house
(Bourdieu 1973) was subtitled 'the world reversed'. It showed how the threshold
of the house became a hinge point at which a series of structured relationships
became 'reversed'. Deleuze and Guattari see such traditional forms of segmentarity as highly coded yet also more 'supple' than the modern. Despite the identification of modernity with the open plan, they suggest modern life has
introduced a more rigid segmentarity identified with bureaucracy and the state
(Deleuze and Guattari 1987: 210). For Deleuze and Guattari segmentarity is a
socio-spatial division that is immanent to life; when they use Henry James'

novela *In the Cage* to describe segmentarity they could also be illustrating the habitus:

> The heroine, a young telegrapher, leads a very clear-cut, calculated life proceeding by delimited segments: the telegrams she takes one after the other, day after day ... her telegraphist's cage is like a contiguous segment to the grocery store next door, where her fiancé works ... plotting out their future, work, vacations, house. Here, as for all of us, there is a line of rigid segmentarity on which everything seems calculable ... Our lives are made like that ... A whole interplay of well-determined, well planned territories. They have a future but no becoming.
>
> (Deleuze and Guattari 1987: 195)

From this view segmentarity is divided into three main types – the binary, circular and linear – which are outlined in Chapter 2 and diagrammed next to the syntactic types in Figure 7.1. While the concept of spatial syntax is not in Deleuze and Guattari's lexicon, the coded rules for the combination of spatial segments are a key theme of chapter 9 of *A Thousand Plateaus* where segmentarity is fundamentally linked to micropractices of power. The three categories of segmentarity – binary, concentric and linear – are all assembled relationships between segments but only the linear type maps easily against the syntactic types of line, fan and net. The binary type can be linked to the fan as a diagram that effects divisions of class, gender, age, rank, etc. through an architectural division of pathways off a common entry (like the contiguous segments in the quotation above). The fan is also the root of the concentric type in the sense that it is based on a nested hierarchic connection between a segment and the sub-segments within it.

The network syntax does not appear in Deleuze and Guattari's scheme largely because they want to identify segmentarity with the latter side of the smooth/striated, rhizome/tree conceptual oppositions where the smooth and rhizomatic flows are opposed to the stasis of segments. Yet a networked spatial structure is fundamental to the enabling of such flows – the traffic of streets and the exchange of markets cannot occur without richly interconnected but structured and striated movement patterns. The network is clearly more linked to smooth space and rhizomatic practices than the controlled fans and linear sequences. The syntactic types are abstract and when they combine in concrete place assemblages the result is always a mixture. A key dimension of syntactic analysis is the degree of rhizomatic connectivity, also known as 'ringiness', versus a 'tree-like' hierarchy of spatial control. The network structure is defined by a multiplicity of pathways and dispersed control, although such spatial freedom may be nested within larger boundaries and structures of power such as the housing enclave and the shopping mall (Dovey 2008). The network can be a branch of a tree. Tree-like structures control circulation and social interaction in certain key access spaces. Thus a hallway or foyer which is the only access to a cluster of rooms has a high level of control over the flow of everyday life. The permeable network or ringy structure offers many possible pathways and diverse encounters – the flow of life through space is only loosely controlled.

Another key characteristic is the 'depth' or 'shallowness' of any segment from the nearest external entry points and the overall depth of the structure. A deep structure requires the traversing of many segments with many boundaries and points of control. The diagrammatic method shows the spatial segments of the building layered into levels of depth so that the level of a space indicates the shortest route from the exterior. Depth is an important mediator of social relations both between inhabitants (kinship relations or organizational hierarchies) and between inhabitants and visitors. Domestic space is often structured along age (adult/child) and gender divisions in its deeper segments, while mediating contact between insiders and visitors in shallower space. The syntax of disciplinary institutions (prison, hospital, asylum, school and factory) locates subjects under surveillance deep within the structure.[3]

Many contemporary buildings, those of Koolhaas among them, are designed with flowing and fragmented spaces, pursuing deliberate ambiguities of enclosure, visibility and permeability. The diagrams outlined above are scarcely detectable so how does syntactic analysis make sense when space is not clearly segmented? Such analysis cannot be exact or mathematical; the illusion of an exact spatial science that pervades Hillier's work hinders its use in the interpretation of the assemblage. The mappings of specific spatial patterns in buildings are not plans but are designed to reveal patterns of access and control through a spatial structure. These maps have a mimetic relationship to the territory but are not mechanically derived from it – the boxes on the diagrams include both separate rooms and semi-separated spatial fields. They are necessarily interpretive but they have an empirical basis in the flows of movement through the buildings.

What makes such analysis potent as a method is that it maps the ways in which buildings operate as fields of socio-spatial encounter. The spatial structure is what Bourdieu terms a 'structuring structure' of the habitus, the embodied divisions and hierarchies between things, persons and practices which construct the social world. Our positions within buildings lend us our dispositions in social life; the spatial division of our world becomes a vision of the world. The buildings we inhabit, our habitat, our spatial habits, all reproduce our social world. Syntactic analysis of space opens up questions – what kinds of agency are enabled and constrained by the particular building genotype within which it is structured and whose interests are served? How is everyday life bracketed and punctuated into socio-spatially framed situations and locales? How does architecture frame the social gaze through structured realms of visibility? What regimes of normalization are enforced and in whose interest? What prospects or freedoms are enabled, and again, in whose interests?

The structural distinctions between controlled and networked structures on the one hand, and between deep and shallow structures on the other, can be mapped against Deleuze and Guattari's distinction between smooth and striated space. Strictness of control through spatial structure is a form of striation and, in general terms, linear and branching structures are more striated, while ringy networks can be identified with smooth space. A permeable network of spaces and the open plan have long been linked to practices of social freedom, yet any conflation of physical enclosure with social constraint, or of open space with liberty, is a dangerous one. Buildings are increasingly called upon to produce an illusion of freedom coupled with the reality of control and surveillance. Freedom of association within a particular social group can build the social capital of that group vis-à-vis other groups. This is what Hillier and Hanson (1984: 255–261) term the 'correspondence' model in which spatial zones correspond to social groupings – those who share a spatial zone also share a social label. Thus an exclusive private school may be a highly permeable zone of social encounter with a rhizomatic spatial structure at the local level yet also also an elite branch of the social tree at a global level. A spatial assemblage that mixes people of different social identities is in general less likely to reproduce those identities and more likely to promote new identity formation. Such spaces are much more characteristic of the urban public realm than the private interior. Interior space is more rigidly segmented and deterministic with primary functions of social reproduction. Thus two kinds of spatial assemblage are counterposed: the more open and smooth networks of public space and the more closed and striated private spaces.

Public and private realms have a symbiotic relationship, and it is the ambiguous zone between them that is often the most interesting and vital part of a city. In general terms the random encounter and open access of the public realm is a threat to the social reproductive function of private space and the determinism of interior structures is a threat to urban diversity. One of the key characteristics of current spatial production involves the emergence of a private realm that generates the illusion of diverse and accessible public space. The programmatic innovations of Rem Koolhaas involve an experimentation with this tension between inside and outside, using the encounter structures of urban space to effect innovations in interior space. I now move to a spatial analysis of three completed projects by Koolhaas/OMA: a school, a house and a library.

LEARNING FACTORY

The Educatorium for the University of Utrecht was built in 1997 to house a cafeteria, two large lecture theatres and a cluster of examination rooms. According to the project architect's statement, it was conceived as the hub of a campus servicing 14 faculties and research facilities. It was described as a 'rendezvous and exchange point, creating a new center of gravity' to 'embody the university "experience": the social encounters of the cafeteria space, the learning and exchange in the auditoria/classrooms, and the individual rites of passage played out in the examination halls' (Cornubert 1998: 43). Note the recognition of three

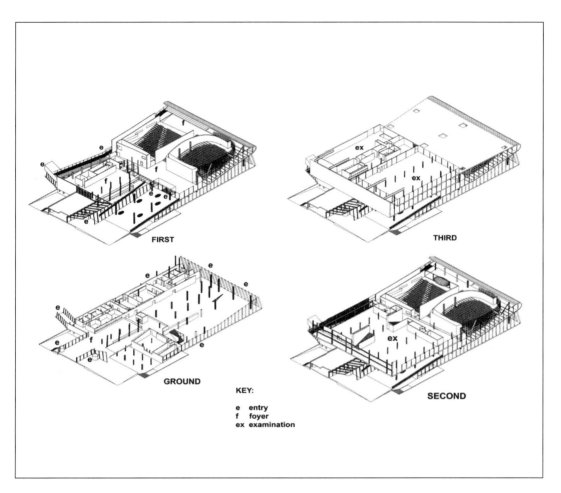

FIRST

THIRD

GROUND

KEY:

e   entry
f   foyer
ex examination

SECOND

Figure 7.2
Educatorium, University
of Utrecht.

different space types: for encounter, for learning and for rites of passage. There was a deliberate attempt to generate diverse forms of social encounter in the building, 'seeking potential overlap between the programs and encouraging exchange between the users of its diverse functions, whilst allowing a pragmatic and nearly autonomous use of individual spaces' (Cornubert 1998: 44).

This project architect's statement introduces a series of key phrases and metaphors that frame the critique of the building. The concept of a 'synthetic landscape' is used to evoke the idea of bringing the outside in. The entry to the building is described by the project architect as a tilted ground plane and 'urban plaza' which then continues as an interior sloping 'field'. This rising floorplate folds upwards and back to become the wall and then roof of the building. It is described by Koolhaas as a 'social magic carpet', an urban landscape of play and social encounter imported into the architecture (Figure 7.2). The floor which folds into a wall has become the iconic image of the building – one of the photographs provided for publication shows a skateboarder 'surfing' the curved surface of the interior folded wall. One of the auditoria has an entire wall open to the view and is described as an 'amphitheater set in the landscape' (Cornubert 1998: 43). Examination rooms are also described as interior landscapes which are able to be flexibly subdivided for different functions. The building as a whole was conceived as a permeable spatial structure, deliberately designed

> to act as a network in which students and users are free to discover their own alternative shortcuts and to 'drift' through [the] building. Rather than attempting to dictate any particular pattern of use, the design of the Educatorium seeks to create a synthetic landscape open to individual choice.
>
> (Cornubert 1998: 45)

Circulation areas are designed as a series of 'pause spaces' for impromptu hanging out between exams or lectures. All of these phrases and metaphors – hub, field, synthetic landscape, interior landscape, fold, drift, pause – come from the project architect's statement. When linked to certain key images of the building they also became the currency for discussion of this building within the discourse of architectural magazines as it was disseminated immediately after completion (Buchanan 1998; Irace 1998; Ryan 1998; van Cleef 1999).

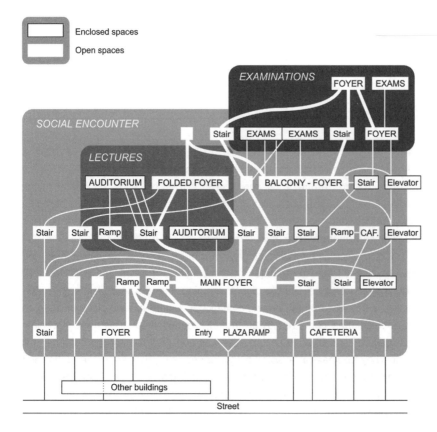

Figure 7.3
Educatorium, spatial structure.

The spatial analysis diagram (Figure 7.3) shows a building which is accessible and highly permeable. The building is accessed publicly through 11 entry points from the exterior and other buildings. For a building of this size and complexity this is a very shallow spatial structure indeed – all major spaces within it are accessible within six levels of depth. With the exception of service spaces (which have been omitted for clarity) there are no dead-ends whatever. In terms of the diagrams in Figure 7.1 the design involves a relentless deployment of the net and an avoidance of both the line and the fan. The spatial structure of the building is intensely rhizomatic. The building has three major functional attractors in the auditoria, examination rooms and the cafeteria, each of which is coupled with a major social circulation space. These three zones are organized vertically with the cafeteria on the ground floor, auditoria above, and the examination rooms occupying the upper levels. The major circulation spaces and routes between them are unenclosed (spaces enclosed by doors are marked by dark frames on the map). There are four major foyers, the aforementioned 'pause spaces' which form a series from the ramped plaza on the exterior to the main foyer which leads upwards to the folded foyer and then back to a balcony foyer outside the examination rooms. While the plan has a high level of permeability with a multiplicity of pathways, the main foyer also operates as a control space through which all of the open circulation systems within the building pass.

The Educatorium is repeatedly described in the literature as a 'factory of learning', a phrase which resonates with Koolhaas' aesthetic and his machinic metaphors. Importantly, here it is also an acknowledgement of the role of the university as a knowledge factory. While knowledge is produced in the research centres and staff offices deeper in the university (in the spokes that surround this building as hub), fragments of this knowledge are revealed in the spectacle of the lecture theatres, discussed in the foyers and cafeteria spaces and examined in the enclosed rooms above. Markus (1993) has shown how the spatial syntax of the lecture theatre surrounded by a field of highly permeable social space dates from the Enlightenment, based on the idea that knowledge is brought into the light from a deeper spatial source (the lab or study), revealed in the ritual of the lecture and then subsequently discussed in the open foyer. Knowledge is legitimated in part by locating its sources in deep spatial programmes. Examination rooms are a little like a reverse lecture, where students perform for teachers and knowledge is tested under ritual conditions of surveillance. Both the lecture and the examination are highly choreographed rituals embodying strong forms of spatio-temporal control. Each has a different kind of diagram (or abstract machine) as its immanent cause.

The lecture produces a spectacle with the theatre as a diagram, where the one is seen by the many. The examination by contrast is derived from the reversed spatial syntax of disciplinary institutions which place subjects under surveillance deep within the spatial structure. Its diagram is the panopticon. In the sense that this building is seen as the hub of the university one would expect to find staff offices and laboratories (the production of knowledge) on the branches of the tree-like structure. The spaces where student performance is legitimated are found deep within the hub. Here the Educatorium becomes partially reversed – inducting its subjects into regimes of normalization and surveillance in relatively deep space. The examination zone is five to six levels deep within the building; it does not receive the level of architectural attention of the shallow zones and is missing from the published photographs in magazines. This is not a field of social or symbolic capital, but rather the site where cultural and intellectual capital are legitimated. Here the field of play abruptly stops and work begins. The architectural treatment of lecture space as part of the synthetic landscape, the smoothing of the lectures, does not extend to examinations. While all examination rooms have multiple points of entry they are each end points to spatial movement. The shortest routes of access and egress to these levels are not through the open foyers but via the enclosed stair and the elevator (Figure 7.3). The fold of this building as it literally folds upwards is one of smooth folding into striation.

One can read the Educatorium as a highly innovative building at its shallow levels that becomes more conservative with depth. The socialization of students, contact between students and staff, and the delivery and sharing of ideas takes place in the relatively shallow network of social spaces. Yet the grading of student performance, the legitimation of institutional knowledge, remains deeply embedded in the spatial structure. The two key metaphors of 'synthetic landscape' and 'factory of learning' reflect the ways that the field relations of the landscape have been imported into the factory in order to urbanize the building. Yet the synthetic landscape of the folded floor/wall/roof does not encompass the examination rooms, and here the building more closely resembles the instrumentalism of the factory. The circulation system in this building is in many ways a masterful piece of design, but it achieves this by integrating such programmatic innovation with entrenched spatial genotypes. Its freedoms of movement and encounter urbanize its interior, but only to the point that it does not threaten the knowledge/power regime, and the diagram, that produces the building in the first place.

HEART MACHINE

This second project is a single-family house on a hilltop setting outside Bordeaux in northern France; it was completed in 1998 with an immediate splash in the architectural press.[4] The client was a family where the father became confined to a wheelchair and the house was largely designed around his needs. Koolhaas suggests that it is not a house for an invalid but an architecture which denies invalidity. The family's previous house in the medieval section of Bordeaux was described by Koolhaas as a 'prison' and the father himself described the new house as his 'liberation' (Colomina and Lleó 1998).

The house is organized with a total of four vertical movement systems connecting three formally distinct floors: a highly transparent living floor sandwiched between the heavy mass of lower (kitchen/entry) and upper (sleeping) floors

Figure 7.4
Bordeaux House.

(Figure 7.4). The base level is an entry courtyard with car access, framed by the house on one side with guest and servant quarters on the other. At this level the house is excavated from the hillside and likened (by Koolhaas) to a sequence of caves or cellars housing the entry, kitchen, wine cellar and television room (Emery 1999). The middle level is a fully transparent glass-enclosed slice of living/dining and gallery/study areas structured into one large field of visual and functional encounter (Figure 7.5). A motorized glass wall slides away to erase the boundary with the outdoor terrace, landscape and commanding views across Bordeaux. Just as the interior is opened to the landscape, so the exterior was to be furnished with artworks using a special tracking system in the ceiling – the bourgeois drawing room (once the 'withdrawing' room) slides out from the house. The bedroom accommodation on the top level is enclosed in a horizontal slab, pierced with porthole-sized windows and designed to appear as if suspended above the transparent living zone. The figure of the house is that of a void sandwiched between two solids.

The four vertical movement systems are three stairways and an open elevator. The elevator provides the wheelchair access: a platform of 3 × 3.5 m which rises and descends on a hydraulic column to align with each of the three floors. There are no walls or balustrades to the platform which becomes a part of each room it aligns with. As Koolhaas puts it: 'The movement of the elevator changed, each time, the architecture of the house. A machine was its heart' (quoted in Colomina and Lleó 1998: 42). At the ground floor the platform becomes an alcove off the entrance/kitchen and provides the access to a wine cellar. At the middle floor it becomes an unenclosed part of the living/dining areas with views

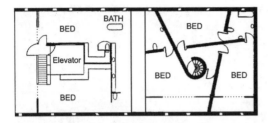

UPPER LEVEL

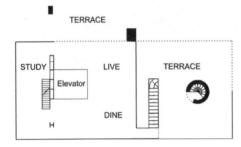

TERRACE

LIVING LEVEL

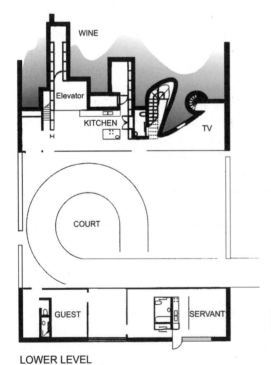

Figure 7.5
Bordeaux House plans.

LOWER LEVEL

out to the landscape and terrace. At the top floor it becomes an alcove off the father's bedroom. The bookshelves which line one side of the platform can only be accessed from the elevator. As in the Educatorium, Koolhaas deploys the metaphor of the machine, privileges trajectories of movement (both up/down and in/out) as the exterior is folded into the interior and vice versa.

The four vertical movement systems generate a highly interconnected spatial structure for the lower floors (Figure 7.6). However, they are also organized for specialized use – the mother's stair to the east, the guest stair near the entry and the children's stair to the west. Koolhaas regards the elevator as a liberating technology and here it is the elevator platform which renders the house accessible by wheelchair. Unlike the urban elevator which is shared by wheels and feet, here it is the domain of one person since use by others would leave the father stranded. This machine is the 'heart' of the house and it places the father in charge. The father controls the architecture, and the position of the elevator becomes a signifier of his presence and absence. When the father is out, on the ground floor or in bed, then the main living space is left with a central void. This void has no handrails and at least one reviewer has suggested that the space produces a sense of genuine insecurity and risk (Davies 1998). This void (reminiscent of Eisenman's famous gap in the floor between the twin beds) can be read as a deconstructive

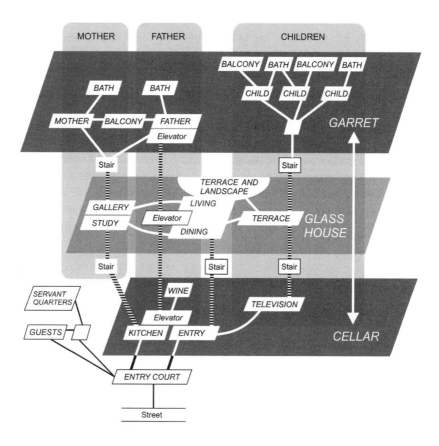

Figure 7.6
Bordeaux House, spatial structure.

challenge to the traditional idea of house and home as reinforcing ontological stability. Yet the void is created and erased in a gender-specific manner – the central living space of the house is only secure when the father is present.

The elevator is furnished in some photographs as a study with a desk and lamp. Since it is lined with bookshelves and controls all access to the wine cellar, it can be interpreted as a reconstruction of the male 'den' brought into the light and mobilized, transposed from deep to shallow space with the walls removed. However, when the platform retreats to the top floor it seals the gap to create a fully enclosed space, deep within the spatial structure. This adult bedroom zone is structured in a long loop with the two bedrooms at once separated and connected by a bathroom and a balcony (Figure 7.6). The children's bedrooms form a more traditional tree-like cluster on the same level but entirely severed from the adult zone and inaccessible to the father. Surveillance over children is the only function not afforded the father.

The Bordeaux house is in many ways a reconstruction of the bourgeois house with its servant quarters and 'cellar' dug into the hillside, surmounted by the *piano nobilé* with commanding views and the attic storey with tiny windows. The design embodies a series of references to domestic prototypes. At one level it is a play on the Bachelardian 'archetype', itself firmly based in the French bourgeois house, with its 'cellar' and 'garret' framing the everyday life of the middle floor (Figure 7.6) (Bachelard 1969). However, it is a radically innovative design, both formally and spatially. It combines a rethinking of the dialectics of inside/outside (as in Mies' Farnsworth house) and vertical/horizontal (Corbusier's Villa Savoye), but with greater programmatic dynamism and complexity (as in the Reitveld/Schröder house). The structure of the house is highly porous on the lower levels, it is also conceptually 'tree-like' with the elevator as its stem. While it embodies new forms of both liberation and social control, gender divisions are enhanced rather than challenged. The machine at its heart is a patriarchal prosthesis. While positions could be transposed (with a woman controlling the space) the structure of the house would remain hierarchical. Is this new spatial hierarchy an accidental by-product of Koolhaas' obsession with movement and elevators? Or is it a deliberate tactic of bringing authority into the light rather than resisting it – exposing the 'nerve' as Kipnis puts it. In either case it seems a dangerous move.

ONE-WAY STREET

The Seattle Public Library, completed in 2004, is perhaps Koolhaas' most developed attempt to create an internal culture of congestion through architecture. The programmatic innovations here have a genesis that goes back to earlier library competition designs that were not built, but which incorporated both new understandings about knowledge exchange and a spatial organization around a spiral flow. The building is an 11-storey volume occupying an entire sloping city block of the downtown Seattle grid with main entries on two different street

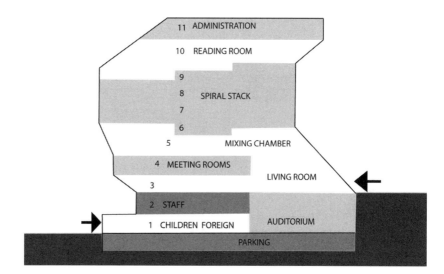

Figure 7.7
Seattle Public Library,
section.

levels. While the external form of the building is not of particular concern here, it has been described as a fishnet stocking that has been crammed with children's building blocks; it has also been described as a stack of books. Figure 7.7 shows a figurative section through the building. The complex interior geography of this building has rendered plans close to useless in navigating the building.

The spatial structure of the building is its key innovation. The lower street entry contains children's and foreign-language sections while the upper street enters directly into a vast 'Living Room'. Connecting the two are both an escalator and public auditorium. Further escalators rise to an information hub ('Mixing Chamber') housing catalogue and internet connections. Sandwiched between is a mezzanine floor of meeting rooms. This cluster of spaces is an extremely smart design which assembles five storeys of programme within two spatial segments deep from the street. The Living Room is effectively one vast floor space extending across the city block with good light and outlook (Figure 7.8); the sense of public accessibility works in both programmatic and representational terms and makes it one of the finest public interiors of its era. This space is effectively the main reading room of the library with generous light and seating. It is open to the auditorium, is overlooked from the mezzanine levels of meeting rooms and Mixing Chamber, and houses a café and small fold-up shop. It incorporates a highly urbanized mix of functions and is integrated with a series of permanent public artworks. This is perhaps the most successful of Koolhaas/OMA's attempts at an urbanized interior.

Beyond the Mixing Chamber the main pathway continues up an escalator to the spiral ramp housing the main collection. From floors six to ten the building floorplate becomes a continuous ramp winding up around the escalator. Books are organized according to the rationalist Dewey system from 0 to 999 with numbers marked on the floor. At the top of the spiral is a grand reading room with a reorientation to the city.

Figure 7.8
Seattle Public Library,
living room, auditorium
and street entry.

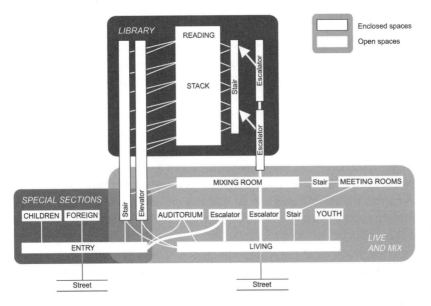

Figure 7.9
Seattle Public Library,
spatial structure.

Figure 7.9 shows how traffic flows through the building with three modes of vertical transport: escalators, elevators and stairs. The sequence of escalators are designed as the primary flow connecting the two street entry levels to the information area (Mixing Chamber) and then up to the spiral collection and reading room. There are two sets of stairs, one for access between levels within the spiral and an enclosed fire escape. The elevators service every level but are less accessible.

This is one of the most disorienting buildings one can imagine. Library management have produced several sectional diagrams to be used as navigational aids by unfamiliar users. The spiral is particularly confusing because while it is very clear where you are within the Dewey system, it is difficult to figure out which floor you are on because there are no boundaries between floors (Figure 7.10). Floors six to ten constitute one continuous pathway from 0 to 999. In a rather literal sense here one becomes disoriented within the building and reoriented towards the books – lost in a world of knowledge. However, there is a problem created by the fact that the escalator going up to the spiral is one way and there is no similar egress (Figure 7.9). Since this is clearly the dominant traffic route, the spiral becomes an effective one-way street for first-time users who can see no way out. There are some fire stairs and the elevators but there is a sense that this violates the very achievements of the building in programmatic terms. With no easy way back to the Mixing and Living Rooms, it is a structure that resembles the shopping mall or department store, generating one-way entries to a world of consumption; where disorientation and reorientation takes place and modes of egress are camouflaged. Without a more detailed evaluation it is difficult to judge the effects of this on local readers, however, conversations with the librarians confirm that many people have to ask to find a way out and makeshift notices direct them to the fire stairs.

This is a very fine public building which reinvents the library as a building type and opens it to the street, but it also seems to divide its public. Some patrons prefer the branch libraries because they find this one too 'industrial' and not 'homely'. While there are regulars who seem very comfortable there is very little sense of enclosure. The shop, café, sitting areas and shelves of the meeting room are all treated as parts of a large open space; one is always and everywhere

Figure 7.10
Seattle Public Library,
spiral stack.

exposed to a public gaze. There are no edges to provide the psychological comfort of prospect and refuge. The sitting spaces along the spiral are placed right on the main pathway and some are exposed on three sides (Figure 7.10). There is a sense that the machinic approach has become an aesthetic ideology embodying a denial of comfort. What is at stake here is an issue of designing for difference – some people want the psychological protection of a nook or alcove and some do not; some people find it difficult to concentrate with strangers looking over their shoulder. So why design a public building for only a part of the population? This is a building designed for a particular kind of cosmopolitan subject: confidently engaged in information exchange rather than quiet reflection. It is a place for a particular kind of being more than it is open to new kinds of becoming.

MAGIC PLACES

> . . . a public accus(es) a trickster of deceiving them. But don't blame the magician for having fooled them, for having given them these sublime moments of illusion.
>
> (Koolhaas 1996: 190)

So what can be made of Koolhaas' desire to unhinge architecture from its role in social reproduction? Koolhaas' goals are generally laudable, especially when he treats interior space as a field of play which resists any simple mimetic relationship with social structure. A permeable spatial network is a primary design tactic. He wants to defy the social logic of space, to free up the programmatic imperatives which lock architecture into the service of a highly choreographed and ritualistic reproduction of social life. The larger project here can be seen as an urbanization of architecture. Urbanity can be defined as an assemblage that produces a high intensity of encounter with difference; for Sennett (1973, 1996) this random encounter is what grants public space its key role in identity formation. Good cities are paradigmatic places of becoming. Yet interior spaces generally serve a very different role than that of the street – much more closely aligned with a strictly striated habitus and functions of social reproduction. Graafland (1998) has suggested that Koolhaas' work is a somewhat Faustian practice which embodies a dialectic between the freedoms he seeks and the tree-like institutional structures in which such practices are embedded; I have argued something similar in relation to his Euralille project (Dovey 2008: chapter 11). This reflects an acceptance of prevailing social and economic forces, a realpolitik wherein the desire for the new is harnessed to make what one can in a difficult world. One of Koolhaas' metaphors for architectural practice is that of 'surfing' the waves of capital, a commitment to taking the opportunities of architectural practice without the illusion of autonomy. The claim to produce certain freedoms is quite distinct from any claim to produce real social change.

One way of understanding this issue is to utilize Deleuze and Guattari's (1987: 220) distinction between a 'connection' and 'conjugation' of flows. A connection, like a new short cut through a building or a city, accelerates the flows of traffic into and throughout an assemblage, increasing the intensity of encounters. Its effect is deterritorializing. A conjugation by contrast is more like a site amalgamation, a joining of segments that performs a reterritorialization (like a marriage). One sees this so often in Koolhaas' work where a programmatic move folds into a formal image that catches the imagination. The folded floor-plate of the Educatorium that is at once ground – ramp – amphitheatre – wall – roof is a good example. Yet these images then circulate through the professional magazines as symbolic capital; programmatic innovation becomes congealed into form and critical thought on spatial practice stops flowing.

Kipnis (1998: 27) suggests that: 'For Koolhaas, architecture is able ... to engender provisional freedoms in a definite situation, freedoms as the experiences, as the sensations, as the effects – pleasurable, threatening, and otherwise – of undermining select patterns of regulation and authority.' While such claims are relatively untestable they need to be considered in the context of everyday experience and social practice, enmeshed in the micropractices of power and liberation that infuse everyday life. Yet such critique of place experience is one which Koolhaas explicitly eschews. One slightly bitter retort to his critics was entitled 'No Grounds for a Non-Place' (Koolhaas 1996) and elsewhere he derides the very idea of local place identity as an obsession with stabilized identity and essentialized meanings (Koolhaas 1995). His view of place is rather opposed to that presented throughout most of this book. His idealized Generic City floats free of any roots, liberated from character and identity. It also often floats free of logic or veracity; in 1995 he wrote that: 'In five to ten years we will all work at home' (Koolhaas 1995).

Koolhaas' work is brilliantly innovative, but it is not always what it seems. Colomina suggests that he operates in the mode of a magician, distracting the eye with one hand, concealing what he is up to with the other (Colomina and Lleó 1998). Koolhaas' formal inventiveness distracts critical attention from his programmatic surgery which at times constructs illusions of freedom which can conceal what has not changed. Programmatic innovation can be reduced to significations of practice. Another way to look at this is that Koolhaas uses the expressive pole of the assemblage to conceal materialistic interventions, and that his expressive mastery distracts attention from any careful critique of the material outcomes. Koolhaas (1996: 190) has alluded to himself as a magician producing 'sublime moments of illusion' and there is no suggestion here that the 'magic' does not work in certain ways. What is missing, however, is an understanding of 'freedom' as a form of practice – something people *do* rather than images they consume. Koolhaas does indeed challenge the primary genotypes of socio-spatial reproduction, yet at the same time he generates illusions that can be a cover for new practices of power or for more of the same.

Chapter 8: Open Court

Transparency and Legitimation in the Courthouse

The state is an assemblage of statutes and standards, of stations and stages, that stabilize practices of power in space and over time. This reiteration of the root *sta* (to stand) is not accidental; the stability of the state has long gone hand in hand with an architecture that stands for authority with its statues and stabilizing images. The state has stamina, staying power; its various chambers and courtrooms are stages for the practice of authority. The various branches of government are organized in a tree-like structure where the uniforms and letterheads resonate with the palaces, houses of parliament and courthouses to legitimate authority. I have argued elsewhere that authority sits alongside force, coercion, manipulation and seduction as primary but overlapping dimensions of power as mediated by built form (Dovey 2008: 14). Authority is defined by unquestioned compliance and is the most efficient means of social control. If we are arrested by the police we may argue about whether we have broken the law, but if the trappings of authority are evident (car, badge, hat) we do not argue the right of the state to enforce the law. Authority is the most pervasive, reliable, productive and stable form of power, yet it needs both the trappings of legitimating imagery and the coercive threat of force – the 'right' of authority is underwritten by the 'might' of force. The key linkage to place identity here is that authority becomes stabilized and legitimated through both spatial rituals and the architectural framing of them. Symbols and rituals of legitimation are effective because one cannot argue with them; they are the way things are done around here. In this regard architecture has a particular capacity to serve this legitimation imperative with spatial assemblages that celebrate and reproduce spatial rituals, symbolize the authority of the state and also embody a sense of intimidation or threat of force in the event of non-compliance.

BEFORE THE LAW

In Kafka's novel *The Trial* the protagonist, Joseph K, is caught in a web of legal machinations which are utterly opaque, he cannot find out either the charges against him or the evidence. A short parable known as 'Before the Law' is inserted into the novel as a story told to K by a priest. In this narrative a man is consumed by a desire to gain access to the law represented spatially by an open gate with a gatekeeper; he is informed by the gatekeeper that he can have access but not yet. Faced with this tantalizing prospect, the man spends his entire life before the gate but access is repeatedly deferred. As he is about to die the gatekeeper tells him this gate was only ever designed for him, but that he will have to close it now.

Contrast this image of an open gate one cannot enter with the late-nineteenth-century Supreme Court building in Melbourne, a rather closed building with open public access (Figure 8.1).[1] This building largely established and anchored the emerging legal district of a booming self-governed British colony. One enters this stone bastion of the law through a neo-classical façade and a sequence of spatial thresholds – steps, loggia, doorways, vestibules, corridors and lobbies – to negotiate a deep, dark and labyrinthine interior. At its centre, under the dome, is the library housing the statutes. The courtrooms are generally deep within this spatial sequence, separated from light and view, with judgment

Figure 8.1
Supreme Court Building, Melbourne, Australia.

dispensed from behind a very high bench. This symbolic separation of the practices of law from the everyday, the sense of solidity and spatial intimidation, were
seen in the nineteenth century as necessary to legitimate the authority of the
law. The neo-classical style of the architecture works in a similar way – stone and
symmetry reinforce the ideal of a timeless institution of law and order. Along
with the wigs and gowns, the books and benches, architecture is a key trapping
of judicial power.

The female statue of Justice that appears above the entry also appears on
the US Supreme Court, the Old Bailey in London and many other Western courthouses. This figure is derived from the Greek and Roman figure of a bare-
breasted female with a balance in one hand and a sword in the other,
representing an open mind and balanced judgement, coupled to the power of
the state to enforce that judgement. A commitment to openness, truth and
reason serve to legitimate the authority of the State. A blindfold was added to
the figure from the sixteenth century as a product of the Enlightenment – Justice
should be 'blind' to differences between those who are equal before the law (Jay
2003). Yet the blindfold also introduced a contradiction in that Justice cannot see
the scales nor where she wields the sword. In Melbourne the Chief Justice of the
day decided that she should have neither blindfold nor scales.

This chapter is an exploration of some of these issues through a critique of
courthouses that seek to transform both the image and spatial practice of the
courts. The 'court' is the stage where justice is performed; the name is derived
from the 'royal court' where it defined an assemblage of people, place and practices at the centre of power. The court is also a place type that sits between
inside and outside, enclosed by walls yet open to the sky. The courtroom is not
literally but conceptually open, reflected by the imperative to hear most cases in
'open court'. It is contrasted with the deeper private chambers on one side and
the street on the other.

The neo-classical image of the courthouse has been linked to a desire to
combine traditional and modern values as a kind of double legitimation. Goodsell (2001) suggests that the traditional American statehouse as a 'temple of law'
embodies paradoxical meanings of both hierarchy and democracy. Yet the classi-
cal still draws its legitimacy from traditions of social class and is widely seen to
have lost capacity to successfully legitimate the State (Brigham 1999). While remnants of the foundations of law in theology and monarchy persist in language
and dress, there is now widespread demand for new architectures of justice.

> The court, like the state, rules by consent, which it earns by its legitimacy and public
> acceptance … in a democratic age public legitimacy ultimately derives from the
> knowledge and understanding that people have of the courts and their processes …
> Architecture is the medium of this communication.
>
> (Mohr 1999)

Architectural programmes for courthouses in recent years have taken on a range
of new symbolic and spatial functions. The idea is that justice be respected but

demystified and transparent. Courthouses must not intimidate and must be accessible. Their circulation systems must provide clear orientation and ease of access. In a multiplicitous society the challenge is that no singular cultural reading can work for all citizens – courtrooms must be sensitive to cultural differences (Tait 1999). They must not generate unnecessary stress, they need relief spaces and in some cases culturally specific settings. They must not exacerbate conflict and must enable processes of reconciliation and healing. Pati *et al.* (2007) identify six dimensions of openness in contemporary court design in the United States: physical access, visibility of the building, transparency of the building, legibility, natural lighting and the inclusion of non-judicial functions into the building. To these could be added those of breaking down the symbolic barriers of belittling scale and inaccessible architectural language.

At the same time as this push for openness there is also a clear imperative to build and maintain confidence in the judiciary. In this regard some things must not change, in particular the clarity of spatial jurisdiction for the courthouse, the courtroom within it and the judge's place within the courtroom. The location of the bench within the assemblage inscribes the authority of the judge who cannot conduct judgment from any other position (Haldar 1994: 169). Authority relies on clear boundaries, identities and practices; it is undermined by any mixing of territories. The courtroom is a space wherein highly codified rules of behaviour and dress apply. It can be described as a form of state habitus: a place with a strong sense of one's place and of the various divisions and hierarchies between things, persons and practices. The courtroom is a strictly striated space where authority is threatened by most forms of smoothness. Mohr shows how tensions and contradictions arise in the conception of an 'open' court as boundaries are controlled to:

> regulate media coverage, to exclude inadmissible evidence, or to control the exercise of judicial power. And yet each of these boundaries must be permeable under the right circumstances: the public must have access to the courts and to their proceedings; admissable evidence must enter the court.
>
> (Mohr 1999)

The architecture of the courtroom stakes out the territorial boundaries of judicial power. The idea of the court as conceptually 'open' co-exists with a clearly enforced spatial closure. At the same time as court architecture produces a rigid spatial segmentarity, it frames a space wherein the legal imperative involves a rigid separation of truth from falsehood, reason from madness and so on (Haldar 1994: 196, cited in Mohr 1999).

The Supreme Court building in Melbourne has over time become the centre of a legal district incorporating seven courthouses, most city law firms and a nearby remand prison. While it remains a much-loved heritage building, the pro-gramming of new courthouses has led to a desire for symbols and practices of openness, transparency, accessibility, enlightenment and equality. The completion of three new major courthouses within this district since 2000 provides an opportunity to assess how the architecture of authority has changed. Each of these buildings was designed with a deliberate intent to move on from the neo-classical idea of the court as a place of hierarchy and intimidation. But what happens when these ideals come into tension with the need to maintain security and a sense of institutional order? How can architects pursue ideals of natural light, view and equality of access yet also provide segregated access and egress for judges, prisoners, juries and the public? How is the architect to avoid closing the courtroom within a spaghetti junction of corridors and lift wells? If courthouse design is to avoid an architecture of intimidation and hierarchy, what happens to the implicit acceptance of authority on which the courts rely? I will begin with a brief description and critique of the three courthouses before proceeding to an analysis of their spatial structure. This work is based on fieldwork conducted in 2003 including interviews with project architects and leading clients, and access to all parts of each building.[2]

THREE MELBOURNE COURTHOUSES

> We wanted to create a courthouse that reflected the place of law in a free society. The courthouse had to be functionally efficient, but it also had to have an ambience reflecting an openness and friendliness of use. It had to reflect light as well as concepts of reconciliation and calm. It was to be dignified but it was not to be intimidating, and certainly not pretentious. It was to have a visible relationship with the outside world, a sense of permanence...
>
> (Black 1999)

The Commonwealth Law Courts were completed in 1998, located on a major city intersection opposite a park.[3] The 14-storey concrete and glass building

Figure 8.2
Commonwealth Law Courts, atrium.

wraps around a small entrance plaza which also houses the entrance to an underground rail station. The building houses all of the national court functions that are located in Melbourne including the High Court, Federal Court and Family Court of Australia; these often involve cases of high political significance. Movement through the building proceeds from the plaza through a security gate to a long and tall atrium space which floods with sunlight and opens views to the park (Figure 8.2). Known as Flagstaff Gardens, the park also has a heritage significance linked to the founding of the colony in the early nineteenth century. The lobby is a fine interior space that operates to mediate the flow of public life from the street through the atrium and its balconies to lobbies and then courtrooms. The ideals of access and transparency have been translated into both visual access to and from the street and parkland and the flow of life to the courts. The courtrooms have been located as close as practical to the main entrance, and the lobby and balcony areas that serve them have been designed in the language of a 'street'. The lobbies are designed as large alcoves hanging off this street – quieter and darker with nearby retreat rooms for private conversations where 'out of court' settlements are often reached.

The most important courtrooms have both windows onto the park and a broad doorway which can be opened to blur the boundary between the court and the lobby. While the street frontage onto the park is minimal, a rear corridor that provides secure judicial access to the courts has been designed with windows on both sides and a diagonal mirror that gives a reflected view of the park to most courtrooms. When judges move through this corridor the high-tech glass switches from transparent to translucent, triggered by movement detectors in the corridor so that the view is periodically replaced by a translucent figure of a passing judge.

The ideal of transparency has also been addressed in the skin of the building where an intricately composed curtain wall plays with the tension between opacity and transparency. Extracts from the Australian Constitution are etched onto the glass walls of the building, melding the architecture and the constitution as frameworks within which the law is practised. The court functions of the building involve a contrast between the Federal and High Courts on upper levels (where the political and economic stakes are often high) and the much busier Family Courts on lower levels (where personal trauma is involved). There is some evidence that this is an uneasy mix – the Family Court engaged a new architect to renovate one section of the building after completion. However, in general terms this is a building where the interior has been enlivened, enlightened and rendered highly accessible in its public zones. The urban presence of the building wraps around the entry plaza with well-composed façades (Figure 8.3). The semi-transparent courthouse floors are surmounted by the bulk of the judges' chambers where senior judges have personal balconies projecting over the street – heroic formal gestures which are windblown and unused. While architects and clients both wanted more integration with the city in the forecourt, this is a lost opportunity as a civic space. The imperative to separate the railway station and court

Figure 8.3
Commonwealth Law
Courts, entry plaza.

entries and to provide a security passage for the law courts has left the public space bereft of public use. The success of the interior atrium is achieved in part by spilling the security functions onto public space.

The second example, the County Court building, completed in 2002, is located directly across the street from the Supreme Court.[4] The building houses 48 courtrooms on eight levels, primarily criminal trials including high-profile cases involving very high levels of security. A primary architectural tactic here was to design the building as three separate blocks with narrow atria between them to bring natural light deep within the building and to echo the public structure and quality of Melbourne's laneway network. However, the building is functionally integrated with a single entrance and the 'laneways' operate mainly as light sources. The plan and wall forms are slightly cranked, tilted and folded in a manner that softens the institutional image of both street façades and interiors. The architectural language here is loosely 'deconstructive' but this is a surface effect rather than a deconstruction of the philosophy of law.

Figure 8.4
County Court, entry.

The building fronts a small public plaza to the south where the entry portico gestures towards the Supreme Court across the street (Figure 8.4). The figure of justice appears on this façade, this time with traditional blindfold and scales. With photography excluded from the courthouse, this plaza becomes an important setting for the televised drama of entry and exit by high-profile figures. The building is more commonly seen on television than in everyday life, its virtual presence outweighing its urban presence. The plaza is more successful as a public interface than the Commonwealth Law Courts. This is achieved, however, at the expense of the entry foyer which is largely filled by security apparatus. The main courtrooms are arranged around a central hall located up a level and deep within the building, where it is lit with slivers of natural light and street view from one of the 'laneway' atria. The separation from the street gives the hall a sense of intimacy and seclusion.

The courtrooms are largely modern re-creations of the traditional courtroom where slightly inclined and timber-panelled walls and coved ceilings generate an almost cavelike sense of both seclusion and theatre. There is a programmatic requirement for up to five categories of segregated access to each court: judge, jury, accused, protected witness and public. The spatial structure required to achieve this is almost impossibly complex and the courtrooms are inevitably located deep within a tangle of corridors and elevators. The strategy of dividing the building into three with 'laneway' atria pays off in the capacity to generate at least borrowed natural light, if not outlook, in the vast majority of courtrooms.

An interesting aspect of the building is that it has a long frontage onto a main street that cannot be used as entry for security reasons; instead a long

Figure 8.5
County Court, blank
frontage with judges'
chambers above.

blank wall covers a large holding area for jurors (Figure 8.5). There was pressure from the local government authority to enliven this urban edge with shops but there was resistance to mixing the institutional image of the courts with commerce. The unfortunate result is an institution of the law which appears somewhat fortress-like. However, above this blank frontage is a key innovation in locating the judges' chambers low in the building to connect visually with the street. This frontage enables a level of public gaze into the traditionally opaque realm of the judges' chambers. Some judges are not amused at the loss of privacy but it enlivens the legal precinct.

At the rear of the County Court on a side street is the Children's Court, completed in 2000 and again driven by a desire for openness, light and transparency.[5] An important issue here is to serve a conciliatory role in children's lives and this court has a history of experimenting with non-adversarial settings – conference tables without barriers or changes of level between magistrates and the public. These spatial settings were perceived to have undermined the authority and legitimacy of the court and exposed magistrates to risk. The new building represented a move back towards a more traditional courtroom layout, but within a more open and transparent public building.

The street frontage is an elegant and broad-eaved, glass-walled pavillion – an entrance foyer to a much larger bulk of courts and office behind (Figure 8.6). This foyer is an accessible extension of the street flanked by courtyards at each end which operate as relief and smoking spaces. Entry to the courts is via open stairways within this foyer which lead to long lobbies which in turn access the courtrooms. This is a very legible plan which maintains a strong sense of

Figure 8.6
Children's Court.

accessibility and transparency from the street to the lobbies. The relationship of the foyer with the courtyards is well-conceived, recognizing how stressful courts can be and the importance of the recuperative effects of gardens and fresh air. The building, however, is compromised by a strict programmatic segregation into the Criminal Division and the Family Division (child protection). This division occurs immediately one enters the foyer and is directed to entirely separate lobbies and courtyards. This is a quite appropriate separation of children at risk from those charged with criminal offences, but the result is to compromise the building architecturally and functionally. The foyer is sliced into three by glass walls and it becomes a bureaucratic place for processing people rather than a social space (Figure 8.7). Thus the identity of the building is based on one social category (children) but is immediately split into two on entry.

The symmetrical plan of the building provides each of the divisions with an identical lobby space servicing a series of courtrooms. The elongated double-height lobbies are well-designed and naturally lit from high windows; they are lined with a series of abstract landscape paintings and intersected with obscure glass bridges for judicial access. The two lobbies, while almost identical in design, are socially quite different. The Family Division lobby is much busier and is a frequent site of trauma. It is difficult to imagine how architecture might be expected to relieve the effects of the legal removal of a child from a parent, or how it could do so any better than this one does. There have been some adaptations of the toilet corridor to avoid hidden dead ends which had become sites for the unleashing of fury.

The courtrooms are designed in a relatively traditional manner but with natural light and outlook in most of them. This is a building which operates in institutional terms to reify an ideal about justice for children, yet its dual role in both punishing and protecting children leaves the architecture torn with an inner contradiction and reinforcing a spatial division between good and bad children. There is, however, an even more crucial distinction between these courts and the

Figure 8.7
Children's Court, foyer.

two buildings discussed above: the Children's Court was constructed with two-thirds of the budget (per square metre) of the adult courts, raising questions about how evenly justice is distributed by age group. While the decision not to mix accused children with those at risk seems sound, this has produced an inflexible building where the Family Division lobby is often overcrowded with people sitting on the floor as they wait for their cases. This is a place where the legitimacy of the court is often called into question because here two quite different institutions of law – the state and the family – intersect. It is hard to see how architecture can address this problem, but reducing the hierarchy between courts may be more effective than removing the symbols of hierarchy within them.

FRAMING JUSTICE

Each of these buildings grapples in its own way with the complexities and contradictions of the architecture of justice. They are successful in different ways, and face different challenges, in forging new relations with the street and in bringing greater light, transparency and access to court proceedings. In terms of public experience the courthouses can be seen as structured sequences of spatial experience from the street to the courtroom. In each case the street entrance has been placed at ground level with a transparent foyer, signifying easy access without the heavy stone and steps of traditional court architecture.

Yet beyond the foyer, levels of accessibility are largely constrained by the spatial programme and in each case there is a requirement for the spatial segregation of different user networks within the building. In the case of the Commonwealth Courts there are only two categories of segregated courtroom access – for the public and the judiciary. The simplified spatial structure in Figure 8.8 shows that all courtrooms enter from a single main foyer/atrium, albeit at different levels, and all are connected to a judicial access system from the rear. It is this programme that enabled the high levels of light and view discussed earlier. All

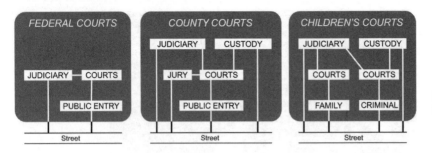

Figure 8.8
Spatial segmentarity.

courtrooms are located within four to six spatial segments from the street: security screen to foyer to stair or elevator to lobby to courtroom. Every stage of this
spatial sequence has light and views back to the city or parkland.

The County Court is a very different proposition where there are four
entirely separate spatial systems serving every courtroom in order to ensure that
judiciary, prisoners, jury and public never cross paths except in the courtroom. At
times there is also a need for witness protection. The logistics of such a programme become highly deterministic of the plan because four modes of access
tend to consume all sides of the courtroom. In order to meet this programme
courtrooms and their lobbies are located deep within the building, ranging from
six to eight spatial segments deep from the street and with relatively little prospect for light and views. The structure of the Children's Court reflects the decision
to combine family and criminal cases and then separate them within the same
building, thus one side of the building needs custody for incarcerated children
and the other does not.

As one travels deeper and higher along these public-access paths to the
courtroom, space becomes more striated. The courtroom is a constellation of
strictly regulated practices centred on the controlling gaze of the judge. While
citizens are deemed equal before the law, the courtroom is not a conference of
equal parties and to allow any such illusion to take root is seen to undermine
legitimacy. A typical courtroom in the County Court shows a single space where
six classes of people interact on three different levels (Figure 8.9). On the floor of
the chamber are the public seating and the lawyers. One step up are the witness
box to one side and the accused at the rear. At the next level up is the jury box
opposite the witness, with the judge one further level up at the front. This assemblage is organized to facilitate face-to-face contact between judge, jury, witness,
barrister and accused. The only face-to-face connection that is not provided for is
that between the public and the accused. This rigid segmentarity of space is the
framework for the rigid distinctions that are established there: between reason
and unreason, truth and falsehood, admissible and inadmissible evidence, justice
and injustice. Courtroom boundaries are reinforced by sound locks; the chance
encounter of public space is excluded.

The choreography of the courtroom is in some ways archaic; its practices
have deep roots in the idea that power speaks from a rostrum and cannot be
questioned or held in contempt. While many of the trappings have been

Figure 8.9
County Courtroom.

discarded there are remnants linking the state to the royal court and religion – 'your worship' or 'your lordship'. In a democracy, power is invested in citizenship, it is immanent in the social body. Yet in practice we elect politicians who appoint judges who then rule from above. The courts are instruments of democracy that deploy the trappings of transcendent power in their practices. The spatial trappings often have more than one mode of justification. The separation of judges from the public with separate entry, higher level, bench and low wall are all justifiable on practical grounds of security, yet they also work symbolically to reinforce hierarchy. They are over-determined in part because the court does not tolerate ambiguity. The line drawn between truth and falsehood, justice and injustice, is echoed in space. Yet they do this only by incorporating some ambiguities – the requirement that the court be 'open' produces a certain closure.

Art is the domain where ambiguity is most effectively expressed and in these courthouses we see a range of examples of public artworks; the ways they are featured gives them a prominent role in the life of the courts. In addition to the glazed etchings of the constitution mentioned earlier, the Commonwealth Courts have a range of abstract sculptures in the atrium and commissioned paintings forming wall panels in the major courtrooms. Abstraction has the advantage of signifying both modernity and an openness of meaning; it can operate as a contemporary counterbalance to the traditions of the law. The artworks in the County Court are generally more figurative. On the main wall of the foyer is a mural entitled 'Land/Law' based on the ideals of Aboriginal law (artist: Judy Watson). Unfortunately the foyer is so consumed by security apparatus that the work cannot be properly viewed. The main hall features a large glass artwork with a translucent, fragmented and fragile figure of Justice entitled 'The Quality of Mercy' (artist: Colin Lanceley). The artworks within the Children's Court are a commissioned series of large paintings hung high on the walls above the foyer – abstract works in bright pastels that generate an air of tranquillity (artist: Bruno Leti). In all of these buildings the artworks have become integrated with the architecture and indeed have been commissioned in service of the same goals as the building – this is not a place for art that challenges or takes sides except on the side of openness, transparency and enlightenment.

There is a broader issue with regard to the architecture of justice that deserves some comment here. In each of these buildings the hierarchical division between the judiciary and everyone else extends well beyond the courtroom to encompass the ancillary spaces, where there are sharp distinctions of comfort, space, light and view. Many of the support staff and jury areas occupy window-less environments which they inhabit for lengthy periods. Part of the Children's Court comprises a psychological assessment centre housed in a substantially win-dowless environment. There is a sense in which the commitment to principles of justice goes only so far. A broader principle that unhealthy environments are assigned on the basis of social hierarchy tends to prevail.

Finally, a question which could use more research: how do these buildings work for their real clients, the hopeful recipients of justice? What are the effects on the perception of justice, equality, access and transparency for the general public? To what degree do they generate illusions of transparency, openness and access without the practice? How do they mediate the sense of injustice that these buildings must house when a case is lost, a child is removed, when the accused is sentenced? The light-filled atrium of the Family Court provides a won-derful sense of relief from the enclosed courtrooms. Leaning on the glass balus-trade, gazing down to the marble floor and out towards the Flagstaff Gardens is the kind of architectural experience that late Modernism, at its best, is all about – the sense of modern justice being administered with flair. But what if a distressed person decided to augment the spectacle by taking a dive (as one barrister sug-gested to me as a possibility)? Outside the Children's Court there is often a small group of teenagers, waiting for court cases, leaving occasional traces of graffiti on the columns. How does the architecture mediate perceptions of the justice they receive, or their chances of graduating to the County Court?

These institutions of authority are open, transparent and accessible, but not beyond the point that legitimacy is eroded. The ideal of an open court paradoxi-cally requires a good deal of security and closure. The deeper dilemma here lies in the quest for an architecture that can legitimate the ideals of democracy – of power as immanent in citizenship. This entails moving on from a reliance on tra-ditional and transcendent ideals of justice dispensed from on high. But it also requires an avoidance of the bureaucratic non-place where justice is the mere administration of rules. The design of the truly open, accessible, enlightened, transparent, democratic and legitimate courthouse may have too many contra-dictions for architects to resolve. But the quest is producing interesting buildings that at their best can reveal the fact that in a democracy the law is never settled.

Chapter 9: Safety Becomes Danger

Drug Use in Public Space

Kim Dovey and John Fitzgerald

This chapter is a socio-spatial analysis of injecting drug use in public space; in a more general sense it is an account of the ways in which marginal spaces of the city are used for marginal activities and the formation of marginalized identities. It focuses on one urban district in Melbourne which became, for a time, strongly identified with heroin sale and use. Selling activities were camouflaged within a diverse streetlife while injecting sites were dispersed throughout laneways, car parks and toilets. These injecting zones occupied liminal places which slide between categories of private and public, mediating complex and paradoxical relations between safety and danger. Those who inject drugs in public space are caught in a dilemma – needing privacy from the public and police yet exposure in the event of an overdose; safety from police becomes danger from an overdose. This contradictory desire to be at once in and out of the public gaze also plays out in the planning and design of supervised injecting facilities where illegal practices are brought under a medical gaze without the gaze of the law.

SMACK STREET

Smith Street is a shopping strip in an inner-city neighbourhood of Melbourne which, in the late 1990s, became strongly identified through the media as a site of heroin sale and use, and was dubbed 'Smack Street'. The trade was incorporated into the diverse streetlife of the retail strip and injection followed in a number of spaces within the surrounding urban fabric. These practices persisted for a number of years despite successive rounds of heavy policing and coincided with an increase in overdose figures. This is part of a much larger assemblage of heroin production, distribution and consumption, together with representational narratives about risk, morality and the socially constructed identity of the 'junkie'. Our focus is on the smaller-scale experience and use of urban space, on the specific mediations of built form and spatial practice.

The study area of about 16 hectares encompassed the major sites of heroin trade and use (Figure 9.1). A brief excursion into the history and social demographics of the context is useful in understanding why such activity became entrenched here. Smith Street developed as a shopping strip during the second half of the nineteenth century (Fitzgerald *et al.* 1998). At this time it was the retail heart of a working-class community. Just beyond easy walking distance from the city, it was serviced with a tramline from 1869 and remained a flourishing retail area into the early twentieth century with major department stores and a vibrant streetlife. The 1950s brought increasing waves of new migrants to the area. Entire blocks of older housing were demolished and replaced with high-rise public housing in the 1960s. These estates of 8–10 hectares each are located within half a kilometre east and west of Smith Street. By the 1970s these estates were occupied by increasing numbers of migrants and refugees. Since the 1980s gentrification has brought an influx of high-income professionals into the broader neighbourhood. During the mid-1990s the public housing estates were publicized in the media as 'hot spots' for the sale and use of heroin. Subsequent police operations displaced the heroin trade from the estates and it re-emerged in the commercial space of Smith Street (Fitzgerald *et al.* 1998).

The heroin trade and use on the estates was linked to domestic space and to the semi-public zones of corridors, shared laundries and stairwells that characterized the modernist structures (Fitzgerald *et al.* 1998). There is a good deal of literature focusing on crime in high-rise public housing estates, much of it concerned with the role of urban spatial structure in mediating crime and socially transgressive behaviour (Newman 1972; Coleman 1985; Franck 1984; Greenberg and Rohe 1984; Hillier 1988). The displacement which occurred in 1995 was to a completely different urban spatial structure – the streets and laneways of the traditional city. Whatever the connections of spatiality to heroin use, the trade and use of heroin was not caused by the spatial dispositions of either the estate or the Smith Street area.

This shift from semi-private to public trading coincided with an increase in both heroin overdose and death across Melbourne. In 1998 there were over 100

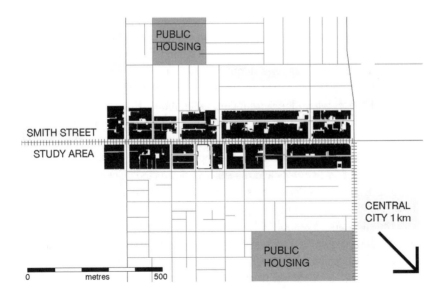

Figure 9.1
Smith Street and context.

non-fatal overdose incidents per month and deaths increased from six to 16 in the two years to 1999 (Fitzgerald *et al.* 1998). Approximately 70 per cent of these incidents occurred in public space.[1] The dangers of overdose are linked to a range of factors including drug quality, predictability, tolerance and multiple drug-use. However, death from overdose generally occurs only when medical assistance is not available.

As an illegal behaviour, heroin use is particularly difficult to document empirically and ethically. The patterns of heroin trade and narratives of spatial experience outlined here were derived from interviews with heroin users.[2] Injecting locations are based primarily on behavioural trace analysis of drug paraphernalia, a reliable method in this case because the containers and syringes are evidence of a crime which are generally discarded immediately after injection. The spatial analysis consisted of a series of layered mappings of the study area including pedestrian access networks, public/private ownership, functional mix and streetlife volume. These analyses were overlaid with maps of trading and injecting locations. Streetlife densities are based on global counts of people visible in public space.[3]

Through the interviews we were concerned to understand both the phenomenology of such practices and places, as well as discursive framings and narratives. We are interested in the formations of identity constructed and performed through marginalized spatial practices. Such places and practices may be best understood in terms of shifting identities, nomadic and rhizomatic practices in the context of a Deleuzian epistemology (Deleuze 1993, 1985). The distinction between smooth and striated space is suggested as one framework of interpretation (Deleuze and Guattari 1987; Moon and Braun 1998).

INSINUATIONS

Our interest is in broad spatial patterns rather than specific causal relations; in how the practices of heroin trade and use insinuate themselves into everyday urban life. Urban street networks can be seen as pedestrian movement patterns which enable and constrain flows of pedestrian life (Hillier 1996). Figure 9.2a shows the accessible pedestrian space network and pedestrian densities in and around Smith Street. This is a mapping of access rather than ownership – roadways are mostly excluded and some privately owned space is accessible.

The Smith Street streetlife is highly diverse in terms of social class, gender, age, behaviour and dress. This is linked to the demographics of the area and the diversity of shops and facilities – a mix of discount stores, supermarket, gaming, video, pawnshop and a range of cafés and restaurants from takeaways to upmarket cafes (Figure 9.3). The diversity of functions produces a variety of behaviour and the area has many of the qualities that Jacobs (1965) has long argued characterize a vital and healthy urban fabric – permeability, mixed use, density and mixed building stock. It is also undergoing a slow decline in diversity through gentrification as everyday goods such as grocers, butchers and furniture are displaced by cafes, restaurants and hairdressers (Fitzgerald *et al.* 1998).

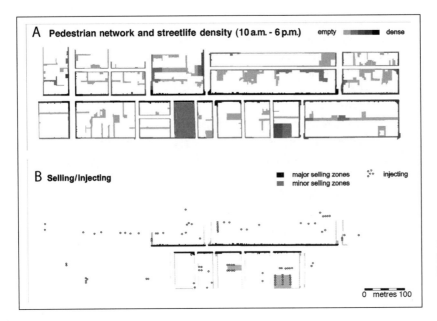

A **Pedestrian network and streetlife density (10 a.m. - 6 p.m.)** empty ▬▬▬ dense

B **Selling/Injecting** ■ major selling zones ⠿ injecting
■ minor selling zones

0 metres 100

Figure 9.2
Pedestrian networks and
injecting.

Figure 9.2b maps the selling and injecting practices during the period of study. It shows the way in which the drug-trading zones co-locate with the density of streetlife, concentrated into the most diverse and downmarket part of Smith Street. This zone was about 400 m long, extending into adjacent side streets since the sale often takes place across time and space. The trade is not stable but a trajectory which may begin with a glance in Smith Street (or an exchange on the telephone) to be concluded in a side street. Only certain sub-groups within the mix are offered heroin, based on a set of coded words, actions and imagery. The identity of the drug user is camouflaged within the diverse streetlife where a mix of identities can be used as masks.

Building functions include four primary categories of office, residential, retail and industrial with different functions often mixed on the same site. Retailing activities occupy nearly all buildings on Smith Street, mostly mixed with office or residential. Only one zone of the street is exclusively retail (unmixed) and this zone coincides with the major drug-trading zone. The side and back streets include residential and industrial uses as well as a mix between them. Industrial uses are located almost exclusively off Smith Street and primarily line the laneways and small streets one block back. There is a strong co-location of such functions with injecting zones.

While the selling of heroin hides in the glare of publicity and in the diversity and anonymity of public space, once the purchase is made users seek a level of privacy away from the public gaze. The opposition between public and private space can be mapped in a variety of ways. The legal division of space between public and private ownership marks the boundaries of governance at the lot line. Yet public spatial practices extend into legally private space. Of interest here are the ways in which these two layers intersect and overlap into zones of public access to legally private space. In the back lanes where the legal boundary is not

Figure 9.3
Smith Street.

Figure 9.4
Laneway.

enforced by walls or fences, where public access flows into car parking bays and open backyards we find many injecting spots in the liminal zones of publicly accessible yet legally private space. Interviews reveal that the users' concern is primarily that of being out of the public gaze:

> 'if you are looking for a place to go and have a shot, you usually find other people have been using it too, a secluded spot that the police aren't likely to drive past ... like it's out of sight from the street where the police might be driving up and down.'

A threshold of streetlife which is crucial in this regard is what Hillier (1996) terms 'continuous co-presence' – those public spaces with a continuous presence of at least two people within each field of view. Hillier suggests that people are alert to this condition of co-presence (linked to passive surveillance) and adjust their perceptions and behaviour accordingly. The condition of continuous co-presence throughout the day is linked to streets which are lined with front entrances, with all their comings and goings. The white areas of Figure 9.5 show these areas of continuous co-presence throughout the day, while the degrees of grey show the degree of seclusion or separation from these areas of co-presence, coded according to the number of spatial turns or 10-metre segments deep into laneways.

Figure 9.5 also shows the injecting zones as white stars which appear most clearly against the deeper and darker sections of public space. A proportion of them (primarily toilets and public car parks) are lost in the zones of co-presence. It is notable that many of the deepest (darkest) segments of laneway are not used for injecting. The degree to which injecting behaviour is under (or potentially under) the gaze of others involves the confluence of several dimensions. First is the way sight lines are mediated by the spatial disposition of buildings, fences, trees and cars. The second involves the way windows and doors (coupled with traces of use) operate as signifiers of potential surveillance because someone could be watching or open the door. Exposure is also mediated by distance – beyond about 20–30 m exposure can protect privacy since intruders will become visible before they get close. Finally, contrasts of sun and shade enable the possibility of hiding in the glare.

This quest for privacy is a dialectic process which mediates the spatial construction of social identity; the public location of drug use shapes the social identity of the user. The risk of disclosure is more than simply a risk of prosecution; exposure while injecting in public entails being labelled with the abject social identity of the 'junkie' which many users regard with some shame: 'it makes me feel like I'm a, I'm a scumbag to be shooting up on the street.' It is not only the act of injecting but also the location which constructs this identity through its connections of derelict space to derelict identity, homelessness and social marginality.

Figure 9.5
Exposure, seclusion and drug use.

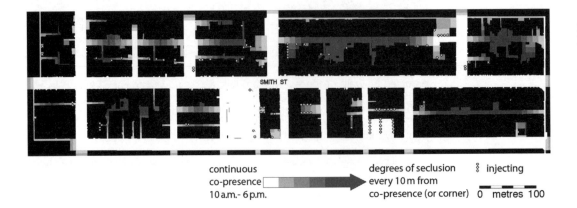

continuous
co-presence
10 a.m.- 6 p.m.

degrees of seclusion   injecting
every 10 m from
co-presence (or corner)   0   metres 100

INJECTING ZONES

As is clear in Figure 9.5, primary injecting zones range from about 10 m to 100 m from the Smith Street selling zones. Injecting zones range in size from tiny alcoves to long linear strips; they are often neither centred nor bounded. The only thing that they all have in common is minimal degrees of seclusion. They are also prone to cycles of use and displacement as resident or police action is taken to stop them being used and as the street trade rises and falls with supply, media publicity and police operations. Figure 9.6 shows more detailed patterns of use. Areas of continuous co-presence are again shown in white, grading to dark grey with degrees of seclusion; injecting zones are shown as white stars. While there is no dominant type of injecting place, the zones can be loosely categorized into public toilets, laneways and car parks.

There were two public toilets accessible within a few metres of the selling zone on Smith Street. The toilets offer public access with private control, public identity with private behaviour. So long as the general public continue to use the toilets then they act as camouflage for heroin use. The toilets, however, are not safe in the event of an overdose, as is recognized by users:

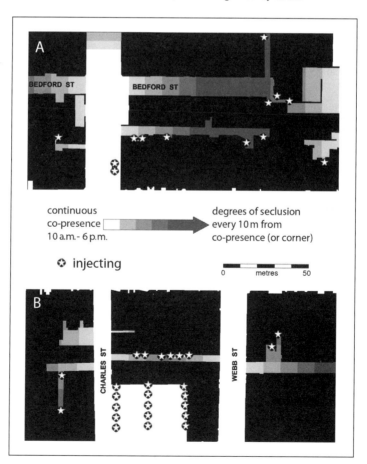

Figure 9.6
Injecting zones.

'people are going into the cubicles and use, and if they're gonna OD they're gonna sit down, and no one's there to help them … and that's a real big risk I suppose, they could be there for a long time before someone notices.'

Since the door is locked from the inside and the drugs can be flushed, the toilets are quite safe from police. Yet this safety becomes acute danger in the event of an overdose – the door locks have been smashed on occasion in the attempt to save lives. These toilets have been demolished since this study and were not replaced.

Injecting in laneways is the most common practice and tends to saturate all sites within about 100 m of the selling zone which satisfy minimal conditions of seclusion. Such sites occupy both public and private land in the legal sense, and where functions are intermittent or time dependent (like storage, garbage or private car parking). Often this is a section of unenclosed private space at the rear of a property. Thus these injecting zones are 'derelict' in the sense that they are less ordered, appropriated and controlled than the fully private or fully public space. These are smooth spaces without the strict territorial controls of the stricter and more striated streetscapes: 'cracks in the existing order' of the city (Massumi 1993: 104) or breaches in the habitus. They are liminal zones which often straddle the legal and social boundaries between public and private space, often zones where legally public space comes to seem private since the public have no reason to be there. This liminality or fluidity of spatial and social identity is a key attribute of many injecting zones. Injecting does not occur in many of the deepest spaces in the urban fabric. It is as if some spaces are just too deep, too secluded, with no routes of escape from police, no excuse to be there and little chance of being discovered after an overdose.

One dead-end laneway (near Webb Street in Figure 9.6b) is overlooked by a building which looks a bit like a factory but is in fact an office. Notices taped to the windows say: 'this lane is under video surveillance', but there are no cameras. The fictional panoptic regime was established by the occupants of the offices who have a good view of the lane and found it distressing to see people inject-ing. This is a relatively safe place to inject since an overdose during the day is highly likely to be reported, yet those who make it safer are acting to eradicate its use. It is the ambiguous identity of the adjacent building that makes it safer, sliding between office and factory. The illusion of privacy makes it safer from overdose but it is used because it seems private and not because it seems safe. The realization, or even the illusion, of surveillance may displace the injecting to a more dangerous location.

On the corner of another laneway is a small garage with an open entrance. This alcove is very close to the zone of co-presence yet hidden from overlooking by both walls and darkness. A slogan was written in chalk on both outside and interior walls: 'Junkies we are watching you – Residents'. Here two identities are affirmed – the legitimate, stable 'resident' and the transgressive, nomadic 'junkie'. The message on the walls carries multiple and conficting meanings. If it were true that residents were watching it may render the location safer in the event of an overdose (if they call an ambulance) or more dangerous (if they call the police).

Figure 9.6a shows an area where Bedford Street almost becomes a dead end and then jogs twice through a small gap to connect with a laneway lined with industrial uses. The three small corners created through the zig-zag were injecting zones. This is an interstitial zone which connects the street to the lane – it is almost, but not quite, possible to see from street to lane and vice versa. This space has the dual quality of being both deep and yet permeable; it is a fluid space from where one can easily disappear into the opposite street or lane if anyone comes. However, the degree of visual control over the approach is not high. The chances of being disturbed during injection or discovered after an overdose are high since the injecting zone is used as a through path.

Some injecting sites are relatively exposed to view from the zones of co-presence yet protected by distance. Figure 9.6b shows an injecting zone in the middle of a straight lane connecting Charles and Webb Streets. This site is fully visible from both streets but gains privacy as a site which offers the chance to detect intruders from a considerable distance. It is safe from sudden interruption with an escape route, and any overdose is likely to be quickly detected.

Car parks are used for injecting based on the camouflage offered by pedestrian presence, the permeable or ringy spatial structure, the visual cover offered by the cars, and the cover offered by the shade of trees in a context of the glare of sunlight. The spatial structure shifts from completely open in the early morning to a highly ringy structure as it fills up with cars. The cars create a shifting visual field where the fluidity of movement camouflages individual behaviour. The injecting spots tend to be located along the edges and under trees, with patterns of drug use varying with the disposition of cars. Car interiors are also used as injecting locations along many of the side streets and in car parks. Private car parks tend to have a stronger sense of enclosure than the public car parks, often with enclosed corners hidden from the street. Many are gated during the evening but with full public access during the day.

SAFETY/DANGER

What are the range of dangers and their priorities as perceived by drug users in relation to spatial forms and practices? How does the perception of safety and danger become inscribed in urban space through drug-use practices? There is clearly a 'dis-ease' associated with injecting in the public gaze and the safer users feel and the further they are from the police and the public gaze, the more relaxed they will be. Seclusion can be achieved through distance; through the enclosure of laneways and stairwells; through the camouflage of car parks and sunshading; and through the lockable doors of the toilets. The danger of being suddenly interrupted by police or passers-by is pronounced in some zones but none of the public injecting zones are completely safe from overlooking and/or interruption.

Figure 9.7 diagrams some of the spatial practices and dilemmas outlined here within the context of a Deleuzian epistemology. The socio-spatial pairs of safety/danger and exposure/seclusion are mapped against each other with a focus on the zones between categories and the vectors and trajectories across them. Each end of the exposure/seclusion trajectory has its dilemma: more exposed means safer in the event of an overdose yet more danger from police; more secluded means safer from police yet more danger from an overdose. The retreat to one kind of safety (in privacy) leads to another kind of danger. The meaning of 'safety' slips across contexts: the 'safe' strength of the drug; 'safe' from police and the public gaze; 'safe' in the event of an overdose. The interviews with users reveal some of the nuances of these experiences: 'users, young people full stop, are indestructible, invisible and indestructible you know, it's like the dog who rolls in dog shit and thinks you can't see them because they've covered up their scent.' Such an illusion of invisibility may be protective in overdose terms since it may lead to a belief in safety from surveillance coupled with the reality of help in an emergency. Safety is also perceived within a context of speed and urgency: 'out on the street, you know, it's just a big rush, and you don't really take care of everything' (cited in Fitzgerald and O'Brien 1999: 46). This 'rush' is at once the rush to score and inject, the rush to be rid of the evidence and the rush of the drug experience. Scoring and injecting are not separate acts so much as different phases of a single trajectory that encompasses economic, symbolic, chemical, spatial and experiential consumption. The rush associated with using in public space can lead to unsafe practices including the sharing of needles: 'there have been times when I shared [needles] in public because it's been, like you just want to get it done as quickly as possible you know.' The speed of this trajectory needs to be understood both as a whole and as a cluster of issues. It begins with the speedy nature of the deal, the glance which initiates

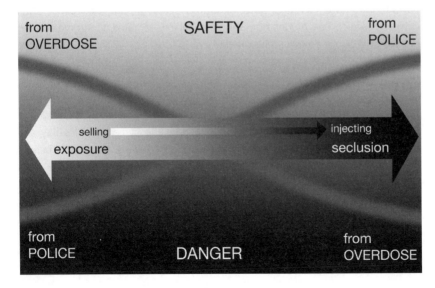

Figure 9.7
Dilemmas of public injecting.

it and the exchange which concludes it. The risk of being seen by police ensures that the period of possession between scoring and injection is a time of legal vulnerability which increases the urgency to inject. The hurry to inject is also driven by the need to ease the sickness; injecting in public when they would prefer to use at home is one indication of a habit one cannot control: 'you'll go and use in public places because you need a shot now, 'coz usually like you're sick you know … it becomes a necessity more than anything.' Yet at the same time scoring and using in public is also seen by some as an exciting urban experience which is enmeshed in social constructions of identity:

> 'I don't know a junkie who doesn't love scoring off the street … there's always this bit of a thrill of anticipation, like you know you're doing this … exchange in front of people who, you believe anyway, aren't really hip to what's going on at all … you feel sort of like separated from the mainstream, you feel like you're part of … a club sort of trip…'

This desirable risk is linked to changes in the social meaning of heroin use and the social identity of drug users. Some users see public injecting in terms of a form of performance, framed within the mainstream media's portrayal of Smith Street as 'Smack Street': 'I shot up on the stairwell of a car park which was great, I loved it, it was like I was a character in a movie.' For many younger users the narrative is one of navigating a terrain of risk and pleasure in a difficult world of socially constructed performances in the public gaze:

> 'I can go without heroin entirely and then I'll walk down the street and I'll think to myself no I'd rather be on heroin and enjoying my life than trying to do the right thing by the public eye because the public eye really is, um, a blind eye anyway ah, and to perform for the public eye I might as well just be performing for yourself because the public eye is not ever going to see what's really going down in the world anyway … the public eye don't care about kids on heroin.'

The dilemma for drug users lies in having to play off competing risks and desires when they inject in a public space. However, there are also dilemmas for the community and for public policy. Attempts to control public injecting have important implications for urban design, public expenditure and the vision we have for civil life in public space. The identity of the 'street junkie' has a very low social status as a stereotype constructed by a larger community in order to identify and thereby stabilize a perceived threat. The spatial shift of injecting from relative privacy to the publicity of the street would appear to be permanent, even if the particular streetscapes upon which these practices focus may change.

An interesting dimension of the spatiality of public injecting is that it shares such liminal zones with practices of graffiti writing. Graffiti is also illegal and is torn between the desire to be visible to the public gaze and the desire to find a vacant surface and to execute the work unobserved. Graffiti writers have been found to disparage heroin use (Halsey and Young 2006) and while there is an overlap in spaces used by both groups the content of graffiti sometimes operates as an injunction against heroin use and a reification of the 'junkie' identity.

Beyond the chalked graffiti produced by residents mentioned earlier ('junkies we are watching you') there was a labelling of a laneway as a shooting gallery and also a bold injunction: 'bash a junkie a day'; a more recent version is: 'junkie cunts die'. These liminal sites of injecting drug use are not simply derelict but are contested in terms of both spatial practices and discourses, operating to both construct and denigrate the identity of the 'junkie'.

Rose (1993) and Butler (1990) have shown how social identities are produced and reproduced through the repetition of performative acts in public. This has the capacity to lend legitimacy to such acts, but also to destabilize social identities such as the stereotypic 'junkie' (Nelson 1999). These are places of becoming in the sense that while using a drug is something someone does, a 'junkie' is something someone 'is'. Having a fix in public also fixes ones identity. So what are the opportunities to intervene in a manner that reshapes the social meaning of heroin use – as something some people do rather than what they are?

The conundrum presented here is part of a large assemblage wherein heroin is likely to remain illegal and of unpredictable quality and strength. There are no really safe places for injecting in public. There are many interventions which can be made to displace dangerous behaviour from some of these places. These include fences, cameras, lights and other design interventions. Some of the laneways in this study have since been fenced. However, it is not at all clear that such displacement would be to safer locations and difficult to predict where it might be displaced to. Many of the urban design practices which occur under the slogan of 'designing out crime' could be better termed 'redistributing danger', the displacement of unwanted behavior and perceived threat into someone else's neighbourhood (Dovey 2000b).

SUPERVISION

While public injecting practices cannot be rendered safe, supervised injecting facilities offer prospects for alleviating the dangers – places where users are guaranteed both safety from police and help in the event of an overdose. The effectiveness of supervised injecting in saving lives is well-established and based on the fact that death from overdose is very rare when treatment is administered. The challenge in terms of the programming and design of such places is to avoid responses which construct or reproduce negative social stereotypes. As we have argued, the spatial transition from selling to injecting is a fluid trajectory of experience and behaviour which moves from the camouflage of publicity to the seclusion of privacy. For Deleuze and Guattari (1987) this is a 'line of flight' – an experience of tension, thrill, rush and danger; a time (and place) when (and where) users run the risks of being arrested, of being identified as a 'street junkie' and of death through overdose. The injecting zones are smooth spaces of flow and movement rather than places of stabilized identity – we suggest that supervised injecting facilities should embody similar qualities. Yet the task of supervised injecting is specifically to attract the injecting practices into the panoptic gaze of medical supervision – a paradigm case of striated space. The traditional role of architecture has been to create and stabilize identities in urban space. Can there be a set of tactics for designing such facilities which mirrors the patterns of injecting drug use outlined here? The challenge here runs counter to the traditional role of architecture as a stabilizer of spatial relations and built forms. Architecture stabilizes the spatial practices of the habitus; our spatial 'habit' geared to 'habitat' (Bourdieu 2000). Indeed, stabilizing and controlling a habit is precisely what supervised injecting is designed to achieve. How can this be done without also reinforcing a negative identity of the 'street junkie'? And a further dilemma here is that the public gaze of the media on such facilities may drive users away as they become subject to both medical and public supervision.

If such places are to mirror the existing practices of drug use in public space then we suggest some approaches to their location and design. First, they should be liminal places which attempt to overcome the binary logic (in/out; either/or) of spatial thinking; the excessive segmentation of space which infuses most facility programming, embodied in the very language of supervised injecting 'rooms'. Sites of supervised injecting could be located in a manner that parallels the liminal locations of existing injection zones – occupying zones between functions and categories; between dead ends and shallow shopfronts, between inside and outside, between public and private. The facilities could be designed with diffuse boundaries in urban space, avoiding thresholds, portals or doorways at which the identity of the place, and therefore the user, is signified. Spatial screening could ensure that entrance transition occurs over a distance or through several spatial turns. Multiple entries could be used so there is no single threshold. The facility could be construed as a 'field' where the gaze of supervision extends beyond a medical core, perhaps with decreasing levels of supervision/safety. The facility could be co-located or nested with other facilities and functions such that its identity becomes blurred. There could be a diversity of types of facility mixed with a variety of functions: chemist shops, medical facilities, vacant buildings, gaming arcades, car parks and train stations. The signage may deploy codings whereby it is labelled as one thing yet understood (by some) to be another. Finally, the location and design of supervised injecting places may need to be ephemeral or mobile – even the best designed and located facilities may have a short-lived success if the market moves or the location is exposed in the tabloid media.

Having said all this, it is worth considering a further dilemma in this politics of visibility. If supervised injection facilities are designed to mirror existing marginalized practices of injecting drug use, do we run the risk of institutionalizing this marginality through the very tactics of liminality, diffusion, multiplicity and ephemerality outlined above? Is it not in the user's interest to normalize injecting practices under clear forms of governance? Normalization of injecting drug use will at once render such practices more safe and less thrilling. But then will it meet its market? If such facilities are really places of becoming then they must work with and between the desires for the drug and desires to control its use.

Chapter 10: New Orders

Monas and Merdeka Square

Kim Dovey and Eka Permanasari

> The course of history … can really claim the thinker's attention no more than the kaleidoscope in the hand of a child, where all the patterns of order collapse into a new order with each turn … The ideas of those in power have always been the mirrors, thanks to which the picture of an 'order' came about …
>
> (Benjamin 1972: 660)

The National Monument in Jakarta is a giant obelisk constructed by Indonesian President Sukarno in 1961 as a representation of the new nation. It stands on the vast expanse of the former colonial King's Square, renamed Merdeka Square ('Freedom Square'), where it is now surrounded by national institutions. The open spaces of the square distance the monument from the crowded city, but were infiltrated from the beginning by various prohibited users – beggars, prostitutes, illegal vendors and homeless people. These rhizomatic practices of everyday life tended to cut across the idealized nationalist symbolism of the square. The demise of Suharto's 'New Order' in 1998 coincided with the rise of another kind of order in Merdeka Square which is now fenced and purified. This chapter explores the changing meanings and uses of this place in both nationalist politics and everyday life.[1]

Jakarta was founded as a port city that was first colonized by the Portuguese in the sixteenth century. The Dutch then established the city of Batavia as a walled city and the centre of the Dutch East Indies in the seventeenth century. As the city expanded southwards under French rule in the early nineteenth century, about 90 hectares of open field was laid out as a military training field named *Champ de Mars* (Field of War) (Heuken 1982: 45). After the Dutch resumed control, the square was renamed *Koningsplein* or King's Square (Figure 10.1). A Governor General's residence was built across the street to the north in 1820 with a palace added in 1879. Various public institutions were constructed facing onto the square: the National Museum to the west (1868) and two Christian churches to the east (Heuken 1982: 45). The City Governor's residence and office was added to the south in 1909. A railway line was cut through the eastern edge in the 1870s and a major train station in 1937. The vast square itself also began to fill with functions: a horse-racing track, market place, police station and

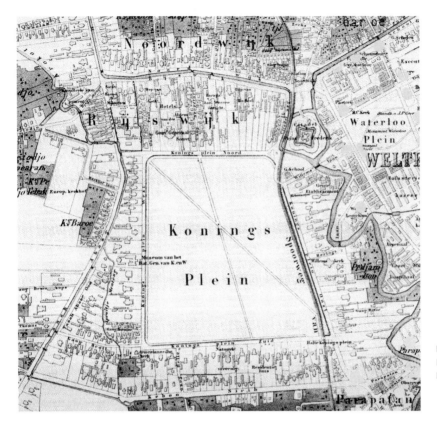

Figure 10.1
Koningsplein under the
Dutch colonial order.

telephone office. The police and telephone buildings defined an open space in front of the Governor's Palace in the north-west corner which became the key centre of power in both symbolic and practical terms, framed by symbols and practices of authority, force and communications. When the Japanese took control from the Dutch in 1942 the square was used primarily as a sporting venue with an athletics stadium and sporting halls.

When independence was first secured in 1949, a rally and flag-raising was held in front of the Governor's Palace facing the Koningsplein. Sukarno appropriated the palace as a Presidential Palace and the square was renamed Merdeka Square and used for political rallies. Merdeka had two meanings here: freedom from the Dutch but also the democratic freedom from a feudal land system (McVey 1996). At this time the open space was confined to the north-west corner in front of the palace. The traditional centre of Javanese power, as established in the Javanese kingdom of Yogyakarta, is located on the axis between mountain and sea facing inland (Legge 1973). The colonial palace in Jakarta already loosely incorporated this structure.

The nation that Sukarno inherited was defined by that part of a vast archipelago colonized by the Dutch; its outer boundaries with Malaysia, the Philippines, Papua New Guinea and Portuguese Timor were fluid and contested. The nation forged by the force of colonial power was primarily held together by the solidarity of the struggle for independence. Keeping the nation together once the common colonial enemy was gone was Sukarno's biggest challenge. One response was to stir up external threats and confrontation with Malaysia but the internal divisions were more substantial. From the beginnings of independence there were secessionist movements in the outer islands and provinces – Ambon, Aceh, Kalimantan, Bali, Batak, Flores. These regional uprisings were at times supported by Britain and the United States who were alarmed at the growing power of the Communist Party in Sukarno's cabinet. Sukarno was under pressure from the Communist Party to institute land reform, but also from Javanese and Muslim majorities to set up either an Islamic or Javanese state (Macdonald 1995). In addition to this, the military largely opposed democracy and threatened a coup. Sukarno's approach was one of inclusion, driven by ideals of secular nationalism common to a range of non-aligned newly emerging post-colonial nations. When he was finally forced to rule with martial law after an uprising in 1957, Sukarno promoted the contradictory ideal of 'Guided Democracy', based on the idea that the nation needed an enforced harmony between conflicting desires for military, communist, Islamic and democratic versions of the new nation.

Sukarno was a great orator with a capacity to bridge differences and construct a language that held contending forces in balance (Legge 1973). He coined the acronym NASAKOM to represent his proposed unity between nationalism, religion and communism. CONEFO was the name for his global Conference of Newly Emerging Forces and GANEFO for the Games of Newly Emerging Forces, both of which he hosted. The national monument that Sukarno built on Merdeka Square is called MONAS in a similar vein and, like the acronym, the monument melds a range of intended meanings into a single form.

MONAS/MERDEKA

The construction of Monas and Merdeka Square was commenced in 1961 – the entire site of the former King's Ground was cleared of racetrack, markets, police station and radio station – but it was not completed until 1976, well after his demise. Sukarno had studied architecture at university and his role in the design of the monument was central; he was often referred to more broadly as the architect of the nation. A design competition was held in 1959, followed by a further competition in 1960, but Sukarno found no appropriate design and no winner was announced. Architects were then asked to draw up sketches made by Sukarno which became the basis of the final design.[2] The design of the square was based on a plan initially developed in 1892, with diagonal streets radiating from the monument bringing traffic to the monument directly from each corner.[3] The vast open spaces were designed with fountains, gardens and smaller monuments.

The monument is formed of a basement surmounted by a broad cantilevered terrace from which a vertical obelisk with a golden flame on top rises to a height of 132 m (Figure 10.2). There was a measure of megalomania about

Figure 10.2
Monas, Jakarta.

Sukarno's nation building; Monas was to be larger than the Eiffel Tower and higher than the Javanese Buddhist monument of Borobudur (Legge 1973). It was also to be the tallest building in Jakarta; with its broad cantilevered terraces in reinforced concrete it was a demonstration of the nation's industrial and engineering capacities. Sukarno saw his own mixed (Balinese/Javanese) heritage as symbolic of the mixed unity of the nation; wary of accusations of Javanese or Islamic domination of the nation, he was careful not to use specifically Javanese or Islamic forms in the monument. It is at once a heroically modernist form with some very specific local references. The form of the obelisk is an echo of the Western histories of nationalism and empire, from Egypt via Paris and Washington. During the 1950s the vast expanse of Tiananmen Square had been cleared with a new obelisk constructed as a symbolic centre of the new China. The use of a vertical form as a stabilizing centre of power also has the symbolic advantage of providing an axis connecting territory/cosmology, and earth/sky. In another echo of so many monuments Monas was also a memorial to the revolutionary moment. Numbers representing the date of independence (17 August 1945) were embodied in the monument dimensions; the revolution as a moment in time was fixed into urban space. Architecture was deployed to keep the moment alive, space was deployed to hold time.

In addition to its role as an object in space, the monument also operates as a museum and lookout with a carefully choreographed spatial sequence. The entrance is through the basement museum containing an officially sanctioned history of the nation in a lengthy series of dioramas. One enters the monument as a kind of ground to the nation; the nation is literally grounded in this constructed history (Sutrisno 1999: 65). The pathway then rises first to the broad terrace and then via an elevator to a balcony under the flame; thus the journey through the monument proceeds from the past to the present where one occupies the centre of the nation. In his famous theory of nationalism Anderson suggests that the nation is an imagined community that cannot be sustained by face-to-face contact but rather is marked by the style in which it is imagined (Anderson 1983: 6). Monas became a key way in which Indonesia was imagined and embodied, just as climbing the Washington obelisk, the Statue of Liberty or the Eiffel Tower are keys to imagining the United States and France.

For Anderson the forms of post-colonial nationalism that emerged in the mid twentieth century are often best understood in terms of the belief systems they seem to oppose. And Geertz has argued that Sukarno was engaged in a revival of the 'theatre state': the pre-colonial Balinese state which was governed through court ritual and spectacle rather than force (Geertz 1968: 107). The broad terrace and the obelisk that rises from it are identified with the traditional Hindu symbolic dyad of *yoni* and *lingga*. This linkage represents both female/male and mortar/pestle, the vertical form of the *lingga* (male) emerges from the horizontal bowl of the *yoni* (female). The *lingga* symbolizes the fertility of a sacred phallus representing both virility and power. As Anderson puts it: 'Fertility of the ruler was seen as simultaneously evoking and guaranteeing the fertility of the land, the prosperity of the society and the expansionist vitality of the empire' (Anderson 1972: 18). Sukarno was not blind to the sexual connotations and referred to the monument as 'a symbol of virile grandeur and bravery ... an emblem of the people's will to soar on high' (quoted in Leclerc 1993). By the time it was complete Sukarno's power was gone and the monument is still widely referred to as Sukarno's last erection.

The gold-plated image of fire at the apex was intended to represent at once an eternal flame, the fighting spirit of revolution and a radiant figure of power, enlightenment and democracy. Fire was a key trope of Sukarno's speeches where it was linked to the spirit of revolution, nationalism and freedom. He claimed that: 'revolution does not work without people who have the spirit of fire' and that there was a need to 'fire up the people's spirit' (cited in Djenar 1994).

Throughout the 1950s and 1960s he repeatedly used the metaphor of fire in his Independence Day speeches. In 1954 he stated: 'the fire of nationalism is still raging' and in 1956 referred to the 'fire of idealism … The fire of initiatives, the fire of struggle … The burning campfire of national unity' (Sukarno, cited in Djenar 1994). Like the mortar and pestle, fire was a symbol that spoke of everyday life around the hearth, of the kitchen fire and campfire as a place of gathering. Sukarno was concerned that with the end of colonialism the spirit of revolution 'has cooled and has no fire' (cited in Djenar 1994).

While the architectural forms are primarily derived from a mix of modernist, Western and Hindu sources, Monas also incorporates the traditional Javanese conception of power as a form of concentrated heat or energy that animates the world:

> Perhaps the most exact image of the ordered Javanese polity is that of the cone of light cast downwards by a reflector lamp … The gradual even diminution of the radiance of the lamp with increasing distance from the bulb is an exact metaphor for the Javanese conception not only of the structure of the state but also of center–periphery relationships and of territorial sovereignty.
>
> (Anderson 1972: 22)

Such power is conceived to radiate and can be absorbed by subjects in proportion to their proximity to the centre of power (Anderson 1965). Merdeka Square was conceived by Sukarno as a place of gathering, his charismatic power was linked to face-to-face presence and he portrayed himself as one of the people, as *Bung* or brother (Kusno 2000: 107). Merdeka Square and the monument were designed as an assemblage that concentrates the spirit and power of the new nation and radiates it across the archipelago. Power is seen as concentrated in both places and people, and the corollary is that a diffusion of power (as in democracy) can be seen as a loss of national power and unity. In this traditional view questions of morality and legitimacy do not apply to the use of power; there is a sense that possession indicates legitimacy (Anderson 1972). In this context then Monas is not a legitimating image of authority so much as it is a literal concentration of power. Power is strongly hierarchical, flowing from centre to periphery; to seize the centre is to gain power. The radiant effect of Monas was accentuated by the circulation of its imagery on stamps, a circulation of political, symbolic and economic capital that also links the imagined nation with everyday life.

Sukarno was ejected from power after an attempted coup in 1965 and the monument and square were not completed until 1976. The new President Suharto made two significant changes to the monument's design. The first was to utilize the basement museum to construct a false history of his own rise to power. Dioramas portray a legal transition of power from Sukarno to Suharto that is clearly untrue.[4] The monument was also originally designed to have buffaloes guarding each corner on large podia (Figure 10.2). These images, linked to peasant agriculture, animist belief and Sukarno's political party, were deleted by Suharto during construction since images of farming were also seen as links to communism. Suharto did not live in the Presidential Palace and did not use Merdeka Square for political purposes during the 32 years of his rule. The square retained a symbolic role and continued to become framed by political and social institutions. The national mosque at the north-east corner, originally initiated and sited by Sukarno, was completed. According to Macdonald (1995: 288) the placement of this mosque adjacent to two existing Christian churches along the eastern edge of the square symbolizes two things: 'Islam is tremendously important in Indonesia: Indonesia is not an Islamic State.' During the 1970s and 1980s, other key locations were filled by the military and the US Embassy, reflecting the power base of Suharto's New Order.

The regime change from Sukarno to Suharto involved a fundamental shift in the role and imagery of public space. All talk of fire, revolution and movement was halted, to be replaced with images of stability and disciplinary order (McVey 1996). The dynamism of the nation was henceforth to be commercial rather than political, represented by office buildings and shopping malls rather than monuments. Public space was emptied of emancipatory capacity and became a place of discipline and fear (Kusno 2000: 104–105). The fire of Sukarno's tongue was replaced by the quiet calm of Suharto who rarely appeared in a crowd; *Bung Karno* (brother) was replaced by *Pak Harto* (father). Merdeka Square as a place for political gathering became a spectacle of the new order. Suharto was also greatly in need of legitimation because his rise to power was swiftly followed by the orchestrated murder of about half a million communists and sympathizers (Abeyasekare 1987; Anderson 2000; Legge 1973; McVey 1996). The trauma of this massacre was repressed under Suharto and continues to haunt the national psyche. Suharto's key claim to legitimacy was that he saved the nation from chaos; the spectacle of urban order was thus a fundamentally important legitimating image.

In 1987 Suharto added a new monument to the boulevard that runs along the western edge of Merdeka Square. This monument depicts a scene from the Hindu story of the Mahabharata. In this story the half-brothers and warriors Arjuna and Karna fought a battle. When Karna's chariot became stuck in the mud, Arjuna killed his brother at the urging of the god Krishna. The monument, located in the centre of the boulevard, is a bronze statue of Arjuna riding in a chariot driven by Krishna heading south down the axis of the main commercial strip of Jakarta. Indonesian culture is steeped in Hindu history and this story is well-known and understood. In this urban field the monument works as an allegory of the relationship between Suharto and Sukarno. Sukarno was part Hindu and widely known as *Bung* (brother) *Karna*; in Javanese *Karna* is pronounced *Karno*. The monument does not portray Karna or the battle itself but evokes the idea of moving on after a necessary struggle; it is a legitimating image for the transfer of power from Sukarno to Suharto and for the symbolic killing of *Bung Karno*. Anderson (1983) argues that modernity erodes the divine right to rule and creates a breach between cosmology and history; the Arjuna statue is a symbolic re-welding of that breach that marks Suharto's order as both new and old.

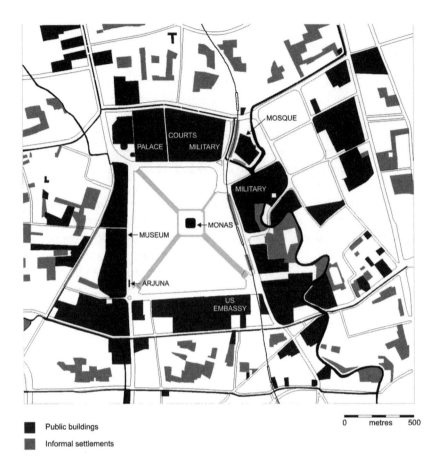

Figure 10.3
Merdeka Square under
Suharto.

0   metres   500

■ Public buildings

■ Informal settlements

This was the only monument of the Suharto era that intrudes into the urban space of Monas and its surrounds. It remains identified with Suharto and its renovation in 2000 was read publicly as a pro-Suharto act.[5] The urban location lends the statue a particular potency with the dynamic chariot in the middle of a modern boulevard connecting the Presidential Palace to the citadels of capital, and bypassing Merdeka Square.

EVERYDAY NATIONALISM

Everyday life in Merdeka Square has never matched its ideals. From the beginning of liberation Jakarta was subject to a massive influx of rural migration to the city. The population increased from less than a million in 1948 to 3.8 million in 1965 and squatter settlements proliferated with internal densities of up to five people per room (Abeyasekere 1987). Under Suharto, images of urban disorder were a serious problem for a regime known as the New Order. In the 1970s many informal settlements were razed without notice and fences were built to hide others. Rural to urban migration was banned and beçak drivers, pedlars, prostitutes and the homeless were moved off the main streets. However, hidden behind the state institutions and prestige sites surrounding Merdeka Square there remains a good deal of impoverished housing in back lanes and a 20-hectare informal settlement lining the Ciliwung River to the south-east of the square (Figure 10.3).

The daily infiltration of Merdeka Square by traders, beggars, prostitutes, and homeless people dates from its inception, increasing in volume during the 1980s and 1990s. Street hawkers and vendors of drinks, food and tourist items would follow visitors around the square and cluster outside the entry to the monument. Beggars and homeless people often used the square as their home base, sleeping under the trees and using the fountains for washing. After dark, the square became a site of prostitution and illegal markets, often combined through the selling of drinks as camouflage for selling sex. These marketing activities were focused under the shade of trees, near the fountains and the monument. The symbolism of national unity and order was undermined by images of poverty, chaos and transgression.[6]

During the uprisings against Suharto in May 1998, the prominent opposition leader Amin Rais planned to use Merdeka Square for a major political rally. The army (under General Wiranto) immediately blockaded the square and Rais was warned of violence if he persisted (Forrester 1999: 84). Rais relocated the demonstration but it was clear that the square and monument retained considerable potency (Nas and Sluis 2000: 85). Demonstrations in the square can be seen at once as opposing the President yet supporting the nation with overtones of a return to democracy. The motives during these weeks of 1998 are complex because the army was controlled by Wiranto who wanted to replace Suharto. It served Wiranto's interests to allow enough urban chaos to develop to legitimate military rule. He allowed widespread riots and looting to continue and gave the demonstrators open access to the parliament building while blockading the square (Young 1999). The fall of Suharto which followed in late 1998 was played out on the freeways and in the parliamentary precinct, but the blockade of Merdeka Square suggested that it retained potency as a site of democratic ideals. The people were permitted to take over the parliament building but were not permitted anywhere near the real centre of power.

The overthrow of Suharto did bring a return to democracy in 1998 and also a revitalization of political engagement to the streets. However, demonstrations remained banned on Merdeka Square which was controlled by the Governor of Jakarta, Sutiyoso (also a Presidential aspirant). In 2002, after Sukarno's daughter (Megawati) was elected President, Sutiyoso built a high fence with gates and guards to enclose the entire square (Figure 10.4). Visitors can access the square without charge but beggars, vendors, prostitutes and the homeless are excluded. An army encampment was set up within the compound to enforce the new order.

Sutiyoso's arguments for the fence were aesthetic; that the national monument and square should present an image of national order, requiring it to be cleared of prohibited users.[7] The fence was seen by some as a ploy by Sutiyoso to win Megawati's support by cleaning up the image of her father's monument

Figure 10.4
Fencing the flame.

(Sukanto 2002). However, the fence was initially opposed by many citizens, urban planners and architects on the basis that 'Freedom' Square should have free public access (Jhonny 2002). At this time street rallies were being mounted against both Megawati and Sutiyoso and some suggested the fence was to prevent political activity (Junaidi 2002).

The fence dramatically changed everyday life in the square, although some transgressive uses continued. The homeless people and beggars were forced out of the square and many moved to derelict land along and under the adjoining railway line. A newly fenced area for vendors was created near the south-west entry, but with little passing trade. Informal vendors have relocated to the railway station, car parks and entry areas outside the gates. Some vendors camouflage themselves as visitors, carrying their goods inside their bags and selling their wares surreptitiously. The prostitutes primarily work at night outside the fence, trading off the passing traffic. Some enter the compound camouflaged as part of a couple; the 'boyfriend' leaves once the connection is made. The market for informal activity has also been sharply reduced within the square because the fence has reduced the flow of visitors to the monument. On weekdays it is largely deserted except for a small army of gardeners and cleaners, and a real army of security guards who live in a camp on the west side of the park and police the gates. The fence necessitates a 600-metre walk across a hot and humid open space from the gate to the monument – a gap that has been partially filled with a horse-and-cart taxi service. On weekends and evenings locals enjoy the fresh air, jogging and walking, and young people use it as a lovers' lane. The monument is floodlit at night lending colour and flicker to the flame.

Most of the real urban life now occurs outside the fence. Political demonstrations are permitted on a small strip of sidewalk opposite the Presidential Palace on the north-west corner. The area in front of the palace has a long history of resistance and is guarded by a pedestrian exclusion zone that encompasses the entire street. On the eastern edge of the square substantial areas beneath and around the train line are utilized for a mix of mobile hawkers, roadside stalls (with people living behind) and homeless encampments. In the car park near the south-east corner of the square is a row of trailers storing razor wire spirals which are designed to unfurl as instant blockades in the event of public insurgency. The trailers have been appropriated by locals as solar clothes driers (Figure 10.5). Their concentration here suggests the target of insurgency is less the monument than the US Embassy across the street – a heavily fortified compound with two lanes of the boulevard closed as a buffer zone with concrete barriers and razor wire.

REFLECTIONS

...history may be half-made because it is in the process of being made; and the image of cultural authority may be ambivalent because it is caught, uncertainly, in the act of 'composing' its powerful image.

(Bhabha 1990: 4)

The ideas of those in power have always been the mirrors, thanks to which the picture of an 'order' came about...

(Benjamin 1972: 660)

While the centre of the Indonesian archipelago is clear, the boundaries are fluid; secessionist forces at the edge of the nation (Aceh, Ambon, Timor, Papua, etc.)

Figure 10.5
Instant barricades and
informal edges.

are at times in danger of slipping out of the fold. For Bhabha this is the dominant story of nationalism, the other is also within. The nation is always ambivalent and Janus-faced, looking both out and in; torn between acknowledging internal differences and repressing them (Bhabha 1990). The figure of the nation is ambivalent and slippery with a discourse connected to the way the details of everyday life emerge as national metaphors. The nation is a narrative performance, which is why the infiltrations of homelessness, prostitution and hawking are such potent images – they tell a truth that is not the official truth.

The figure of Monas with its history and its fenced void invites a psychoanalytic reading. In Lacanian theory identity is constructed in infancy – the well-known 'mirror-phase' when the child identifies the figure in a mirror as both 'real' and 'imaginary' (Lacan 1977). From this view we invent unified symbols and images of self-identity in order to overcome internal division; we construct a semblance of original unity that is also a fantasy of origins (Žižek 1991: 197). This links also to the Balinese notion of the theatre state where the hierarchy of the state is portrayed as a mirror of the harmony of the cosmos (Legge 1973; Geertz 1980). Such notions can be useful in understanding spatial configurations like Monas/Merdeka that play a dominant role in the national psyche. Symbols of unified identity also operate at the political level through stabilized symbols of unified identity and authority. Phallic signifiers are privileged in this field because they connect the imaginary to the stability and authority of power. Monas and Merdeka operate as legitimating images, verifying the integrated ideal of the Indonesian state and citizenry. Monas symbolizes the fire at the heart and hearth of the nation, the shared everyday life of Indonesian citizens and the ideals of freedom and democracy. It resonates at once with Javanese and Hindu traditions, and progressive secular nationalism. Merdeka is the symbolic order of an imaginary nation which the real practices of poverty and disorder contradicted and interrupted. The emptiness that is left after the real has been fenced out is at once a fantasy of wealth and harmony and also a collective void from which the search for national identity proceeds. The fence is the mediator in this assemblage, the screen we are not supposed to see but merely look through.

The Indonesian nation is engaged in a new era of grounding authority in democracy. The state of Merdeka Square reflects the tensions and contradictions of this struggle and it embodies some of the opportunities. The monument and square encodes the egalitarian ideals and hopes of a new nation, but they are reframed as a spectacle to be looked at rather than a place of political participation. Images of poverty are erased from the spectacle where possible while the reality continues in the back lanes and informal settlements nearby. After some initial opposition to the idea of freedom square being fenced off, the middle classes of Jakarta have appropriated the square as a protected and purified park. But much of the time Merdeka Square is something of a void in this vibrant city. The size of the square was set by the former King's Ground and is far too large for an effective urban space. At 75 hectares it is over five times the size of Tiananmen Square, and 12 times the size of Place de la Concorde. The excess of space within the square is exemplified by the fact that about 6 hectares of the southern section has been turned into a deer park – an ironic return to the idea of a 'royal' park on the site of the colonial King's Ground. In its current form it will continue to symbolize a colonial and grandiose past rather than a dynamic future.

It is not hard, however, to imagine a future when the fence will be torn down and the square becomes a place of genuine civic and political engagement. The monument has been framed and reframed several times and its meanings are far from exhausted. The giant podia still stand bare at its corners where the buffalos were deleted. There is at least a case for new development within the square and opportunities to reimagine the nation. Imaginative architects and urban designers could forge new connections with the surroundings – particularly the President's Palace and railway station. While there is respect for the ideals and legacies of Sukarno there is also considerable scope to explore options for the use and development of the square, opening it up to a new era of democracy while transforming the symbols of a difficult past. New development could help to intensify the life of the square while leaving a huge open space clear around the monument. The north of the square on axis could be considered as a site for a new parliament, establishing a new symbolic triangle of power between President, Parliament and Monas. This would bring democracy to centre stage on axis between sea and mountains. Other buildings could be added over time reinforcing the conception of Monas as a symbolic mountain or volcano and Indonesia as an archipelago of differences. It is important that any such redesign incorporate the interests of the poor into the centre of the national symbol; the flexible everyday economy of the street need not be fenced out. In this sense there is also a case for a memorial to those slaughtered in 1965.[8] The Suharto ascendancy and its accompanying violence remains an unspeakable trauma that haunts the national psyche, but it will at some point be acknowledged in the authorized national narrative. Such a redesign would entail a rethinking of public space for Indonesia, without reduction to any essentialized version of Indonesian unity or history. The nation was invented a mere 60 years ago and remains an unfinished project.

Chapter 11: Urban Slippage

Smooth and Striated Streetscapes in Bangkok

Kim Dovey and Kasama Polakit

The typical inner-city neighbourhood of Bangkok is dense, diverse and subject to continuous pressure for change due to traffic, freeways, modernization, commerce, tourism and migration.[1] One of the key characteristics is instability: the identity of the place can be defined by its slippages, by the fluidity of forms, practices and meanings. A variety of proprietors, residents, hawkers and others use and appropriate public space for a broad range of functions, desires and practices. The use and meaning of public space is subject to both local and global flows of time and space with shifting meanings of secular and sacred, private and public, legal and illegal. This looseness is linked to a high population density and demand for the use of space; but also to negotiable forms of governance and urban planning. Much of urban Bangkok has a multiplicitous urban character, held in place by the inertia of a robust urban morphology and a certain strictness of cultural coding.

Our intention here is to use the smooth/striated conceptual opposition of Deleuze and Guattari as a framework for understanding the use and meaning of urban space in Ban Panthom – an inner-city neighbourhood of Bangkok. Our point is more practical than theoretical: such concepts are tools for rethinking urban space, for prising open the question of how a complex urban assemblage works. Such concepts may be useful for understanding labyrinthine urban districts such as Ban Panthom that do not submit easily to the gaze of urban analysis. The conception of smoothness focuses attention on the slippages and movements of use and meaning, on the zones between categories and on the relationship between rhizomatic practices of everyday life and hierarchical systems of spatial control.

The looseness of public space in Ban Panthom can be construed as a conjunction of loose forms (or loose parts), loose practices (behaviours, functions) and loose meanings. Looseness of form is primarily linked to the loose parts which move around this neighbourhood with a high level of flexibility – food stalls, hawker trolleys, chairs, tables, washing, retail goods and vehicles. The looseness of function is closely linked to the loose parts, the manner in which the same space is used for a multiplicity of functions either at the same time or different times. One function may slip into another or be camouflaged within it. Loose meanings are in turn linked to loose relations between forms and functions.

LAYERED SPACE

One of the traps in a study such as this is the tendency is to see Bangkok through the lens of Western theory as an example of a more general order of Asian cities or streetscapes. Yet such Western theory has long been engaged in deconstructing its own limits; the Asian city is one of the products of what Said (1978) terms 'orientalism', a discourse that orients and stabilizes the identity of the West against the orient. Edensor (1998) bravely enters into this West/Other dichotomy with his description of the 'Indian street' that he contrasts with the increasingly regulated, desensitized and over-determined Western street. He celebrates the Indian street as a tangle of spatial forms and practices, smells, values and representations situated in opposition to the 'Western' street in the context of theories of the *flâneur*, Foucault's heterotopic spaces and de Certeau's resistant walker. But to what extent is such disorder a mythic construction of the Western gaze, and what is the value of Western theory to its interpretation? While Indian and Thai streetscapes may be no more alike than those of North America and Australia, if there is a thread that unites many of the poorer streets of what Seabrook (1996) calls the 'cities of the south' it is the relative weakness of the state in controlling a vibrant (if at times desperately poor) local economy. One effect is a sense of slippage or looseness.

These slippages are accentuated in the cultural context of Thailand. While we have no desire to reduce this context to any kind of essentialism, the meanings of its urban places and the various spatial practices within them need to be considered in light of local nuances of culture, nationalism, religion and authority (Askew 1994). Thai social structure is strongly ordered by hierarchical oppositions of older/younger, parent/child and higher/lower social status. Principles of deference permeate social practice at every level from the family to the nation (Morell and Chai-anan 1981). At the top of the hierarchy is a triangular formation of nation–religion–monarch. The King is 'father' of the nation, and Buddhism is the national religion and the source of moral order and merit. The authority of the state and the military has long been based in a capacity to harness governance to this legitimating triumvirate (Reynolds 1991). The authoritarianism of hierarchy is, however, strongly mediated by a Buddhist belief in community, justice and the sanctity of life (Jackson 1991). The social hierarchy is geared to a conceptual opposition of order versus confusion (Morell and Chai-anan 1981). Confusion (*woon wai*) is a state of nuisance, instability or anarchy which upsets the social order. The high value placed on a stable social order links to a belief that only rigid and authoritarian forms of governance can maintain stability (Dhiravegin 1992; Hindley 1976). One might expect such a social structure to produce a highly ordered and rigidly controlled urban morphology. Yet in many ways it is the opposite: urban regulations are widely transgressed and the Thai streetscape can be very confusing, especially as viewed from the West.

Thailand has generally been very open to Western ideas and technologies (Reynolds 1998) and the culture is characterized by a remarkable capacity to absorb new ideas, beliefs, names and meanings without displacing existing ones. Through layering and juxtaposition one can have both the traditional and the modern, Thai and Western, both the rule and its transgression (Wilson 1962). There is a great deal of slippage in spatial discourse and places often have several names which persist in common usage. Such different names can service different interests with different meanings that are often left unclear (O'Connor 1990). In the Thai context, oblique communication is often more effective than direct language; conflicts and contradictions are often avoided rather than resolved. New ideas, forms and spatial practices tend to form layers and juxtapositions rather than displacements. The social order and the urban order are at the same time both strongly hierarchically controlled and highly fluid.

The tension between spatial practices and codes of control can be explored through the theoretical lens of Delueze and Guattari's (1987) distinction between smooth and striated space as introduced in Chapter 2. Striated space is where identity has become stabilized, as opposed to the smooth spaces of becoming. Smooth space is linked to rhizomatic modes of practice – migrating horizontally within the interstices of a larger order – and contrasted against structures of hierarchical control. Smooth space is a field of vectors on which we ride or slide, where power is practised through camouflage and the blurring of identity and authority. Smooth and striated are not types of space or place so much as tools for thought; every real place is a mixture of the two in a reciprocal relation (Deleuze and Guattari 1987: 486) where each is folded into the other; for our purposes here this entails the enfolding of public/private, sacred/secular, temporary/permanent and legal/illegal.

BAN PANTHOM

Ban Panthom is about 17 hectares, a short walk north of the tourist neighbourhood of Khao San Road in Banglamphu and ten minutes east of the Chao Phraya River. It is bounded by an elevated freeway on the north-east, the traffic artery of Samsen Road on the north-west, with a derelict canal and minor street on the south-west and south-east respectively (Figure 11.1). The area is primarily residential at a density of about 100 dwelling units/hectare, however, densities are difficult to measure since official figures are quite inaccurate and there is a significant floating population who officially live elsewhere. The area is well served by public transport with many bus lines passing nearby. Like all of Bangkok this was once a water-based settlement with a dense network of canals (*khlongs*), nearly all of which are now replaced by streets. While the site remains bordered by one of the city's largest surviving *khlongs* (Khlong Banglamphu), the last water taxi operated there in 1996, and while it is used a little for fishing and swimming, it is heavily polluted.

The district is centred on the temple and school compound of Wat Mai. In the south-west of the district are the remains of one of the city's major marketplaces which has long attracted entertainment functions and transgressive

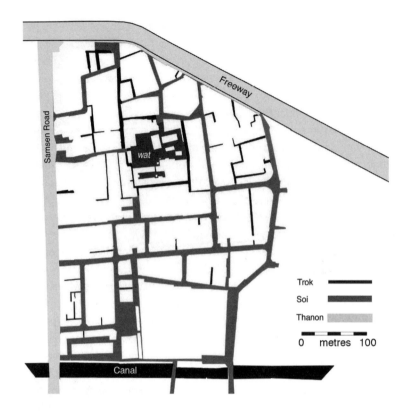

Figure 11.1
Ban Panthom – street
network.

activities such as prostitution and drug use. Ban Panthom has been subject to many major disruptions and changes during the twentieth century – a series of fires, subdivisions, filling of canals, road widening, new construction, migration (from north-east Thailand), new factories (including a large water-treatment plant), growing tourism, removal of the marketplace and persistent attempts by authorities to eradicate illegal activities.

The street and pedestrian network of Ban Panthom, can be divided into a street hierarchy of *thanon* (main street), *soi* (side street) and *trok* (pedestrian street or lane).[2] The neighbourhood is bordered by a major *thanon* to the south-east, and is penetrated by a network of *sois* and *troks* before opening into the *wat* compound at the centre with a range of temples, religious buildings, a school and monks' quarters (Figure 11.1). The *soi* is defined by being secondary to a main street and by carrying vehicular traffic (Figure 11.2). *Sois* often have no sidewalk, indeed many of them have been formed by an enforced widening of the narrower *trok* by removing the front section of the adjoining houses. The definition of a *trok* is linked to the width of pathway (extending from half a metre to 3 m wide) and to the exclusion of cars (Figure 11.3). The definition of a *trok* spans the English terms 'laneway', 'alley' and 'walkway', except that the *trok* is generally lined with buildings and main entrances – it is not a back, except in the sense of being internal to the block structure. It is the absence of cars and the capacity for a richer streetlife that most characterizes the *trok*. *Troks* are

Figure 11.2
Typical *sois*.

widely used for children's play, watching television and a broad range of economic and social activities (Figure 11.3 lower). Yet there is often a slippage – 'troks' have become 'sois' as they have been widened for cars and appropriated for parking, retail and commercial functions. A number of streets with car parking and traffic (such as Figure 11.2 lower) are referred to by those in the community over about 40 years of age as 'troks', after their former name, character and use. Community members over about 60 years of age tend to refer to all of the streets in the area as 'troks'.

The public circulation network is also identified by places known as *paksoi* and *paktrok* – the entry points to the *soi* or *trok* – node points with a concentration of

Figure 11.3
Typical *troks*.

commercial and social life. At lower levels of this street hierarchy, access becomes ambiguous. The smaller *troks* are often difficult to pass due to width or blockages. Some *paktrok* locations function as control points for the community within: strangers are asked their business and who they are looking for. The boundary between public and private is often ambiguous in both the legal and access senses.

At the centre of the neighbourhood, Wat Mai is a temple compound of about a hectare incorporating temples, monks' quarters, cremation hall, school, community facilities and open space. The compound is enclosed within a 3-metre-high fence, with two entries for cars and two for pedestrian – usually these are left open. *Wats* in Thailand are divided hierarchically into 'royal' versus 'common' types; Wat Mai is a common *wat*. Much of the surrounding residential land is owned by the *wat*, inhabited by poorer residents and regarded as a slum.

The built form of Ban Panthom comprises a very broad range of building types: these include the traditional architecture of the *wat* compound, two-storey detached teak houses, modern apartments and hotels, shophouses in various styles, factories and modern detached houses behind high walls. There is also a good deal of makeshift housing in concrete, timber, corrugated steel and plastic. The row-house type, 4 m wide and two to five storeys high, dominates the study area, particularly along the main roads and *sois*. The housing in smaller *troks* is less formal and more makeshift. The functional mix includes residential, office, retail, industrial, educational, religious and entertainment uses, with a predominance of residential on the interior of the neighbourhood. However, functions are impossible to map fully. First, because activities are often mixed on the same site, especially a mix of residential, retail, industry and services; and second because there is considerable blurring between functions within the same space.

PUBLIC/PRIVATE

The boundary between private and public space is subject to continuous negotiation, particularly with regard to the ways in which private activities spill onto edges of the *sois* and *troks*. Local unwritten rules play a key part in the control and use of public space, increasingly so as one moves deeper into the *soi* and *trok* network. Most *sois* do not have defined sidewalks, yet in the section near the main streets the pavement is marked with yellow stripes to mark the extent to which shops are permitted to appropriate the space, ensuring space for vehicles and pedestrians (Figure 11.2 upper and centre). As one moves deeper into the neighbourhood, however, these striations disappear and the boundary is managed in a fluid and local manner based on a shared understanding that the traffic, both pedestrian and vehicular, must continue to flow. The zone of ambiguous space on the *sois* is generally up to 2 m wide and is used for domestic and retail activities as well as car parking. There is a tacit, but loose, agreement that this space in front of buildings is controlled by proprietors. Domestic activities include washing and drying clothes, gardening, dish washing, cooking, conversing and watching television. Retail activities include dining, product display and car-repair workshops. When traffic eases, the streets are used for ball games and exercise.

Car parking on busy Samsen Road (on the north-west edge of the site) is regulated by police, yet within the Ban Panthom neighbourhood it becomes subject to a set of tacit local rules, framed in turn by the prospect that if traffic were blocked then the authorities would act. Property owners have a tacit right to park in front of their building, however, this is not a legal right and there are no car-parking spaces marked. Control over such parking is generally enforced by the use of territorial markers such as small screens and steel frames (often doubling as clothes driers) when the household car is not there (Figure 11.2 lower). This system is reinforced by the prospect of having one's car scratched if it is violated. Beyond the semi-private zones in front of dwellings there is also a tacit right to park anywhere that does not block traffic. This rule has the tendency to turn the larger intersections into small parking lots. Those wishing to park often compete for this space with mobile street vendors. Some intersections are almost entirely appropriated by cars under repair from nearby workshops – businesses whose 'public' space far exceeds that of their private shop. Car parking on intersections often competes on a first come first served basis with a busy breakfast market in food stalls and hawkers (Figure 11.4).

The loose parts of this urban ecology can be construed as a continuum, from the almost continuously moving hawker trolleys to stalls that have become almost permanent. Itinerant street vendors range from those carrying goods, pushing carts and riding tricycles to those driving mini pick-up trucks at very low speed. They move along the *sois* and *troks*, but also gather to wait at the *paktrok*

Figure 11.4
Intersection competition.

and *paksoi* intersections. Some of the mobile trolleys are set up in regular locations as temporary stalls for various periods of the day and night; this may include a seat and umbrella for the vendor, and it may extend to seats and tables for customers (Figure 11.4). This system may be ad hoc or thoroughly organized, as with those that are wheeled or trucked into specific sites on a regular schedule. In some cases such furniture and goods remain in public space permanently, where they may become extensions to the architecture which become fixed over time. In these ways, loose parts gradually become almost permanent, yet camouflaged among the mobile stalls and trolleys. The booth to the right of Figure 11.4 is a trolley that has become a permanent part of the building.

At a larger scale this blurring between architecture and furniture becomes a blurring between renovations and new buildings. In a bid to create space for public sidewalks and cars, building regulations require new construction to be set back 2 m from the property line. The effect, however, has been to stimulate an elaborate camouflage whereby buildings are 'renovated' until they are completely replaced without setback. On one large site encompassing ten row-houses and a hotel, all of the façades were replaced with a single façade and no setback; then all the buildings were demolished and replaced with a factory (Figure 11.5). This enabled the process to be defined as a 'renovation'. Immediately across the street from this factory a car workshop uses the public space for vehicle repairs during the day, yet in the early evening they are cleared away and it becomes a café.

DAY/NIGHT

Some sidewalks are appropriated on a rhythmic cycle by different restaurants. One piece of sidewalk in front of a corner shophouse is the site for three different enterprises. In the morning from 6 a.m. to 9 a.m. the shophouse is closed

Figure 11.5
'Renovated' factory
(right) and workshop/
café (left).

but on the sidewalk is a breakfast stall selling fast-food (coffee and pastry). From 10 a.m. to 4 p.m. the breakfast stall is replaced by another food stall and the shop opens to sell beverages and snacks. From 5 p.m. to 10 p.m. it is replaced by an evening restaurant while the shop remains open for drinks. The sidewalk stalls pay the proprietor for space, water and electricity, as well as paying a 'fee' to local government officers, part of which disappears as graft. Thus the income from this public sidewalk flows in six different directions – the adjacent proprietor, three restaurants, the local authority and its officers.

Samsen Road, the major artery lining the north-western edge of the neighbourhood, shows dramatic daily transformations of use. During the day the two-and-a-half-metre-wide strip of sidewalk is lined with shops about every 4 m (Figure 11.6 upper). The traffic is heavy and noisy, making sidewalk conversation difficult during the day. The produce from some shops is displayed on the adjacent sidewalk and an occasional stall may be set up, but itinerant vendors are not permitted. After 6 p.m. this spatial regime changes as shops close their roller doors and mobile restaurant stalls are wheeled out from storage in the *trok* network. By 7 p.m. Samsen Road becomes a busy strip of evening restaurants that are nearly all independent of the shops which line the footpath (Figure 11.6 lower). The spatial pattern is a series of fold-up tables and chairs lining the shopfronts, with the food stalls occupying the outer edge of the footpath and a narrow walkway between them. Due to the narrow sidewalk, the gutter is used by vendors as serving space, food preparation and washing up. As the evening traffic eases on Samsen Road, cars are permitted to park there and the 'kitchens' compete with cars which then park further into the street.

This evening dining strip is technically illegal and is sustained by regular 'fines' paid by vendors to the local authorities. Some of this payment is creamed off as graft and the remainder operates as a form of rent. Despite its illegality, this is a sustainable system where the 'fines' are matched to the food market, the vendors' profits and the regulators' salaries. The fine is also a fee in the sense that it is calibrated to ensure that the flow of money continues. This slippage between a fine, a bribe and a fee keeps the fluid urban order under loose control. A stricter and fairer regime would legitimate the practice, establish a licence fee and eliminate the graft. However, such a regime could eliminate the incentive for enforcement, as it establishes a much more stable spatial order with striations on the pavement and higher prices. Beyond the edges of the sidewalk, the local jurisdiction ends and the appropriation of the roadway becomes a matter for the police. Yet police control over parking diminishes, along with the traffic, after 6 p.m., when parked cars begin to appropriate the traffic lanes. While the gutter and traffic lanes establish very clearly marked boundaries between both jurisdictions and functions, as the night wears on these striations become dissolved. Shop owners also have tacit rights over the use of the sidewalk and many of the evening vendors also pay them for rent and electricity. Other shop owners have lined the sidewalk edge with large and immovable potted plants that operate to screen the traffic and prevent food vendors from using the sidewalk during the evening.

Figure 11.6
Diurnal/nocturnal
transformations.

LEGAL/ILLEGAL

With a history as one of Bangkok's major market and entertainment districts, Ban Panthom has long been the site of a range of illicit activities, such as prostitution, gambling and drug use, which have proven difficult to eradicate. The sex industry in Ban Panthom was traditionally geared to the working classes with more recent influence from tourism. The industry here developed through a series of motels which have long operated as camouflage for prostitution – single men who register are asked if they want a woman. These are primarily modern buildings of about five storeys occupying large sites, surrounded by walls which offer high levels of privacy (Figure 11.7). They were originally designed as 'curtain motels'

Figure 11.7
'Hotel' strip.

where a curtain is drawn around the parking space adjacent to the room to secure complete privacy. Camouflage is provided by the fact that they are also called hotels and are used for regular accommodation and as 'love hotels' with rooms available by the hour.

Since the proliferation of AIDS in the 1980s, attempts have been made to close down the industry and the greatest effect in this neighbourhood has been the transformation of a number of hotels into 'apartments'. Being single rooms without kitchens, these apartments fill a need for cheap accommodation (often rented by students) and they stimulate the local market in cheap street food. The sex trade continues in the hotels along a major *soi* which extends east from Samsen Road south of the *wat*. This *soi* has a distinctly different character from the rest of the district and forms a semantic barrier between the north and south of the neighbourhood; many locals are fearful of the area and distrustful of its inhabitants. Some restaurants on Samsen Road are geared to the sex trade through a certain slippage in the services of the waitress. Tourism has had a major impact on the sex trade in recent years, most of the hotel signs are now in English and the car park curtains have largely disappeared.

While the sex trade extends from Samsen Road deep into the Ban Panthom neighbourhood, other illegal activities tend to locate in the *troks* located at the greatest depth from the busy *sois* and *thanon*. The deepest public spaces in Ban Panthom constitute the *troks* immediately to the south of the Wat Mai compound, contiguous with it yet without direct access. This is a small area that encompasses the intersection of three *troks*. Most of the illegal drug use and gambling in Ban Panthom is perceived to occur here. Groups of children playing at the outskirts often operate as lookouts for the gambling. The only group of homeless people in the neighbourhood are also based here, sleeping in semi-permanent beds beside the *trok*. While their place is scarcely secure, this is their home; they have an occupation making garlands and are accepted in the community. Indeed, many of the homeless once lived on a canal lining the eastern edge of the *wat* before it was filled in 1989 to create a rather derelict *soi*. On this *soi*, close to the deepest intersection, a small corner has been screened off with a curtain and a makeshift public urinal has been installed. These deepest parts of the *trok* network are easy to bypass and often avoided by other members of the community. An interesting dimension of this deepest space of the Ban Panthom area is that it is unclear just whose police jurisdiction it lies within. The boundary between two juridictions runs somewhere down the middle but its location is unclear. Those running the gambling pay graft to both police authorities and the ambiguity enables each to act as if the problem belongs to the other. Transgressive activities slip through smooth urban spaces between jurisdictions.

SACRED/SECULAR

The central compound of Wat Mai establishes a conceptual opposition between the notionally sacred centre of the *wat* compound and the notionally secular space of the streets. While the compound has gates to control vehicle access, it is permanently accessible by pedestrians. The grounds within constitute the largest open space in the neighbourhood and are generally packed with car parking which at times blocks the entry to the sacred space within the buildings. The open space is used by neighbourhood children when the parking eases and is cleared for festive occasions. The *wat* is surrounded by the poorest parts of the neighbourhood, often makeshift housing on land owned by the *wat* where the poor have long taken sanctuary in Buddhist benevolence. Until relatively recently the *wat* was also seen to be surrounded by brothels in a manner that made royal patronage difficult – the royal family could not visit. As a result a number of the former hotel/brothels surrounding the entrance to the *wat* have been converted into apartments. The main entry *soi* has been transformed with an entry gateway on the main road, parking has been regulated along much of this *soi* which is lined with large potted plants.

The slippage between sacred and secular space extends throughout the street network. In the early morning the streets have a semi-religious character as monks in saffron robes walk through the street network where they accept food offered by residents, an exchange known as 'merit-making' with benefits to both monks and residents. The streets are subject to dramatic shifts of meaning and behaviour at particular annual festivals. During the celebration of the Chao Phor Nu shrine in September, the car park of an entertainment complex becomes a sacred space and the entire *soi* network of Ban Panthom becomes a dragon pathway as parades move through the *sois*, past temporary altars set up in front of shophouses.

There are a number of smaller sacred sites dotted throughout the neighbourhood, mostly comprising sacred trees festooned with fabric, garlands and small shrines. The location of these ranges from the smallest *troks* to the most

Figure 11.8
Shrine and workshop.

public spaces. These sacred sites also have spin-offs for other activities. A sacred phallic image with its associated tree and shrines partially blocks the footpath on busy Wusut Kasat Road. The adjacent proprietors, a restaurant and car repair shop, have taken the opportunity provided by this sacred blockage to extend it for secular uses, and much of the street is blocked by cars under repair (Figure 11.8).

STATUS

Social status – a mix of wealth, social class and ethnicity – is a key lens through which Ban Panthom is seen by its residents. The poorest residents are homeless and occupy the deepest levels of urban space as outlined earlier. In general terms all of the poorest areas on the neighbourhood are located in a ring that encircles the *wat* compound. However, this does not mean that all of the housing in this zone is low income. Indeed most of the wealthiest housing is located in a zone to the south of the *wat* that substantially overlaps the poorer areas and extends along the hotel district.

Ethnic differences are perceived to occur along two axes. Thai nationals are distinguished between 'Thais' on the one hand and Chinese, Indian and Isaan (north-east Thailand) 'migrants', all of whom are conceived in varying degrees as 'other' to mainstream Thai culture. Such identities are loosely linked to districts within Ban Panthom: the wealthier Chinese are largely identified with the southern district and the Muslim Indian population is identified (largely as landowners) with the south-western corner near the former marketplace. The people from

Isaan are identified with the poorer areas surrounding the *wat* and are often referred to as 'migrants'. There is also a considerable population of students who are not identified with particular groups. The second social distinction is between Thai nationals (all the groups above) and *Farang*, which translates loosely as 'Western foreigners', together with others such as Japanese or other Asian foreigners. The incursion of foreigners into Ban Panthom is considerable as tourist activity spills over from the nearby Kao San Road area, as the sex trade becomes more global, and as cheap guesthouses open for backpackers.

SMOOTH/STRIATED

Ban Panthom is a highly complex urban landscape that is easy to characterize as chaotic, but at the same time it is a highly structured neighbourhood with a stable experience of home and community for most of its inhabitants. It also has a strong sense of resilience and resistance embodied in the labyrinthine spatial structure. It is enmeshed in the cross-traffic of a giant city but is also resistant to many aspects of urban change. The district is subject to the flows of tourists but does not have a sufficient level of symbolic capital to be transformed by them. It is subject to considerable vehicular traffic and would certainly be safer and more liveable if it were more protected.

The theoretical lens of smooth and striated space is translated here in terms of various forms of slippage or looseness – loose parts, loose practices and loose meanings. In many ways the character or place identity is defined by these slippages: by a slipping between categories, and by the movements through which one thing, practice or meaning becomes another. Functions slip from house to shop to factory; from hotel to brothel; from sidewalk to restaurant to shrine to car park; from laundry to café to gambling house. Hawker trolleys become building renovations and renovations become demolitions. Boundaries between districts, practices, meanings and social classes are blurred. Meanings slip from sacred to profane, from public to private; exchanges of money slip from a fine to a licence to a bribe; *troks* become *sois* as domestic reproduction slips into market production and local becomes global.

These forms of smoothness, looseness or becoming are not all of a kind. The looseness of urban space can be construed as different kinds of juxtaposition between loose parts, loose practices and loose meanings. Some slippages may be characterized as unstable boundaries as in the limits to parking and between police jurisdictions. In other cases two or more forms, actions or meanings may combine to form a hybrid: the house that is also a shop; the television in the *trok*. Hybrid spaces may operate asymmetrically where one serves as camouflage for the other: the fine/bribe and hotel/brothel are of this order. Differences of form, practice and meaning may be serial where one becomes another over time as the renovation becomes a new factory.

Despite the focus on slippages, our point is not to suggest that this is primarily smooth space; all space is always being striated and becoming smooth in varying degrees and ways (Deleuze and Guattari 1987: 474). The character of Ban Panthom can be understood as a continuously negotiated tension between smooth and striated. But not all urban space is equally smooth: one characteristic here is that the forms of striation become weaker, and urban space becomes smoother, as one moves deeper into the neighbourhood. The urban spatial structure is at one level hierarchical, with its structure of *thanon*, *soi* and *trok*, yet the lower levels of this hierarchy are increasingly rhizomatic rather than tree-like.

The control of the state does not saturate the city; the smoothness of urban space increases with depth from the major streets. It is interesting to compare this with the Foucaultian model of the panopticon as a disciplinary technology that spatializes the power of the state by generating maximum visibility deep within a socio-spatial structure while eliminating social contact between subjects. In many ways Ban Panthom does the opposite – a deeper realm of relatively free circulation (for locals) and high levels of social capital becomes relatively invisible and protected from state control.

Tensions between globalization and local tradition are played out along this continuum of shallow (main streets) and deep (*wat*, *soi* and *trok*) – reflected in the Western name of the main 'road' and the ambiguously named and defined *sois* and *troks*. Both the *wat* compound with its traditional architecture and the everyday life of the *troks* are strongly identified with local Thai urbanism together with Buddhist values of benevolence and justice. These deeper urban spaces contrast with the branded franchise stores on the main street. The rhizomatic practices in the deeper spaces – the 'migrating' hawkers and residents, children's play, the homeless, the illicit activities – are strongly linked (for better and worse) to the livelihood of the poor.

Any simple opposition between smooth and striated is confounded by the fact that the striated morphology of the *trok* network clearly plays a key role in both enabling slippage and resisting change. The inertia of urban morphology and particularly the street hierarchy is geared to many of the slippages, some of which in turn enable resistance to the erosion of that morphology. This protection serves at once to protect the local community and the various transgressive practices. As one moves deeper into urban space it becomes less urban with less traffic, less random encounter and greater private appropriation of public space. The higher levels of social capital and lower levels of symbolic capital serve to demarcate and protect the deeper space almost like a housing enclave. Yet Ban Panthom is not an ideal neighbourhood, and in this it contrasts markedly with the middle-class housing developments that proliferate on the outskirts of Bangkok: local variations on the global production of instant place identity enclosed both literally and symbolically. There is no room for nostalgia in Ban Panthom – the traditional canal settlement is long gone. With its fragments, juxtapositions, slippages, and without a dominant metanarrative, Ban Panthom can be construed as a postmodern urban landscape. Yet it remains distinctly 'other' to most imagery of global urbanity.

Finally, Ban Panthom can be seen as a complex web of flows. At one level these are flows of people, vehicles, trolleys and furniture, linked in turn to flows of goods, services and money. At a deeper level these flows can be seen as based in flows of desire. Desires for food, services and goods leads to a movement economy of stalls, hawkers and pedestrians. Spiritual desires are evident in the *wat* and other sacred sites, in the parades of monks and seasonal festivities. Desires for sex and the necessary privacy it entails are evident in both the built form and semiotics of the hotel strip; these are linked in turn to flows of customers and money, and then to the flows of sex workers from rural areas, to which the money flows in return. Desires to consume the ambience of the 'place' and its food are increasingly evident in the flows of tourists. Desires of car owners and traffic engineers are evident in the push to turn *troks* into *sois*; countered by the desires of residents to protect the social space of the *troks*. Desires of authorities to create and maintain a higher degree of urban order is evident in regulations over parking and construction. These desires in turn intersect with, and are often countered by, the desires of residents to survive, to make a life and to make a profit.

There is a sense in which all cities are slippery in varying degrees, an insight that owes much to a range of great urban theorists from Benjamin (1978) through Jacobs and Alexander to Sennett (1996), among others. One way of construing a city like Bangkok is to see it within a double duality of both the orientalism of East/West (Said 1978) and the economic divide construed as North/South (Seabrook 1996). While there are inherent problems with casting a Western gaze upon the Eastern city, we hope to have shown it possible to use some Western theory as a lens for examining Eastern urbanism without essentializing it. Yet the economic divide is also fundamentally linked to the critique of smooth space. In Benjamin's famous account of a city from a different 'south' – Naples of the early twentieth century – he exalted a property he termed 'porosity' where:

> The stamp of the definitive is avoided. No situation appears intended forever, no figure asserts its 'thus and not otherwise' … one can scarcely discern where building is still in progress and where delapidation has already set in. For nothing is concluded. Porosity results … above all from the passion for improvisation … Even the most wretched pauper is sovereign in the dim dual awareness of participating, in all his destitution, in … Neapolitan street life.
>
> (Benjamin 1978: 166–168)

The property of porosity that Benjamin exalts has a lot in common with the smoothness and slippage outlined above. Slippage co-exists with poverty because it enables those without a place in the larger order to make a place in the interstices and cracks within it. There is a great deal at stake in our understanding of urban districts such as Ban Panthom and of mega-cities like Bangkok. It is easy to see Ban Panthom, like much of Bangkok and other cities of the south, as a problem that needs to be fixed. Yet this desire to fix it, whether it flows from the global expert or the local planner, may run counter to the way the place operates for, and is experienced by, its inhabitants. Urban place identity and practices of everyday public life are not easily tied down and understanding them requires a loosening up of our thinking. While there is no easy way to overcome the problems of orientalism or of poverty, it is possible to analyse and understand Eastern urbanism without essentialism, and southern urbanism without paternalism.

Notes

Chapter 2: Place as Assemblage

1 See, for instance, Fisher (2007).
2 Originally published in 1972.
3 The terminology of the *genotype* and the methods of spatial syntax analysis can run against the grain of Deleuzian analysis; this issue will be explored more in Chapter 7.

Chapter 3: Silent Complicities: Bourdieu, Habitus, Field

1 Perhaps the most accessible general reference is Bourdieu (1990a). Useful secondary sources on Bourdieu include Jenkins (1992) and Swartz (1997).
2 Stevens' (1998) book remains the most potent critique of the architecture profession from this perspective. He has more recently conducted this critique from outside the academy through a highly contentious website where he has become a marginalized and contentious figure. See www.archsoc.com.

Chapter 4: Limits of Critical Architecture: 'I Mean to be Critical, But...'

1 See also responses from Eisenman *et al.* in the following issues of *Progressive Architecture*.
2 See also Dovey (2008: ch. 5, 6, 7) and Dovey (2001).
3 See also Dovey (1999).
4 See Eagleton (1990), Jay (1973), Adorno and Benjamin (1999).
5 The company was BHP, the case against the Ok Tedi mine in Papua New Guinea was eventually won by the indigenous community.

Chapter 5: Slippery Characters: Defending and Creating Place Identity

1 This project is part of a funded Australian Research Council project entitled 'What is Urban Character?' For other publications from this project see: Dovey *et al.* (2006, 2008), Wood *et al.* (2006) and Woodcock *et al.* (2008). The full project involved six case studies and over 50 in-depth interviews.
2 The work of urban theorists such as Jacobs (1965), Lynch (1972) and Alexander (1977) from the 1960s and 1970s was supplemented by both a phenomenology (Relph 1976; Seamon and Mugerauer 1985) and psychology (Rapoport 1982) of 'place'. An international research conference in Melbourne in 1985 was focused on the theme of 'Place and Placemaking' where both Relph and Rapoport were keynote speakers.
3 For a more complete account of the rise of urban character discourse in Victoria, see Woodcock *et al.* (2004).
4 For a full account of the Camberwell case study, see Dovey *et al.* (2005).

5 Boroondara City Council (1996), *Residential Urban Character Study*, Consultant's report by Urban Initiatives, Neighbourhood Character Area 104.

6 City of Yarra (1997) Urban Character Strategy, Mike Scott and Associates, Melbourne.

7 The developer of Beacon Cove was Mirvac. A series of 12-storey towers on the waterfront were included as part of this project but our focus here is on the hinterland.

8 Delfin are now amalgamated as Delfin Lend Lease (www.delfin.com.au).

Chapter 6: Becoming Prosperous: Informal Urbanism in Yogyakarta

1 The universities were the University of Melbourne (Kim Dovey) and Universitas Islam Indonesia (Wing Raharjo). Access to the community was negotiated through the NGO Yayasan Pondok Rakyat (People's Shelter Foundation). YPR Collaborators: Ignatius Hersumpana, Yoshi Murti, Enok Rusmanah, Tri Suhartini, Sani Widowati, Muklas Setiawan, Nining Suhartiningsih, Abdillah Yusuf, Budi Setiawan, Kusen Hadi, Ratih Sukma, Heru Slamet, Eko Prawoto. Community Artist: Samuel Indratma.

2 These maps were the collective work of the following students: University of Melbourne: Ammon Beyerle, Nick Bourns, Richard Chandler, Gwyneth Choi, Gethin Davison, Keith Diamond, Lin Fan, Akihito Hatayama, Natalie Kirschner, Jacinta Li, Leanne Marshall, Anna Maskiell, Timothy Moore, Sophie Nicholau, Lochlan Sinclair, Anastasia Victor and Joan Wheelahan. Universitas Islam Indonesia: Rizeki Raharja, Danang Mahardhika, Faruq Haqi, Lucky Oktavianto, Nova Nanda, Meidan Fidelia, Satriaramadhan, Nindya Putri, Paramitha Sekartaji, Galuh Kartika, Ulfah Catlya, Ibnu Wibowo, Lastika Pintriany, Nensi Yuli.

3 See also Chapters 2 and 3 of this volume.

4 This project won an Aga Khan Award for development architecture in 1992: www.akdn.org/akaa_award5_awards.asp#indonesia.

Chapter 7: Urbanizing Architecture: Rem Koolhaas and Spatial Segmentarity

1 An earlier publication involved a critique of two of these buildings (Dovey and Dixon 2002); I want to acknowledge the work of Scott Dixon on this earlier paper.

2 For a more lengthy introduction to my approach in a different context, see Dovey (2008: 23–31). For other uses of spatial analysis, see Markus (1993).

3 See Hillier and Hanson (1984) '*The Social Logic of Space*'; Markus (1993) *Buildings and Power*; Dovey (2008) *Framing Places*, ch. 2.

4 See *OMA* (1998); Colomina and Lleó (1998); Davies (1998); Emery (1999); Nesbit (1998). For an account of the role of architectural media in the construction and reception of new architecture, see Dovey (2000).

Chapter 8: Open Court: Transparency and Legitimation in the Courthouse

1 The Supreme Court was designed in 1884 by Melbourne architects A.L. Smith and A.E. Johnson (http://supremecourt.vic.gov.au).

2 My thanks to the architects Paul Katsieris of Hassell, Bob Sinclair of Jackson Associates and Roger Poole of Bates Smart; also to Judges Michael Black and Michael Strong for assistance.

3 The architects were Hassell Architects (Project Architect: Paul Katsieris). See also Lyon (1999).

4 This building is the result of a Public Private Partnership where the building is constructed, owned and maintained by a private corporation yet has no conceivable function other than as a court building. This is an important issue in relation to design but there is no scope to explore it here. The architects were Daryl Jackson Associates (Project Architect: Bob Sinclair) and Lyons Architects (Hamish Lyon).

5 The architects were Bates Smart Architects.

Chapter 9: Safety Becomes Danger: Drug Use in Public Space

1 Turning Point Alcohol and Drug Centre, personal communication (Fitzgerald). These figures relate to a statistical zone which is broader than the study area. Specific figures for overdose or death which correlate exactly to specific sites within the study area are unavailable.

2 A total of 54 in-depth interviews with heroin users were recorded and transcribed; informed consent was recorded without identification.

3 This research was funded by the National Health and Medical Research Council of Australia and approved by the University of Melbourne Human Research Ethics Committee and the Victoria Police Research Committee. The area is well-known to police, including its selling and injecting locations.

Chapter 10: New Orders: Monas and Merdeka Square

1 The fieldwork upon which this chapter is based was mostly undertaken as PhD research by Eka Permanasari, see Permanasari (2007).

2 There is dispute over authorship of the design but it is likely that several architects had a role, including Soebandrio (Nasional 1978) and Soedarsono (Nas 1993; Leclerc 1993).

3 This design, by Treub, established the figure of paths connecting corners to the centre but without the elaborate beaux-arts layout that followed (Nasional 1978).

4 The history of the coup has never been clearly resolved but it is clear that all of the generals who could have been rivals to Suharto were killed and that Suharto met with the coup leader on the night before the coup (Anderson and McVey 1971, 1978; McVey 1996; Anderson 2000).

5 See 'Kereta Arjuna Wijaya akan Digusur', *Kompas*, 10 March 2000.

6 For a more detailed account, see Permanasari (2007).

7 See 'Kecolongan Soal Pemagaran Taman Monas', *Kompas*, 11 December 2002.

8 For Žižek (1991: 204–208), an important role of the symbolic order of the state is to conceal the violence on which it was established.

Chapter 11: Urban Slippage: Smooth and Striated Streetscapes in Bangkok

1 This chapter is based on PhD fieldwork conducted by Kasama Polakit from 2002 to 2004 and a follow-up visit in 2006. The initial fieldwork involved many interviews, observations and detailed mapping over a two-month period. See Polakit (2004).

Bibliography

Abbott J. and Douglas D. (2003) 'The use of longitudinal spatial analyses of informal settlements in urban development planning', *Development Southern Africa*, 20 (1): 3–19.

Abeyasekere, S. (1987) *Jakarta: A History*, Singapore: Oxford University Press.

Adorno, T. (1974) *Minima Moralia*, London: New Left Books.

Adorno, T. and Benjamin, W. (1999) *The Complete Correspondence*, London: Polity.

Alexander, C. (1964) *Notes on the Synthesis of Form*, New York: Oxford University Press.

—— (1965) 'A City is not a Tree', *Architectural Forum*, 122 (April–May); Reprinted in Stout, F. and LeGates, R. (eds) (1996) *The City Reader*, London: Routledge, pp. 118–131.

—— (1979) *The Timeless Way of Building*, New York: Oxford University Press.

Alexander, C., Ishikawa, S. and Silverstein, M. (1977) *A Pattern Language*, New York: Oxford University Press.

Allen, S. (1997) 'From object to field', *Architectural Design*, 127: 24–31.

Alsayyad, N. (2004) 'Urban Informality as a "New" Way of Life', in Roy, A. and Alsayyad, N. (eds) *Urban Informality*, New York: Lexington, pp. 7–30.

Anderson, B. (1965) 'Mythology and the tolerance of the Javanese', Ithaca, NY: Dept of Asian Studies, Cornell University.

—— (1972) 'The idea of power in Javanese culture', in Holt, C. (ed.) *Culture and Politics in Indonesia*, Ithaca, NY: Cornell University Press, pp. 1–69.

—— (1983) *Imagined Communities*, London: Verso.

—— (2000) 'Petrus Dadi Ratu', *New Left Review*, 3 (May–June).

Anderson, B. and McVey, R. (1971) *A Preliminary Analysis of the October 1, 1965 Coup in Indonesia*, Ithaca, NY: Cornell University Southeast Asia Program.

Appadurai, A. (2000) 'Spectral housing and urban cleansing', *Public Culture*, 12 (3): 627–651.

Askew, M. (1994) 'Bangkok: transformation of the Thai city', in Askew, M. and Logan, W. (eds) *Cultural Identity and Urban Change in Southeast Asia*, Melbourne: Deakin University Press.

Bachelard, G. (1969) *The Poetics of Space*, Boston: Beacon.

Baird, G. (2004) ' "Criticality" and its Discontents', *Harvard Design Magazine*, 21.

Barthes, R. (1982) *A Roland Barthes Reader*, London: Vintage.

Bateson, G. (2000) *Steps to an Ecology of Mind*, Chicago, IL: University of Chicago Press.

Benjamin, W. (1968) *Illuminations*, New York: Schocken.

—— (1972) 'Zentralpark', in Thiedemann, R. and Schweppenhauser, H. (eds) *Gesammelte Schriften*, Frankfurt.

—— (1978) *Reflections*, New York: Harcourt, Brace & Yovanovich.

Bhabha, H. (1990) 'Narrating the nation', in Bhabha, H. (ed.) *Nation and Narration* London: Routledge, pp. 1–7.

Black, M. (1999) 'Representations of justice – introduction', *Journal of Social Change and Critical Enquiry*, 1 (1), available online: www.uow.edu.au/arts/joscci/joscci1/black&kastieris.html (accessed 30 October 2008).

Bourdieu, P. (1973) 'The Berber house', in Douglas, M. (ed.) *Rules and Meanings*, Harmondsworth: Penguin, pp. 98–110.

—— (1977) *Outline of a Theory of Practice*, London: Cambridge University Press.

—— (1984) *Distinction*, London: Routledge.

—— (1986) 'The forms of capital', in Richardson, J.G. (ed.) *Handbook of Theory and Research for the Sociology of Education*, New York: Greenwood, pp. 241–258.

—— (1990a) *In Other Words*, Cambridge: Polity.

—— (1990b) *The Logic of Practice*, Cambridge: Polity.

—— (1991) *Language and Symbolic Power*, Cambridge: Polity.

—— (1993) *The Field of Cultural Production*, New York: Columbia University Press.

—— (2000) *Pascalian Meditations*, Cambridge: Polity Press.

Brigham, J. (1999) 'Architectures of justice', *Journal of Social Change and Critical Enquiry* 1 (1), available online: www.uow.edu.au/arts/joscci/joscci1 (accessed 30 October 2008).

Buchanan, P. (1998) 'Rem Koolhaas/OMA: Educatorium at University of Utrecht', *Architecture and Urbanism*, 336: 24–45.

Butler, J. (1990) *Gender Trouble*, New York: Routledge.

Carroll, L. (1998) *Alice's Adventures in Wonderland and Through the Looking Glass*, London: Penguin.

Colebrook, C. (2002) *Understanding Deleuze*, Sydney: Allen & Unwin.

Coleman, A. (1985) *Utopia on Trial*, London: Hilary Shipman.

Colomina, B. and Lleó, B. (1998) '"A Machine was its Heart": House in Floirac', *Assemblage*, 37: 36–45.

Conley, T. (2005) 'Sensation', in Parr, A. (ed.) *The Deleuze Dictionary*, Edinburgh: Edinburgh University Press, pp. 244–246.

Corner, D. (1999) 'The agency of mapping', in Cosgrove, D. (ed.) *Mappings*, New York: Reaktion, pp. 213–252.

Cornubert, C. (1998) 'Educatorium, Utrecht, Holland', *Domus*, 800: 42–47.

Cresswell, T. (2004) *Place*, Oxford; Blackwell.

De Bono, E. (1969) *The Mechanism of Mind*, Harmondsworth: Penguin.

de Certeau, M. (1984) *The Practice of Everyday Life*, Berkeley, CA: University of California Press.

De Landa, M. (2006) *A New Philosophy of Society*, New York: Continuum.

Deleuze, G. (1985) 'Nomad thought', in Alison, D. (ed.) *The New Nietzsche*, Cambridge, MA: MIT Press.

——(1988) *Foucault*, Minneapolis, MN: Minnesota University Press.

—— (1990) *The Logic of Sense*, New York: Columbia University Press.

—— (1993) *The Fold*, Minneapolis, MN: University of Minnesota Press.

—— (2007) *Two Regimes of Madness*, New York: Semiotext(e).

Deleuze, G. and Guattari, F. (1987) *A Thousand Plateaus*, London: Athlone.

Derrida, J. (1974) *Of Grammatology*, Baltimore, MD: Johns Hopkins University Press.

de Soto, H. (2000) *The Mystery of Capital*, New York: Basic Books.

Dhiravegin, L. (1992) *Demi Democracy*, Singapore: Times Academic Press.

Djenar, D. (1994) *Sukarno's Fire*, Melbourne: La Trobe University, Asian Studies Paper #3.

Dovey, K. (2000a), 'Myth and media', *Journal of Architectural Education*, 54 (1): 1–6.

—— (2000b) 'Redistributing danger: Enclosure and encounter in urban design', *The Australian Planner*, 37 (1): 10–13.

—— (2001) 'Memory, democracy and urban space', *Journal of Urban Design*, 6 (3): 265–282.

—— (2005) *Fluid City*, London: Routledge.

—— (2008) *Framing Places: Mediating Power in Built Form*, 2nd edn, London: Routledge.

Dovey, K. and Dickson, S. (2002) 'Architecture and freedom: Programmatic innovation in the work of Rem Koolhaas', *Journal of Architectural Education*, 55 (4): 268–277.

Drew, P. (1992) *Harry Seidler*, London: Thames & Hudson.

Durand-Lasserve, A. (2006) 'Market-Driven evictions and displacements', in Huchzermeyer, M. and Karam, A. (ed.) *Informal Settlements*, Cape Town: University of Cape Town Press, pp. 207–227.

Eagleton, T. (1990) *The Ideology of the Aesthetic*, Oxford: Blackwell.

Edensor, T. (1998) 'The culture of the Indian street', in Fyfe, N. (ed.) *Images of the Street*, London: Routledge, pp. 205–224.

Eisenman, P. (2004) 'Liberal views have never built anything of value', interview by Robert Locke, 27 July 2004, available online: www.archinect.com/features/article.php?id=4618_0_23_0_M (accessed 11 March 2006).

El Kadi, G and Bonnamy, A, (2007) *Architecture for the Dead*, Cairo: American University in Cairo Press.

Emery, M. (1999) 'House at Floirac, Gironde', *Architecture d'Aujourd Hui*, 320: 24–33.

Evers, H. and Korff, R. (2000) *South East Asian Urbanism: The Meaning and Power of Social Space*, Singapore: Institute of Southeast Asian Studies.

Fairclough, N. (1995) *Critical Discourse Analysis*, London: Longmans.

Featherstone, M. (1991) *Consumer Culture and Postmodernism*, London: Sage.

Fisher, K. (2007) 'Pedagogy and architecture', *Architecture Australia*, 96 (5): 55–58.

Fitzgerald, J. and O'Brien, M. (1999) *Health in Larger Terms*, Research Report, Dept of Criminology, University of Melbourne.

Fitzgerald, J., Broad, S. and Dare, A. (1998) *Regulating the Street Heroin Market in Fitzroy/Collingwood*, Research Report, VicHealth, Melbourne.

Florida, R. (2005) *Cities and the Creative Class*, New York: Routledge.

Flyvberg, B. (2004) 'Five misunderstandings about case study research', in Seale, C. *et al.*, *Qualitative Research Practice*, London: Sage, pp. 420–434.

Forrester, G. (1999) 'A Jakarta diary', in Forrester, G. and May, R. (eds) *The Fall of Suharto*, Singapore: Select.

Foucault, M. (1979) *Discipline and Punish*, New York: Vintage.

—— (1980) *Power/Knowledge*, New York: Pantheon.

—— (1997) 'Space, power and knowledge', in Leach, N. (ed.) *Rethinking Architecture*, London: Routledge, pp. 367–379.

Franck, K. (1984) 'Exorcising the ghost of environmental determinism', *Environment & Behavior*, 16 (4): 413–435.

Gamma, E., Helm, R., Johnson, R. and Vlissides, J. (1995) *Design Patterns*, Reading, MA: Addison-Wesley.

Geertz, C. (1980) *Negara: The Theatre State in 19th Century Bali*, Princeton, NJ: Princeton University Press.

Ghirardo, D. (1994) 'Eisenman's bogus avant-garde', *Progressive Architecture*, November: 70–73.

Giddens, A. (1984) *The Constitution of Society*, Cambridge: Polity.

—— (1990) *The Consequences of Modernity*, Stanford, CA: Stanford University Press.

Gilloch, G. (1996) *Myth and Metropolis*, Cambridge: Polity.

Goldberger, P. (2004) *Up from Zero*, New York: Random House.

Goodsell, C. (2001) *The American Statehouse*, Lawrence, KS: Kansas University Press.

Graafland, A. (1998) 'Of rhizomes, trees and the IJ-Oevers, Amsterdam', *Assemblage*, 38: 28–41.

Greenberg, S. and Rohe, W. (1984) 'Neighborhood design and crime', *Journal American Planning Association*, 50 (1): 48–61.

Habermas, J. (1984) *The Theory of Communicative Action: Volume 1*, trans. T. McCarthy, Cambridge: Polity.

Hays, C.M. (1984) 'Critical architecture', *Perspecta*, 21: 15–28.

Haldar, P. (1994) 'In and out of court: On topographies of law and the architecture of court buildings', *International Journal for the Semiotics of Law*, 7 (20): 185–200.

Halsey, M. and Young, A. (2006) ' "Our Desires are Ungovernable": Writing graffiti in urban space', *Theoretical Criminology*, (10) 3: 275–306.

Heidegger, M. (1962) *Being and Time*, New York: Harper & Row.

Heuken, A. (1982) *Historical Sites of Jakarta*, Jakarta: Gpta Lota Caraka.

Heynen, H. (1999) *Architecture and Modernity*, Cambridge, MA: MIT Press.

—— (2007) 'A critical position for architecture', in Rendell, J. *et al.* (eds) *Critical Architecture*, London: Routledge, pp. 48–56.

Hillier, B. (1988) 'Against enclosure', in Teymur, N., Markus, T. and Wooley, T. (eds) *Rehumanising Housing*, London: Butterworths.

—— (1996) *Space is the Machine*, Cambridge: Cambridge University Press.

Hillier, B. and Hanson, J. (1984) *The Social Logic of Space*, Cambridge: Cambridge University Press.

Hindley, D. (1976) 'Thailand: The politics of passivity', in Neher, C. (ed.) *Modern Thai Politics*, Cambridge, MA: Schenkman, pp. 172–191.

Hochman, E. (1989) *Architects of Fortune*, New York: Weidenfeld & Nicholson.

Huchzermeyer, M. (2006) 'Policy, Data and Civil Society', in Huchzermeyer, M. and Karan, A. (eds) *Informal Settlements*, Cape Town: University of Cape Town Press, pp. 19–40.

Huchzermeyer, M. and Karan. A. (2006) 'Introduction', in Huchzermeyer, M. and Karan, A. (eds) *Informal Settlements*, Cape Town: University of Cape Town Press, pp. 1–18.

Hyatt, P. (1993) 'Northern Light', *Steel Profile*, 46 (December): 2–11.

—— (1994) *Touch the Earth Lightly* [Video], Melbourne: Discovery Video International/BHP.

Irace, F. (1998) 'Educatorium: OMA a Utrecht', *Abitare*, 379: 104–114.

Jackson, P. (1991) 'Thai-Buddhist identity', in Reynolds, C. (ed.) *National Identity and its Defenders*, Melbourne: Monash Papers on Southeast Asia No. 25: 191–232.

Jacobs, J. (1965) *The Death and Life of Great American Cities*, Harmondsworth: Penguin.

Jameson, F. (1984) 'Postmodernism or the cultural logic of late capitalism', *New Left Review*, 146: 53–92.

Jameson, F. and Speaks, M. (1992) 'Envelopes and enclaves: The space of post-civil society', *Assemblage*, 17.

Jay, M. (1973) *The Dialectical Imagination*, Boston: Little Brown.

—— (2003) *Refractions of Violence*, London: Routledge.

Jenkins, P. (2006) 'Informal settlements: Infernal and eternal?', in Huchzermeyer, M. and Karan, A. (eds) *Informal Settlements*, Cape Town: University of Cape Town Press, pp. 84–102.

Jenkins, R. (1992) *Pierre Bourdieu*, London: Routledge.

Jhonny, T. (2002) 'Memagari Monas Tidak Logis dan Mangada-ada', *Kompas*, April 24.

Junaidi, A. (2002) 'City council supports Monas fence', *Jakarta Post*, 11 May.

Kant, I. (1974) *Critique of Judgement*, trans. J. Bernard, New York: Hafner.

—— (1979) ' A theory of esthetic experience', in Rader, M. (ed.) *A Modern Book of Esthetics*, New York: Holt, Rinehart and Winston, pp. 336–346.

Khudori, D. (1987) *Towards a Community of Liberation*, Research Report #1298, Rotterdam: Institute of Housing Studies.

—— (2004) *Menuju Kampung Pemerdekaan*, Yogyakarta: Yayasan Pondok Rakyat.

Kipnis, J. (1998) 'Recent Koolhaas', *El Croquis*, 79: 26–31.

Koestler, A. (1964) *The Act of Creation*, London: Hutchinson.

Koolhaas, R. (1978) *Delirious New York*, New York: Oxford University Press.

—— (1995) 'Generic city', in Koolhaas, R and Mau, B. (eds) *Small, Medium, Large, Extra-Large*, New York: Monacelli Press, pp. 1248–1264.

—— (1996) 'No grounds against a non-place', in *Euralille*, Basel: Birkhauser, pp. 51–71.

Koolhaas, R. and Mau, B. (1995) *Small, Medium, Large, Extra-Large*, New York: Monacelli Press.

Kusno, A. (2000) *Behind the Postcolonial*, London: Routledge.

Kwinter, S. (1996) 'Flying the bullet, or when did the future begin?', in Kwinter, S. (ed.) *Rem Koolhaas: Conversations with Students*, Houston, TX: Rice University, School of Architecture, pp. 68–94.

Lacan, J. (1977) *Écrits: A Selection*, New York: Norton.

Leclerc, J. (1993) 'Mirrors and the lighthouse', in Nas, P. (ed.) *Urban Symbolism*, Leiden: Brill, pp. 38–58.

Lefebvre, H. (1991) *The Production of Space*, Oxford: Blackwell.

—— (1996) *Writings on Cities*, Oxford: Blackwell.

Legge, J. (1973) *Sukarno: A Political Biography*, London: Allen Lane.

Lewis, M. (1999) *Suburban Backlash*, Melbourne: Bloomings.

Lynch, (1972) *What Time is this Place?* Cambridge, MA: MIT Press.

Lynn, G. (ed.) (1993) 'Folding in architecture', *Architectural Design Profile*, 102.

Lyon, H. (1999) 'Hassell's law', *Architecture Australia*, September–October: 58–62.

Macdonald, G. (1995) 'Indonesia's Medan Merdeka: National identity and the built environment', *Antipode*, 27 (3): 270–293.

McKenzie, E. (1994) *Privatopia*, New Haven, CT: Yale University Press.

McVey, R. (1996) 'Building behemoth: Indonesian constructions of the nation state', in Lev, D. and McVey, R. (eds) *Making Indonesia*, Ithaca, NY: Cornell University, Studies of South-East Asia #20, pp. 11–25.

Malpas, J. (2006) *Heidegger's Topology*, Cambridge, MA: MIT Press.

—— (2008) 'New media, cultural heritage and the sense of place', *International Journal of Heritage Studies*, 14 (3): 197–209.

Markus, T. (1993) *Buildings and Power*, London: Routledge.

Martin, R. and Mathema, A. (2006) 'Clash of civilizations', in Huchzermeyer, M. and Karan, A. (eds) *Informal Settlements*, Cape Town: University of Cape Town Press, pp. 126–145.

Massey, D. (1994) *Space, Place and Gender*, Cambridge: Polity.

—— (2000) 'Space-time and the politics of location', in Read, A. (ed.) *Architecturally Speaking*, London: Routledge, pp. 49–61.

Massumi, B. (1992) *A User's Guide to Capitalism and Schizophrenia*, Cambridge, MA: MIT Press.

Meldrum, A. (2006) 'A tsunami of demolitions', *New Internationalist*, January–February: 16–17.

Merleau-Ponty, M. (1962) *Phenomenology of Perception*, London: Routledge.

Mohr, R. (1999) 'In between power and procedure', *Journal of Social Change and Critical Enquiry* 1 (1), available online: www.uow.edu.au/arts/joscci/joscci1 (accessed 30 October 2008).

Moon, G. and Braun, T. (1998) 'Place, space and health service reform', in Kearns, R. and Gesler, W. (eds) *Putting Health into Place*, Syracuse, NY: Syracuse University Press, pp. 270–288.

Morell, D. and Chai-anan, S. (1981) *Political Conflict in Thailand*, Cambridge, MA: Oelgeschlager, Gunn & Hain.

Nas, P. (1993) 'Jakarta, city full of symbols', in Nas, P. (ed.) *Urban Symbolism*, Leiden: Brill, pp. 13–37.

Nas, P. and Sluis, R. (2000) 'Contained student protest', *Social Sciences*, 4 (2–3).

Nasional PPT (1978) *Tugu Nasional*, Jakarta: Pelaksona Pembina Tugu Nasional.

Nelson, L. (1999) 'Bodies (and spaces) do matter', *Gender, Place and Culture*, 6 (4): 331–353.

Nesbit, M. (1998) 'House play', *Artforum*, 37 (3).

Newman, O. (1972) *Defensible Space*, New York: Macmillan.

Norberg-Schulz, C. (1980) *Genius Loci*, New York: Rizzoli.

O'Connor, R. (1990) 'Place, power and discourse in the Thai image of Bangkok', *Journal of the Siam Society*, 78 (2).

OMA/Rem Koolhaas (1998) *Living.Vivre.Leben*, Bordeaux: Birkhauser.

Owen, C. and Dovey, K. (2007) 'Fields of sustainable architecture', *Journal of Architecture*, 13 (1): 9–21.

Panofsky, E. (1967) *Architecture Gothique et Pensée Scholastique*, trans. P. Bourdieu, Paris: Minuit.

Patton, P. (2000) *Deleuze and the Political*, London: Routledge.

Payne, G. (1999) 'Introduction', in Payne, G. (ed.) *Making Common Ground*, London: Intermediate Technology Publications.

Peattie, L. (1992) 'Aesthetic politics: Shantytown or new vernacular?', *Traditional Dwellings and Settlements Review*, 3 (2): 23–32.

Perlman, J. (1976) *The Myth of Marginality*, Berkeley, CA: University of California Press.

Permanasari, E. (2007) *The Use and Meaning of Sukarno's Monuments and Public Places in Jakarta*, unpublished PhD thesis, University of Melbourne.

Pimlott, M. (2007) *Without and Within*, Rotterdam: Episode.

Portes, A. (1998) 'Social capital', *Annual Review of Sociology*, 24: 1–24.

Prigge, W. (2008) 'Reading the urban revolution', in Goonewardena, K., *et al.* (eds) *Space, Difference and Everyday Life*, London: Routledge, pp. 46–61.

Putnam, R. (1995) 'Bowling alone: America's declining social capital', *Journal of Democracy*, 6: 65–78.

Rajchmann, J. (1998) *Constructions*, Cambridge, MA: MIT Press.

Rajchmann, J. and Koolhaas, R. (1994) 'Thinking big', *Artforum*, December, pp. 47–51.

Rapoport, A. (1982) *The Meaning of the Built Environment*, Beverly Hills, CA: Sage.

Relph, E. (1976) *Place and Placelessness*, London: Pion.

Reynolds, C. (1991) 'Introduction', in Reynolds, C. (ed.) *National Identity and Its Defenders*, Melbourne: Monash Papers on Southeast Asia, No. 25.

—— (1998) 'Globalization and cultural nationalism in modern Thailand', in Kahn, J. (ed.) *Southeast Asian Identities*, Singapore: Institute of SEA Studies, pp. 115–145.

Rose, G. (1993) *Feminism and Geography*, Minneapolis, MN: University of Minnesota Press.

Roy, A. (2004) 'Transnational trespassings', in Roy, A. and Alsayyad, N. (eds) *Urban Informality*, New York: Lexington, pp. 289–317.

Royston, L. (2006) 'Barking dogs and building bridges', in Huchzermeyer, M. and Karan, A. (eds) *Informal Settlements*, Cape Town: University of Cape Town Press, pp. 165–179.

Rüedi, K. (1998) 'Curriculum vitae: The architect's cultural capital', in Hill, J. (ed.) *Occupying Architecture*, London: Routledge, pp. 23–38.

Ryan, R. (1998) 'The new Dutch school', *Architecture*, 87 (3): 136–143.

Said, E. (1978) *Orientalism*, London: Routledge.

Seabrook, J. (1996) *In the Cities of the South*, London: Verso.

Seamon, D. and Mugerauer, R. (eds) (1985) *Dwelling, Place, and Environment: Towards a Phenomenology of Person and World*, Boston, MA: M. Nijhoff.

Sennett, R. (1973) *The Uses of Disorder*, Harmondsworth: Penguin.

—— (1996) *Flesh and Stone: The Body and the City in Western Civilization*, New York: W.W. Norton.

Smit, W. (2006) 'Understanding the complexities of informal settlements', in Huchzermeyer, M. and Karan, A. (eds) *Informal Settlements*, Cape Town: University of Cape Town Press, pp. 103–125.

Sola-Morales, I. (1994) 'Terrain vague', in Davidson, C. (ed.) *Anyplace*, Cambridge, MA: MIT Press, pp. 119–123.

Somol, R. and Whiting, S. (2002) 'Notes around the Doppler effect', *Perspecta*, 33: 72–77.

Sorkin, M. and Zukin, S. (eds) (2002) *After the World Trade Center*, New York: Routledge.

Speaks, M. (1994) 'Bigness', *Any*, 9: 60–62.

—— (2005) 'After theory', *Architectural Record*, June: 72–75.

Stevens, G. (1998) *The Favoured Circle*, Cambridge, MA: MIT Press.

Sukanto, I. (2002) 'Monas and Gpinang', *Jakarta Post*, 14 October.

Sutrisno, M. (1999) 'Estetika Ruang', in Sutrisno, M. (ed.) *Kisi-Kisi Estetika*, Yogyakarta: Kanisius.

Swartz, D. (1997) *Culture and Power: The Sociology of Pierre Bourdieu*, Chicago, IL: University of Chicago Press.

Tafuri, M. (1976) *Architecture and Utopia*, Cambridge, MA: MIT Press.

Tait, D. (1999) 'Boundaries and barriers', *Journal of Social Change & Critical Inquiry*, 1 (1), available online: www.uow.edu.au/arts/joscci/joscci1 (accessed 30 October 2008).

Turner, J. (1976) *Housing by People*, London: Marion Boyars.

United Nations (2003) *The Challenge of Slums*, London: Earthscan.

Van Cleef, C. (1999) 'Campus landscape', *Architectural Review*, 1225 (March): 50–53.

Webster, C. (2002) 'Property rights and the public realm', *Environment and Planning B*, 29 (3): 397–412.

Wilson, D. (1962) *Politics in Thailand*, Ithaca, NY: Cornell University Press.

Wittgenstein, L. (1967) *Philosophical Investigations*, Oxford: Blackwell.

Woodcock, I., Dovey, K. and Wood, S. (2004) 'Limits to urban character', in Edquist, H. and Frichot, H. (eds) *LIMITS: SAHANZ Proceedings, Vol. 2*, Melbourne: 545–550.

Young, K. (1999) 'The crisis', in Forrester, G. and May, R. (eds) *The Fall of Soeharto*, Singapore: Select, pp. 104–129.

Zaera, A. and Koolhaas, R. (1992) 'Finding freedoms: Conversations with Rem Koolhaas', *El Croquis*, 53: 6–31.

Žižek, S. (1991) *For They Know Not What They Do*, New York: Verso.

Zukin, S. (1991) *Landscapes of Power*, Berkeley, CA: University of California Press.

Index